PRACTICAL
CRITICISM

A Study of
LITERARY JUDGMENT

BY

I. A. RICHARDS

Fellow of Magdalene College, Cambridge
Author of " Principles of Literary Criticism "

1930

PREFACE

A CONVENIENT arrangement for the parts of this book has not been easy to find. A friendly reader will, I think, soon see why. Those who are curious to discern what motives prompted me to write it will be satisfied most quickly if they begin by glancing through Part IV, which might indeed have been placed as an Introduction.

The length of Part II, and a certain unavoidable monotony, may prove a stumbling-block. I have included very little there, however, that I do not discuss again in Part III, and it need not be read through continuously. A reader who feels some impatience will prudently pass on at once to my attempted elucidations, returning to consult the facts when a renewed contact with actuality is desired.

The later chapters of Part III will be found to have more general interest than the earlier.

I am deeply indebted to the living authors of some of the poems I have used for their permission to print them ; a permission which, in view of the peculiar conditions of this experiment, witnesses to no slight generosity of spirit. Some contemporary poems were necessary for my purpose, to avoid the perplexities which ' dated ' styles would introduce here. But in making the selection I had originally no thought of publication. The interest of the material supplied me by my commentators and the desire that as many types of poetry as possible should be represented have been the only reasons for my choice. But in those instances in which I have not been able to form a high opinion of the poems I must ask the forgiveness of the authors and plead as excuse a motive which we have in common, the advancement of poetry.

My acknowledgments are due also to the publishers of these poems. Details of these obligations will be found in Appendix C, in which I have hidden away, as far as I could, particulars as to the authorship and date of the poems. For obvious reasons the interest of these pages will be enhanced if the reader remains unaware of the authorship of the poems until his own opinions of them have been formed and tested by comparison with the many other opinions here given. I would, therefore, earnestly counsel an intending reader not to consult Appendix C until a late stage in his reading.

I. A. R

CAMBRIDGE,
April 1929.

CONTENTS

PART I

INTRODUCTORY

PART II

DOCUMENTATION

PART III

ANALYSIS

PART IV

SUMMARY AND RECOMMENDATIONS

PART ONE
INTRODUCTORY

A

INTRODUCTORY

I HAVE set three aims before me in constructing this book. First, to introduce a new kind of documentation to those who are interested in the contemporary state of culture whether as critics, as philosophers, as teachers, as psychologists, or merely as curious persons. Secondly, to provide a new technique for those who wish to discover for themselves what they think and feel about poetry (and cognate matters) and why they should like or dislike it. Thirdly, to prepare the way for educational methods more efficient than those we use now in developing discrimination and the power to understand what we hear and read.

For the first purpose I have used copious quotations from material supplied to me as a Lecturer at Cambridge and elsewhere. For some years I have made the experiment of issuing printed sheets of poems—ranging in character from a poem by Shakespeare to a poem by Ella Wheeler Wilcox—to audiences who were requested to comment freely in writing upon them. The authorship of the poems was not revealed, and with rare exceptions it was not recognised.

After a week's interval I would collect these comments, taking certain obvious precautions to preserve the anonymity of the commentators, since only through anonymity could complete liberty to express their genuine opinions be secured for the writers. Care was taken to refrain from influencing them either for or against any poem. Four poems were issued at a time in groupings indicated in the

Appendix, in which the poems I am here using will
be found. I would, as a rule, hint that the poems
were perhaps a mixed lot, but that was the full
extent of my interference. I lectured the following
week partly upon the poems, but rather more upon
the comments, or protocols, as I call them.

Much astonishment both for the protocol-writers
and for the Lecturer ensued from this procedure.
The opinions expressed were not arrived at lightly
or from one reading of the poems only. As a measure
of indirect suggestion, I asked each writer to record
on his protocol the number of ‘ readings ’ made of
each poem. A number of perusals made at one
session were to be counted together as one ‘ reading ’
provided that they aroused and sustained one single
growing response to the poem, or alternatively led
to no response at all and left the reader with nothing
but the bare words before him on the paper. This
description of a ‘ reading ’ was, I believe, well
understood. It follows that readers who recorded
as many as ten or a dozen readings had devoted no
little time and energy to their critical endeavour.
Few writers gave less than four attacks to any of
the poems. On the whole it is fairly safe to assert
that the poems received much more thorough study
than, shall we say, most anthology pieces get in the
ordinary course. It is from this thoroughness,
prompted by the desire to arrive at some definite
expressible opinion, and from the week’s leisure
allowed that these protocols derive their significance.

The standing of the writers must be made clear.
The majority were undergraduates reading English
with a view to an Honours Degree. A considerable
number were reading other subjects but there is no
ground to suppose that these differed for this reason
in any essential respect. There was a sprinkling of
graduates, and a few members of the audience were
non-academic. Men and women were probably

included in about equal numbers, so, in what follows ' he ' must constantly be read as equivalent to ' he or she'. There was no compulsion to return protocols. Those who took the trouble to write—about 60 per cent.—may be presumed to have been actuated by a more than ordinarily keen interest in poetry. From such comparisons as I have been able to make with protocols supplied by audiences of other types, I see no reason whatever to think that a higher standard of critical discernment can easily be found under our present cultural conditions. Doubtless, could the Royal Society of Literature or the Academic Committee of the English Association be impounded for purposes of experiment we might expect greater uniformity in the comments or at least in their style, and a more wary approach as regards some of the dangers of the test. But with regard to equally essential matters occasions for surprise might still occur. The precise conditions of this test are not duplicated in our everyday commerce with literature. Even the reviewers of new verse have as a rule a considerable body of the author's work to judge by. And editorial complaints are frequent as to the difficulty of obtaining good reviewing. Editors themselves will not be the slowest to agree with me upon the difficulty of judging verse without a hint as to its provenance.

Enough, for the moment, about the documentation of this book. My second aim is more ambitious and requires more explanation. It forms part of a general attempt to modify our procedure in certain forms of discussion. There are subjects — mathematics, physics and the descriptive sciences supply some of them—which can be discussed in terms of verifiable facts and precise hypotheses. There are other subjects—the concrete affairs of commerce, law, organisation and police work—which can be handled by rules of thumb and generally accepted conventions. But in between is the vast *corpus* of problems, assumptions, adumbrations, fictions, prejudices, tenets; the sphere of random beliefs and hopeful guesses; the whole world, in brief, of abstract opinion and disputation about matters of feeling. To this world belongs everything about which civilised man cares most. I need only instance ethics, metaphysics, morals, religion, æsthetics, and the discussions surrounding liberty, nationality, justice, love, truth, faith and knowledge to make this plain. As a subject-matter for discussion, poetry is a central and typical denizen of this world. It is so both by its own nature and by the type of discussion with which it is traditionally associated. It serves, therefore, as an eminently suitable *bait* for anyone who wishes to trap the current opinions and responses in this middle field for the purpose of examining and comparing them, and with a view to advancing our knowledge of what may be called the natural history of human opinions and feelings.

In part then this book is the record of a piece of field-work in comparative ideology. But I hope, not only to present an instructive collection of contemporary opinions, presuppositions, theories, beliefs, responses and the rest, but also to make some suggestions towards a better control of these tricksy components of our lives. The way in which it is hoped to do this can only be briefly indicated at this point.

There are two ways of interpreting all but a very few utterances.

Whenever we hear or read any not too nonsensical opinion, a tendency so strong and so automatic that it must have been formed along with our earliest speech-habits, leads us to consider *what seems to be said* rather than the *mental operations* of the person who said it. If the speaker is a recognised and obvious liar this tendency is, of course, arrested.

We do then neglect what he has said and turn our attention instead to the motives or mechanisms that have caused him to say it. But ordinarily we at once try to consider the objects his words seem to stand for and not the mental goings-on that led him to use the words. We say that we ' follow his thought ' and mean, not that we have traced what happened in his mind, but merely that we have gone through a train of thinking that seems to end where he ended. We are in fact so anxious to discover whether we agree or not with what is being said that we overlook the mind that says it, unless some very special circumstance calls us back.

Compare now the attitude to speech of the alienist attempting to ' follow ' the ravings of mania or the dream maunderings of a neurotic. I do not suggest that we should treat one another altogether as ' mental cases '[1] but merely that for some subject-matters and some types of discussion the alienist's attitude, his direction of attention, his order or plan of interpretation, is far more fruitful, and would lead to better understanding on both sides of the discussion, than the usual method that our language-habits force upon us. For normal minds are easier to ' follow ' than diseased minds, and even more can be learned by adopting the psychologist's attitude to ordinary speech-situations than by studying aberrations.

It is very strange that we have no simple verbal means by which to describe these two different kinds of ' meaning '. Some device as unmistakable as the ' up ' or ' down ' of a railway signal ought to be

[1] A few touches of the clinical manner will, however, be not out of place in these pages, if only to counteract the indecent tendencies of the scene. For here are our friends and neighbours—nay our very brothers and sisters—caught at a moment of abandon giving themselves and their literary reputations away with an unexampled freedom. It is indeed a sobering spectacle, but like some sights of the hospital-ward very serviceable to restore proportions and recall to us what humanity, behind all its lendings and pretences, is like.

available. But there is none. Clumsy and pedantic looking psychological periphrases have to be employed instead. I shall, however, try to use one piece of shorthand consistently. In handling the piles of material supplied by the protocols I shall keep the term 'statement' for those utterances whose 'meaning' in the sense of what they *say*, or purport to say, is the prime object of interest. I shall reserve the term 'expression' for those utterances where it is the mental operations of the writers which are to be considered.

When the full range of this distinction is realised the study of criticism takes on a new significance. But the distinction is not easy to observe. Even the firmest resolution will be constantly broken down, so strong are our native language habits. When views that seem to conflict with our own prepossessions are set before us, the impulse to refute, to combat or to reconstruct them, rather than to investigate them, is all but overwhelming. So the history of criticism,[1] like the history of all the middle subjects alluded to above, is a history of dogmatism and argumentation rather than a history of research. And like all such histories the chief lesson to be learnt from it is the futility of all argumentation that precedes understanding. We cannot profitably attack any opinion until we have discovered what it expresses as well as what it states ; and our present technique for investigating opinions must be admitted, for all these middle subjects, to be woefully inadequate.

Therefore, the second aim of this book is to improve this technique. We shall have before us several hundreds of opinions upon particular aspects of poetry, and the poems themselves to help us to

---

[1] We shall meet in the protocols plenty of living instances of famous critical doctrines that are often thought to be now merely curiosities of opinion long since extinct.

examine them. We shall have the great advantage of being able to compare numbers of extremely different opinions upon the same point. We shall be able to study what may be called the same opinion in different stages of development as it comes from different minds. And further, we shall be able in many instances to see what happens to a given opinion, when it is applied to a different detail or a different poem.

The effect of all this is remarkable. When the first dizzy bewilderment has worn off, as it very soon does, it is as though we were strolling through and about a building that hitherto we were only able to see from one or two distant standpoints. We gain a much more intimate understanding both of the poem and of the opinions it provokes.[1] Something like a plan of the most usual approaches can be sketched and we learn what to expect when a new object, a new poem, comes up for discussion.

It is as a step towards another training and technique in discussion that I would best like this book to be regarded. If we are to begin to understand half the opinions which appear in the protocols we shall need no little mental plasticity. And in the course of our comparisons, interpretations and extrapolations something like a plan of the ways in which the likely ambiguities of any given term or opinion-formula may radiate will make itself apparent. For the hope of a new technique in discussion lies in this : that the study of the ambiguities of one term assists in the elucidation of another. To trace the meanings of ' sentimentality', ' truth', ' sincerity', or ' meaning ' itself, as these terms are used in criticism, can help us with other words used in other

---

[1] A strange light, incidentally, is thrown upon the sources of popularity for poetry. Indeed I am not without fears that my efforts may prove of assistance to young poets (and others) desiring to increase their sales. A set of formulæ for 'nation-wide appeal' seems to be a just possible outcome.

topics. Ambiguity in fact is systematic ; the separate senses that a word may have are related to one another, if not as strictly as the various aspects of a building, at least to a remarkable extent. Something comparable to a ' perspective ' which will include and enable us to control and ' place ' the rival meanings that bewilder us in discussion and hide our minds from one another can be worked out. Perhaps every intelligence that has ever reflected upon this matter will agree that this may be so. Every one agrees but no one does any research into the matter, although this is an affair in which even the slightest step forward affects the whole frontier line of human thought and discussion.

The indispensable instrument for this inquiry is psychology. I am anxious to meet as far as may be the objection that may be brought by some psychologists, and these the best, that the protocols do not supply enough evidence for us really to be able to make out the motives of the writers and that therefore the whole investigation is superficial. But the *beginning* of every research ought to be superficial, and to find something to investigate that is accessible and detachable is one of the chief difficulties of psychology. I believe the chief merit of the experiment here made is that it gives us this. Had I wished to plumb the depths of these writers' Unconscious, where I am quite willing to agree the real motives of their likings and dislikings would be found, I should have devised something like a branch of psychoanalytic technique for the purpose. But it was clear that little progress would be made if we attempted to drag too deep a plough. However, even as it is, enough strange material is turned up.

After these explanations the reader will be prepared to find little argumentation in these pages, but much analysis, much rather strenuous exercise in changing our ground and a good deal of rather intricate navigation. Navigation, in fact—the art of knowing where we are wherever, as mental travellers, we may go—is the main subject of the book. To discuss poetry and the ways in which it may be approached, appreciated and judged is, of course, its prime purpose. But poetry itself is a mode of communication. What it communicates and how it does so and the worth of what is communicated form the subject-matter of criticism. It follows that criticism itself is very largely, though not wholly, an exercise in navigation. It is all the more surprising then that no treatise on the art and science of intellectual and emotional navigation has yet been written ; for logic, which might appear to cover part of this field, in actuality hardly touches it.

That the one and only goal of all critical endeavours, of all interpretation, appreciation, exhortation, praise or abuse, is improvement in communication may seem an exaggeration. But in practice it is so. The whole apparatus of critical rules and principles is a means to the attainment of finer, more precise, more discriminating communication. There is, it is true, a valuation side to criticism. When we have solved, completely, the communication problem, when we have got, perfectly, the experience, *the mental condition* relevant to the poem, we have still to judge it, still to decide upon its worth. But the later question nearly always settles itself ; or rather, our own inmost nature and the nature of the world in which we live decide it for us. Our prime endeavour must be to get the relevant mental condition and then see what happens. If we cannot then decide whether it is good or bad, it is doubtful whether any principles, however refined and subtle, can help us much. Without the capacity to get the experience they cannot help us at all. This is still clearer if we consider the use of critical maxims in teaching. Value cannot be demonstrated except through the communication of what is valuable.

Critical principles, in fact, need wary handling. They can never be a substitute for discernment though they may assist us to avoid unnecessary blunders. There has hardly ever been a critical rule, principle or maxim which has not been for wise men a helpful guide but for fools a will-o'-the-wisp. All the great watchwords of criticism from Aristotle's ' Poetry is an imitation ' down to the doctrine that ' Poetry is expression', are ambiguous pointers that different people follow to very different destinations. Even the most sagacious critical principles may, as we shall see, become merely a cover for critical ineptitude ; and the most trivial or baseless generalisation may really mask good and discerning judgment. Everything turns upon how the principles are applied. It is to be feared that critical formulas, even the best, are responsible for more bad judgment than good, because it is far easier to forget their subtle sense and apply them crudely than to remember it and apply them finely.

The astonishing variety of human responses makes irksome any too systematic scheme for arranging these extracts. I wish to present a sufficient selection to bring the situation concretely before the reader, reserving to the chapters of Part III any serious attempt to clear up the various difficulties with which the protocol-writers have been struggling. I shall proceed poem by poem, allowing the internal drama latent in every clash of opinion, of taste or temperament to guide the arrangement. Not all the poems, needless to say, raise the same problems in equal measure. In most, some one outstanding difficulty, some special occasion for a division of minds, takes precedence.

It is convenient therefore to place here a some-
what arbitrary list of the principal difficulties that
may be encountered by one reader or another in the
presence of almost any poem. This list is suggested
by a study of the protocols themselves, and drawn
up in an order which proceeds from the simplest,
infant's, obstacle to successful reading up to the
most insidious, intangible and bewildering of critical
problems.

If some of these difficulties seem so simple as to
be hardly worth discussion, I would beg my reader
who feels a temptation to despise them not to leap
lightly to his decision. Part of my purpose is *docu-
mentation* and I am confident of showing that the
simple difficulties are those that most need attention
as they are those that in fact receive least.

We soon advance, however, to points on which
more doubt may be felt—where controversy, more
and less enlightened, still continues—and we finish
face to face with questions which no one will pretend
are yet settled and with some which will not be
settled till the Day of Judgment. In the memorable
words of Benjamin Paul Blood, ' What is concluded
that we should conclude anything about it ? '

The following seem to be the chief difficulties of
criticism or, at least, those which we shall have most
occasion to consider here :—

A. First must come the difficulty of *making out the
plain sense* of poetry. The most disturbing and
impressive fact brought out by this experiment
is that a large proportion of average-to-good
(and in some cases, certainly, devoted) readers
of poetry frequently and repeatedly *fail to under-
stand it*, both as a statement and as an expression.
They fail to make out its prose sense, its plain,
overt meaning, as a set of ordinary, intelligible,
English sentences, taken quite apart from any

further poetic significance. And equally, they misapprehend its feeling, its tone, and its intention. They would travesty it in a paraphrase. They fail to construe it just as a schoolboy fails to construe a piece of Cæsar. How serious in its effects in different instances this failure may be, we shall have to consider with care. It is not confined to one class of readers ; not only those whom we would suspect fall victims. Nor is it only the most abstruse poetry which so betrays us. In fact, to set down, for once, the brutal truth, no immunity is possessed on any occasion, not by the most reputable scholar, from this or any other of these critical dangers.

B. Parallel to, and not unconnected with, these difficulties of interpreting the meaning are the difficulties of *sensuous apprehension*. Words in sequence have a form to the mind's ear and the mind's tongue and larynx, even when silently read. They have a movement and may have a rhythm. The gulf is wide between a reader who naturally and immediately perceives this form and movement (by a conjunction of sensory, intellectual and emotional sagacity) and another reader, who either ignores it or has to build it up laboriously with finger-counting, table-tapping and the rest ; and this difference has most far-reaching effects.

C. Next may come those difficulties that are connected with the place of *imagery*, principally visual imagery, in poetic reading. They arise in part from the incurable fact that we differ immensely in our capacity to visualise, and to produce imagery of the other senses. Also the importance of our imagery as a whole, as well as of some pet particular type of image, in our mental lives varies surprisingly. Some minds can do nothing and get nowhere without images ; others seem to be able to do everything and get anywhere, reach any and every state of thought and feeling without making use of them. Poets on the whole (though by no means all poets always) may be suspected of exceptional imaging capacity, and some readers are constitutionally prone to stress the place of imagery in reading, to pay great attention to it, and even to judge the value of the poetry by the images it excites in them. But images are erratic things ; lively images aroused in one mind need have on similarity to the equally lively images stirred by the same line of poetry in another, and neither set need have anything to do with any images which may have existed in the poet's mind. Here is a troublesome source of critical deviations.

D. Thirdly, more obviously, we have to note the powerful very pervasive influence of *mnemonic irrelevances*. These are misleading effects of the reader's being reminded of some personal scene or adventure, erratic associations, the interference of emotional reverberations from a past which may have nothing to do with the poem. Relevance is not an easy notion to define or to apply, though some instances of irrelevant intrusions are among the simplest of all accidents to diagnose.

E. More puzzling and more interesting are the critical traps that surround what may be called *Stock Responses*. These have their opportunity whenever a poem seems to, or does, involve views and emotions already fully prepared in the reader's mind, so that what happens appears to be more of the reader's doing than the poet's. The button is pressed, and then the author's work is done, for immediately the record starts playing in quasi- (or total) independence of the poem which is supposed to be its origin or instrument.

Whenever this lamentable redistribution of the poet's and reader's share in the labour of poetry occurs, or is in danger of occurring, we require to be especially on our guard. Every kind of injustice may be committed as well by those who just escape as by those who are caught.

F. *Sentimentality* is a peril that needs less comment here. It is a question of the due measure of response. This over-facility in certain emotional directions is the Scylla whose Charybdis is—

G. *Inhibition.* This, as much as Sentimentality, is a positive phenomenon, though less studied until recent years and somewhat masked under the title of Hardness of Heart. But neither can well be considered in isolation.

H. *Doctrinal Adhesions* present another troublesome problem. Very much poetry—religious poetry may be instanced—seems to contain or imply views and beliefs, true or false, about the world. If this be so, what bearing has the truth-value of the views upon the worth of the poetry? Even if it be not so, if the beliefs are not really contained or implied, but only seem so to a non-poetical reading, what should be the bearing of the reader's conviction, if any, upon his estimate of the poetry? Has poetry anything to say; if not, why not, and if so, how? Difficulties at this point are a fertile source of confusion and erratic judgment.

I. Passing now to a different order of difficulties, the effects of *technical presuppositions* have to be noted. When something has once been well done in a certain fashion we tend to expect similar things to be done in the future in the same fashion, and are disappointed or do not recognise them if they are done differently. Conversely, a technique which has shown its ineptitude for one purpose tends to become discredited for all. Both are cases of mistaking means for ends. Whenever we attempt to judge poetry from outside by technical details we are putting means before ends, and—such is our ignorance of cause and effect in poetry—we shall be lucky if we do not make even worse blunders. We have to try to avoid judging pianists by their hair.

J. Finally, *general critical preconceptions* (prior demands made upon poetry as a result of theories—conscious or unconscious—about its nature and value), intervene endlessly, as the history of criticism shows only too well, between the reader and the poem. Like an unlucky dietetic formula they may cut him off from what he is starving for, even when it is at his very lips.

These difficulties, as will have been observed, are not unconnected with one another and indeed overlap. They might have been collected under more heads or fewer. Yet, if we set aside certain extreme twists or trends of the personality (for example, blinding narcissism or grovelling self-abasement—aberrations, temporary or permanent, of the self-regarding sentiment) together with undue accumulations or depletions of energy, I believe that most of the principal obstacles and causes of failure in the reading and judgment of poetry may without much straining be brought under these ten heads. But they are too roughly sketched here for this to be judged.

B

More by good luck than by artful design, each poem, as a rule, proved an invitation to the mass of its readers to grapple with some *one* of the difficulties that have just been indicated. Thus a certain sporting interest may be felt by the sagacious critic in divining where, in each case, the dividing line of opinion will fall, and upon what considerations it will turn. No attempt will be made, in the survey which follows, to do more than shake out and air these variegated opinions. Elucidations, both of the poems and the opinions, will be for the most part postponed, as well as my endeavours to adjudicate upon the poetic worth of the unfortunate subjects of debate.

A very natural suspicion may fittingly be countered in this place. Certain doubts were occasionally expressed to me after a lecture that not all the protocol extracts were equally genuine. It was hinted that I might have myself composed some of those which came in most handily to illustrate a point. But none of the protocols have been tampered with and nothing has been added. I have even left the spelling and punctuation unchanged in all significant places.

But another falsification may perhaps be charged against me, falsification through bias in selection. Space, and respect for the reader's impatience, obviously forbade my printing the whole of my material. Selected extracts alone could be ventured. With a little cunning it would be possible to make selections that would give very different impressions. I can only say that I have been on my guard against unfairness. I ought to add perhaps that the part of the material least adequately represented is the havering, non-committal, vague, sit-on-the-fence, middle-body of opinion. I would have put in more of this if it were not such profitless reading.

PART TWO

DOCUMENTATION

But enough of this ; there is such a variety of game springing up before me, that I am distracted in my choice, and know not which to follow. It is sufficient to say, according to the proverb, that here is God's plenty.

DRYDEN on the Canterbury Pilgrims.

Life's more than breath and the quick round of blood.
'Tis a great spirit and a busy heart ;
The coward and the small in soul scarce do live.
One generous feeling, one great thought, one deed
Of good, ere night, would make life longer seem
Than if each year might number a thousand days
Spent as is this by nations of mankind.
We live in deeds, not years ; in thoughts, not breaths ;
In feelings, not in figures on a dial.
We should count time by heart-throbs. He most lives
Who thinks most, feels the noblest, acts the best.

POEM I

HERE, for once, in the opinions maintained about the central point, Nature shows a taste for system, and gives us the rare satisfaction of seeing nearly all the logical possibilities well represented in living and lively form. The central dispute concerned the place and value of the doctrine these verses propound, and whether that doctrine be well or ill expressed. Differing replies upon these matters were associated with high degrees of delight or disgust. That the thought contained is true ; that, on the contrary, it is false ; that, though true enough, it is commonplace ; that it is original and profound ; that, as a commonplace or as a paradox, it is finely or tamely, clearly or confusedly expressed ; these were the questions agitated. The various possible answers were so well represented that it seems worth while making up a table :—

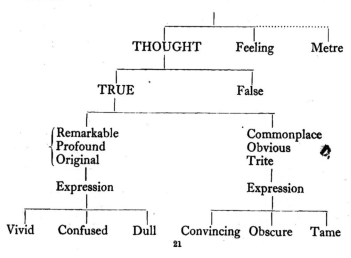

First let the advocates of its excellence be heard.

1·11.[1] Truth is the essence of art, and the outstanding feature of this passage is truth. The poet has expressed in vivid terms his conception of the higher, if not the highest plane of life and we who read his work, cannot fail to appreciate its *nobility of thought*[2] and realise its challenge to mankind. The verse is full of sentiment, but sentiment of the best kind.

Alas ! we often fail to appreciate it, as is lamentably shown in what follows. But let those of more elevated temper continue.

1·12. Here is *noble thought* clothed fittingly and strikingly in *powerful verse*. The first nine lines especially appeal to me, ending, as they do, in effective antithesis.

1·13. A noble message, well conveyed by the form chosen.

' Noble ' seems indeed a key-word to this passage.

1·14. These lines express the thoughts of a lofty soul in a simple yet impressive manner. They are lines which are worth remembering both on account of their thought and their concise and clear expression. The last phrase haunts the mind, but apart from this *the whole passage moves forward with a gentle motion* which tends to infix the words on the memory.

---

[1] This numbering of the protocols is primarily introduced to facilitate reference. But the decimal system allows me also to use it to suggest certain groupings. The number before the decimal point (1'— to 13'—) indicates the poem which is being discussed. The first number after the point suggests, when it remains the same for a sequence of extracts, that the same general problem, approach, or view is being illustrated. Thus 1'11, 1'12, 1'13 . . . have some cognate bearing, but with 1'2 a different general topic has taken its place. Similarly with the later decimal places. For example, 1'141, 1'142 . . . may be especially considered along with 1'14, all being concerned in different ways with the same secondary point. (Here the metrical qualities of the passage.)

But I have not attempted to make this numbering strictly systematic. It is used as a rough indication of the moments when we pass over to a new question ; it is a mere supplement to paragraphing, and any reader may neglect it at his discretion.

Unless otherwise expressly stated a different number implies a different writer.

[2] The italics in all cases are mine and are introduced not to distort the protocols (the reader will become used to them) but to direct the reader's attention without toil to the points with which, for the moment, my commentary is concerned—or to indicate where comparisons may be interesting.

It may seem strange that the phrase ' acts the best '
should haunt the mind, but this is possibly not what
the writer intended.

Not all those who agree about the lofty nobility of
the passage and who most admire its expression are
at one as to why this expression is to be admired.

1·141. The rather rugged metre makes the best possible setting
for the *noble idea* of the poet. It carries one along with it, con-
veying the idea of someone speaking rapidly, his *words almost
tumbling over each other*, in the stress of emotion : an instance
of how a *noble theme* can inspire a poet to clothe it in *noble
diction*, without any of the verbal embroideries often employed
by poets, to make inferior themes palatable.

Words which ' almost tumble over one another '
and yet ' move forward with a gentle motion ' would
seem impossibly versatile if we did not know how
much this kind of movement in verse depends upon
the reader. Several other views about the verse
qualities are also found even among admirers.

1·142. The thought is the most important thing about this
poem. The hint of paradox arrests the reader's attention, the
truth of it gives one a feeling of satisfaction. It is expressed in
plain, straightforward speech which is the best medium for a
didactic poem.

1·143. I admire this because I think the thought expressed is
true and interesting, and original in that it gives the impression
of vivid personal experience, and it is of interest to all since it
concerns all. The choice of common everyday words drives
home the thought, by connecting it closely to ordinary life.
The passage *gains little from* the beauty of *rhythm* and might
with little or no loss have been written in prose.

1·144. A stimulating thought well expressed. The Author
protests against half-heartedness. The theme, dealing with the
true way of living, is naturally of a lofty character, and *blank
verse* suits the subject-matter with peculiar felicity.

1·145. The short phrases in line four and the long sweep in 5,
6 dying away in 7, are magnificent.
The last four lines clinch the argument perfectly.

Let us now hear something of the other side of the case before turning to the extreme enthusiasts.

1·15. The poem is worthless. The underlying idea, that life must be measured by its intensity as well as its duration is a familiar one. Consequently the poem is to be judged by its strength and originality of expression. The author has brought no freshness to his material ; *his thought is flabby and confused ; his verse is pedestrian.* Away with him !

The next writer adds a complaint which looks as though it might apply to much blank verse.

1·16. The moralising of this poem is too deliberate to be swallowed without a grimace. The poet had a few trite precepts of which to deliver himself, and failed to make the pills palatable by poetic wrappings. The metre and necessary accentuations are awkward, and *no relief is offered by any sort of rime scheme.*

Still more severe upon the same point is 1·161 ; it is left to 1·162 to restore the balance.

1·161. Excellent prose but not good verse ; *not even smallest attempt at metre or rhyme.* Writer probably more of a philosopher than a poet : too matter-of-fact, too little Imagination and Fancy.

1·162. It is difficult to express one's attitude to this. The sentiment is very proper, but fails to rouse one to enthusiasm. What does the vague phrase " Spent as this is by nations of mankind ", mean ? And the construction from lines 4 to 7 is very clumsy. The thing could have been said five times more quickly—and would have been so in poetry. *This is prose, chopped up to fit a metrical scheme.* Contrast its rhetorical phrases with the concentration and fullness of No. 3.

An approach through comparisons is also made by 1·163 which is more introspective and shows more emancipation from the tyranny of the ' message '.

1·163. Reminded of the pitched-up movement or strong artificial accent of post-Elizabethans. But this is without their complexity of thought, especially shown in metaphor. Imitative. Here the movement becomes more reflective, less an experience ; a deliberate loading of rhythm—influence of the didactic pretentions. Wordsworth ? Spurious. Mid-Victorian poetic drama ? A collection of commonplace aphorisms on borrowed stilts. I accept the statements with indifference. It might have been written for a Calendar of Great Thoughts. Reading it aloud, I have to mouth it, and I felt ridiculously morally dignified.

Truth, of some kind, has hitherto been claimed or allowed by all, but more than one of the poet's assertions challenged a division.

1·17. On reading this my mind jumps up and disagrees— *if living is measured by intensity of feeling, cowards live as much as heroes.* Line 3 might be parodied with equal truth—

" One wounded feeling, one foul thought, one deed
    Of crime, ere night, would make life longer seem "—

The impression received was one of the self-satisfaction of the author (I do not say " poet ") :—a spinster devoted to good works, and sentimentally inclined, or perhaps Wordsworth.
Large query to the last line.

Why Wordsworth's name should be considered such a telling missile is uncertain.

Still more vigorous is dissent upon the temporal issue.

1·18. Finally I disagree entirely that " great thoughts ", " good deeds " or " noble feelings ", make life seem longer, personally I feel *they make it seem shorter.*

But there are some who refuse to let a little difference like this come between them and the poet.

1·181. This poem expresses for me just that view of the difference between existence and life which seems truest. I never can conceive of time as some measurement indicated " in figures on a dial ". Thought is the chief activity regarded as foolish or with complete indifference by *those with whom one comes in contact oftenest, i.e. " the small in soul ".* I do not speak in any bitterness but from my normal experience. It is this conclusion *to which I seem to be forced* which makes *such a stanza as this* seem to me to be fit to be ' shouted from the house tops '. That is why it appeals to me.

I do not agree however that " one great thought, one deed of good . . . would make life *longer* seem ", than it does to men each humdrum day, *but rather think " shorter " would express the idea better.* I may think of it in a special sense however, which would not appeal to most and which I should find it almost impossible to explain, and in any case metaphysics is banned. I am sorry, for the idea is always the chief joy to me in poetry.

I must have been responsible for the ban on metaphysics by some request that the protocols should deal with the poetry rather than with the Universe. The ' stanza ' remark may offset 1·16 and 1·161. The misanthropy finds a slight echo in 1·182 which again expresses doubt based on the facts of Temporal Perception ; but a balm for disillusionment is discovered by 1·183.

1·182. Good on the whole, though it is doubtful if life really seems longer to the good than to the wicked or to the merely passive.
The lines are worth reading twice because they really do express something instead of just drivelling on like those of number II.

1·183. Suggests Browning to me, and is more interesting for that reason. But there is in this piece a more all-round handling of the idea than Browning would have given it. It seems to be the product of *a man of middle age, who has taken the sweets of life and proved them mere vanity, but who has not turned cynic.* It is at once *healthy and profound.*

Browning figures again in 1·19, where Wordsworth has some amends made to him.

1·19. One thought clearly and forcibly expressed. Idea expressed in the first two lines, amplified in the next seven and finally summed up in the last two. Chief effect—*a familiar thought brought home with new conviction.* The rhythm of blank verse—restraint combined with even flow—expressive of the meditativeness and yet obvious truth of the idea. The passage reminiscent of the whole effort and accomplishment of the greatest poets, and in a secondary way of passages in Shakespeare, Shelley, Wordsworth, Browning, etc.

1·191. The thought a little obvious and *I don't find anything in the expression to drive it home.*

1·192. It is not a new thought, but *the symmetry and perfect meter* makes the old thought more impressive than if said in prose. The meter lends dignity, and makes it serious and profound.

After these jarring voices a more unanimous chorus will make a soothing close. It will be noticed that the central issue, the doctrinal aspect of the passage, becomes less and less prominent and that Mnemonic Irrelevances and the possibilities of Sentimentality take its place.

1·193. I don't know why, but as soon as I read it, I linked it somehow with that poem of Julian Grenfell's, " Into Battle ", and especially with this stanza, which immediately came into my mind.

> " The black-bird sings to him, Brother, brother,
>   If this be the last song you shall sing,
>   Sing well, for you may not sing another,
>   —Brother, sing."

I think this was suggested by " we shall count time by heart-throbs " once again. A phrase of Robert Lynd's also came into my mind " the great hours of life—hours of passionate happiness and passionate sorrow—". And I thought to myself " *how true that is*. These ARE the only hours in life that mean anything. Any why ? Because they lift one to the infinite . . . " *le silence éternel de ces espaces infinis m'effraie !* "

1·194. Appeals to me because it *sums up my creed* as a Socialist, *of service not self*. A further appeal lies in its emphasis of a fact we are too apt to forget, namely, that the real test of life is action and nobility of thought and feeling, not length of years. This amounts to a solemn warning, and as befits the solemnity of the theme the movement is wedded to the thought. The long line and the slow movement, rendered more impressive by the number of long vowels, *hammer the thought into the mind*.

But even the ' lofty ideal ' of the passage has its turn to be challenged.

1·195. This appeals ; not as a passion, not by sympathetic interests nor as beauty, but by its simple truth and teaching— a teaching which *seems to come from a fellow human being*, and one to which we may all attain. *There is no lofty ideal*, the regard of which makes us feel poor creatures and realise the impossibilities of perfection. True it may be judged sentimental if carefully dissected, but some amount of sentiment appeals naturally to the instincts of every one : what moral teaching is successful without some appeal to sentiment ? It is a call not to sense, nor to the soul but to the heart.

A Transatlantic smack[1] now makes itself unmistakably felt and continues through several extracts.

1·2. This is *fine*—a grand appeal to us to make our lives bigger, greater, more sublime, to put aside the petty and material interests which shut in our souls and *let forth our big and generous impulses*. It is an appeal to us to *live*, and not merely to exist, and this appeal culminates in a grand climax in the last two lines.

The superb luxuriance of the style in 1·21 has as characteristic a savour as the looser idioms of 1·22. Nor are the contents less significant in their rendering of one powerful trend of that western world.

1·21. It successfully catches the rythm of the human heart beat—the fundamental rythm of all music and of all poetry. The swing catches the heart and the emotions, *the thought leads the mind on to inspiration*. The more you read the verse the more the rythm and the theme, the two together, catch your soul and carry you completely in tune on to the end ; and you wish there were more.

Even the first reading takes you into its cadence and its spirit. It wears better with each succeeding reading that you really have concentrated òn.

It is *an inspirational bit*, yet full-blooded and perfectly conversant with life as it is in its sorrows, despairs, and its fulfilled and unfulfilled hopes. More than much poetry it has a taste of life—life as Shakespeare knew it and Hugo, not as Shelley or Keats, or a shallow modern novelist know it. In it is a punch, an energy and *the vigour of red-blooded manhood tinged with a deep tone* of " God's in his heaven, all's right with the world " *if you do your own fighting* to live your own full, rich life.

It surely has inspired something here !

1·22. Worldly ideals and philosophy run through it. It is modern, speaking of self-expression. *It says to self-express a full emotional and a rich intellectual life.*

It is clear in parts at first. Subsequent readings show subtlety as well as clarity.

Not poetic in comparison with the Romantic age, it being *too serious and too of the soil and the streetcar for the average romantic.*

[1] I cannot plume myself that my literary acumen alone is responsible for this perception. I have other evidence.

We go back now to English speech-rhythm, but the crescendo of praise does not flag.

1·3. After reading over this passage for the first time, I received one impression—" How much every one of those words *means*,— ordinary words they are, too, such as I myself probably use every day—' every rift loaded with ore' ". And then I read it again. And this impression deepened, and others arose. The vividness of the thing ! What a sure hand guided this pen . . . how strong it is ! And what a gradual rise to the glorious lifting of the veil in the last line but one " *we should count time by heart- throbs* ". The voice has risen for an instant to passion. And then it dies away, firm and masterful to the end.

From this high peak of admiration to the complete union of hearts, with all the appropriate trappings of a romantic attachment thrown in, is a mere *glissade*.

1·31. Yes, intensely. This is first rate. Why ? [in order].

(1) Curious way it suggests immediately great intimacy with the author. FRIENDSHIP. A room at night, curtains drawn, roaring log fire, chimney corner, author musing, old inns, you and him alone.

One of those rare and inexplicable moments which stand out as REAL in a world of phantasms. When your mind seems to touch another's, and you realise that far beyond our being brothers, we are all ONE person.

(2) Most loveable nobility [unconscious] to which I immediately respond.

(3) Artistic reasons

  a. Topping condensation of language. No vapid and ineffectual adjectives. Each word contains multitudes.

  b. Freedom and balance of lines. Like wonderful music.

Could the variety of the human garden be better displayed, even in the sunlight, than in this pot-pourri of academic lucubrations ?

With *Poem I* we have been concerned chiefly with

the problem of the 'message', the truth and worth
of the doctrine embodied in the poem. Discussion
of this general question of the place of 'messages'
and doctrines in poetry is postponed until Part III,
expecially Chapter VII. (The Index may also be
consulted.)   With *Poem II* we pass to a different
group of critical difficulties.

Gone were but the Winter,
    Come were but the Spring,
I would to a covert
    Where the birds sing.

Where in the whitethorn
    Singeth a thrush,
And a robin sings
    In the holly-bush.

Full of fresh scents
    Are the budding boughs
Arching high over
    A cool, green house.

Full of sweet scents,
    And whispering air
Which sayeth softly :
    " We spread no snare :

" Here dwell in safety,
    Here dwell alone,
With a clear stream
    And a mossy stone.

" Here the sun shineth
    Most shadily ;
Here is heard an echo
    Of the far sea,
        Though far off it be."

POEM II

THE adverse comments upon this poem show some interesting uniformities. One particular allegation recurs again and again like a refrain. A very widespread, well-inculcated presupposition may be suspected behind such a confident general agreement.

2·1. The writer has *only got to find twelve rhyming words* to express very trivial thoughts so why 'thrush', 'bush', 'boughs', 'house'.
Whole poem silly.

2·11. It has little merit—parts of it are deplorable.
The first two verses are quite attractive, and the rhyme 'thrush' with 'bush' is *almost bearable*. When 'boughs' and 'house' come next however, the attempt to enjoy the poem fails. There are not only poor rhymes, there is also much poverty of thought, and much real silliness in the poem.

Does this certainty that imperfect rhymes make a perfect indictment arise from any real pain they inflict upon readers' ears ? Or are the reasons for this contempt more subtle ?

2·12. The first 2 lines are not sense. I laughed at the rhyming of thrush and bush ; and boughs and house. *Reminds one quite pleasantly of the " poetry " one wrote when aged ten.*

Probably this brings us nearer to the true explanation. Reminders of our own poetic efforts, not only at the age of ten but even in years closer at hand, have an inevitable influence on our judgment, a useful influence when it keeps within its province, but dangerous when it meddles with matters beyond it. All but a very few beginners in verse find rhyming a great strain upon their verbal ingenuity and atten-

33

tion. Success or failure for the neophyte is very
largely a question of the control of rhymes. More
often than not the strain of finding rhymes and
fitting them together has been so intense that nothing
else has been genuinely attempted. It is probably
true, even of the best writers, that

> Rimes the rudders are of verses
> By which, like ships, they steer their courses,

but most people's first voyages, in command, are
made in vessels that are all rudder, and they fre-
quently retire from the trade before this stage has
been passed. An exaggerated respect for rhyming
ability is the result, and a tendency to great severity
towards verses in which the poet, if concerned only
with making his rhymes perfect, could be charged
with partial unsuccess. That the poet may have had
other, more difficult and more important, tasks in
hand is easily overlooked. And that he could possibly
have *intended* only a partial rhyme, and have pre-
ferred it to a full one, is too bewildering a thought to
be entertained.

Another strong motive for the avidity with which
imperfect rhymes are fastened upon is the desire for
something tangible by which to judge poetic merit.
Normal sensibilities can decide with considerable
certainty whether two sounds rhyme perfectly or
not. The task is nearly as simple as that of a car-
penter measuring planks. It is a grateful relief to
pass from the nebulous world of intellectual and
emotional accordances to definite questions of sensory
fact. By assuming that the poet intended to rhyme
perfectly, we get a clear unambiguous test for his
success or failure. The assumption need not be
explicit and usually is not, but the temptation to
entertain it is very comprehensible.

Details of scansion, opportunities for grammatical
objection, for allegations of descriptive inaccuracy,

for charges of logical inconsistency, share this attraction. To put the point generally, all those features which can be judged without going *into* the poem, all details or aspects that can be scrutinised by the mind in its practical, every - hour, non-poetical capacity, are so many invitations to make short work of the task of critical appraisement. Instead of trying the poem on, we content ourselves with a glance at its lapels or its buttons. For the details are more easily perceived than the *ensemble*, and technical points seem more obtrusive than the point of the whole.

The following extracts may perhaps be considered to illustrate these remarks :—

2·2. I think this is utterly absurd. Sentiment utter rubbish. Poet not in love with nature—merely fed up with life. Idea of peace CAN be made attractive, but *this is a wish for a lazy and " secure " life* rather than a longing for peace.

Who has ever seen a " green " house, or seen the sun shine shadily ?

Why *bring in a line at the end*, to upset, what is at its best but a jingle of a metre, when the whole thing has been said in the preceding line ?

Idea of living with a mossy stone singularly unattractive.

The sternness of the opening finds its complement in a later extract (2·8) ; and some—clearly much needed—elucidations of the ' cool green house' are given in 2·6.

The cavils continue :—

2·21. Green houses not usually cool, though I suppose they might be if anyone was foolish enough to erect them under arches of budding boughs.

What does the air mean when it sayeth softly we spread no snare. What are we ?

The charge of descriptive inaccuracy now spreads to the robin's song, though ' most shadily ' continues to prove a particularly tough morsel to assimilate.

2·22. Full of mistakes. Firstly it is nonsense : moreover it is trite and not " inspired nonsense ". *How can the sun shine " most shadily " ?* Set out to be natural and fresh and has become commonplace and ridiculous. *Though no ornithologist, do robins sing ?* The metre is sing-songy and *the rhymes* such as " boughs " and " house " and " shadily " and " the sea " *require a lot of imagination.* The addition of the 5th line in the last stanza though permissible seems uncalled for.

2·23. First reading produced a feeling of irritation at having to read such silly stuff because it was so senseless. One feels that the poem is meant to be one of musical simplicity and the peace of nature. But in effect it is silly as it is very slight in thought and hideously worded. To begin a poem with such a line as " Gone were but the Winter " gives the show away. Rhymes such as " boughs " and " house " grate on one's ear. When you look into it it is hardly sense, *how can the sun shine shadily ?* and *who wants to live with a mossy stone anyway ?*

2·24. Trivial. Commonplace idea. Ambiguity of the idea of budding boughs arched over a *cool green house.*
In the last verse the phrase " Here the sun shineth most shadily " is stupid and also ambiguous in meaning. *The sun cannot shine shadily, it can only cause shadows to be cast ;* besides, the term " most shadily " might mean that the sun is ashamed of shining when perhaps it had no right to do so.

Grammar has its turn.

2·25. A very light set of verses of very little merit. *The rhyming is poor—e.g.* thrush and bush, boughs and house—and the construction of the whole thing is extremely weak.
The verbs are used badly—e.g. " Singeth a thrush ", but " Sings a robin ",—and *the grammar of verse 4 is quite obscure ;* if, as apparently is the case, both the scents and the air say, " We spread no snare "—obviously " sayeth " is incorrect. How, *again,* can the sun shine shadily ? Altogether, a very slight, futile example.

The ' message ' question (what the poem *says*), also a comparatively external consideration, is noticed in 2·3, which puts forward a devastating view of literary history.

2·3. This poem might have been pleasing to the reading public a few hundred years ago, but *to-day I can see little reason why it should be read, except for historical interest.* It is simple, almost

childish, without being charming. The riming of " boughs "
with " house " is distinctly irritating, *as is a fifth line* on the last
verse. It is rambling, discursive, and *says nothing that matters.*
But there is melody and rhythm, which redeem it slightly.

Moral qualms similar to those in 2·2 appear in
2·4 and 2·41. Such just remarks upon ' make-
believe ' may seem to owe their application here to
Mnemonic irrelevance as much as to Stoicism.

2·4. Communication extraordinarily successful. Experience
most pleasant and refreshing *and consolatory : the last makes
indulgence seem rather childish and cowardly.* Make-believe has
its after-effect of increasing rather than decreasing present dis-
content. To make this experience an end in itself is to ignore
our responsibility to society, etc. etc. and sacrifice the latter
half of life, while temporarily to indulge is mental " dope."
Doubtful whether I like it or not owing to an unfortunate
dislike of the trifling. Pleasure never a strong influence (in
literature).

It seems a pity that this severe critic should be
throwing away such valuable views. May they help
and support some other earnest student, such an
one as the next writer, for example :

2·41. The passage is obviously intended to possess lyrical
simplicity. *Assonance, rather than strict metre,* is used to heighten
effect of simplicity. I may appreciate the poem better in a lighter
moment. A more serious subject fits better my serious working
mood.

The assonance suggestion is probably an attempt
to meet such strictures on the rhymes as we have
noticed above.

It is slightly surprising, in view of the subject-
matter of the poem, that mnemonic irrelevance did
not have more play. One writer was on his guard.

2·5. I fear I am not an impartial judge, as the lines inevitably
associate themselves with a scene and experience which I value.

Its influence elsewhere in the protocols is so great
that mere caution hardly explains its absence. More
probably the explanation is the extreme difficulty so

many writers found in reading (rendering) it so as to yield them any satisfaction. An extremely illuminating account of this difficulty is given in 2·6, a document of capital importance for understanding the reception of this poem.

2·6. An interesting example of the difference made by reading the same poem in different ways. In reading this, one must not let the rhythm become too square-cut. If one does, *the whole thing becomes jerky and amateurish :* one accentuates faults of scansion, and throws *emphasis upon the wrong words.* I read this three times. The first two times, I gave it four accents or three to each line :

> Fúll of frésh scénts,
> Aŕe the búdding boúghs.
> Aŕching hígh óvér,
> A coól greén hoúse,

But this is certainly wrong : it should be

> Fúll of fresh scénts
> Are the búdding boúghs,
> Aŕching high óver
> A coól green hoúse.

This is faster, lighter : it goes with a swing. It reminds one of Morris' lines for his bed-hangings :

> Rest then and rest
> And think of the best,

or however they go. Read like this, the poem is a light little thing, without indeed much intellectual appeal, but expressing certainly the pleasant feeling of joy and peace one feels in the spring. Read heavily, the poem would disgrace some boys of 14 : the scansion is faulty—alternating wildly between 4 feet and 3 : the rhymes (*e.g.* thrush and bush) atrocious. *The sense suffers too :* e.g.

> " *Wíth* a cléar stream
> *Ańd* a móssy stóne.

(instead of

> " With a cleár stream,"
> etc.)

is silly : it suggests the poet saying : " Here, yoü'd better take a stream too : yes, *and* a stone." Again, *with the accent thrown off* " *green,*" *in the 3rd stanza, one is less likely to be worried by thoughts of* " *greenhouses* ", or alternatively (which is worse), of houses of brick and mortar, painted that blatant shade of bright green which is so distressing. *The " cool green house " is of course the place under the trees.* The important points are (1) that it is cool (2) that it is like a house. But if one accentuates " green," these are just the points which do not stand out.

How widely renderings of the same poem may differ is demonstrated by 2·61, where a reply to the earnest student (2·4) is also suggested.

2·61. In writing these lines the author is carried along by *a deep passion for real life, as distinct from mere existence.* The depth of his feeling expresses itself in *the breathless, tumultuous music of the whole.*

Very detailed analyses of correspondences between sound and sense are perhaps always open to suspicion ; but 2·7 is persuasive as well as subtle, and 2·71 does seem to be recording rather than inventing.

2·7. This poem is full of the most delicate changes of metre. There are two accents in every line, but they are so changed about, and the unstressed syllables are so varied in position and number, that there are scarcely any two lines alike.
The vowels are also well arranged.

> " Arching high over
> A cool green house."

The sudden transition to the long i sound gives an impression of height in the arch, set off by the broader vowels on either side.
The whispering air is perfectly expressed by the repeated s's in verse 4.
The echo is wonderfully suggested in the last verse by the quiet additional last line, and by the fact that the third line is an exact metrical repetition of the first line of the first verse. I like " *here the sun shineth, most shadily* ". *It is at once suggestive and concise.*

2·71. The sincerity and spontaneity of this lyric might be contrasted with the muddled sentimentality of IV. *In its own rather tiny way,* it is quite exquisite. One feels the delicate movement of the rhythm as it changes from the clear fine tone of the 3rd and 4th verses to the gravity and steadiness of the last two. The corresponding shift in vowel values might be noticed—the deepening effect given by the long ' a's ' and ' o's.' The adjectives are chosen with a full regard for their emotive

value—in particular,, " mossy stone " which at once produces the
intended atmosphere of quietness and uninterrupted peace.

In the last remark a reminiscence of the principles
of Japanese gardening might be respected. ' Its
own rather tiny way ' supplements the impression.
   With this fine balance and sense of proportion 2·8
may be contrasted.

> 2·8. No thoughts whatever would come to me until I had
> committed these verses to memory. Then I saw that the words
> and the subject were simple enough, *but underneath* lay some-
> thing which I cannot define. It seems to be unutterable sadness,
> the cry of a sensitive heart, betrayed by someone it trusted.
> (Perhaps Tess felt like this). The kindness and solace in nature
> appears to be emphasized, in contrast to the cunning and the
> strife of men. The sound of the echo of the sea seems to me to
> be necessary to make such a scene complete, as it gives a soothing
> sense of the vastness of nature all round us, *that we are not*
> *alone, that there is someone above us, greater and wiser and stronger*
> *than we.* It reminds me of " The Forsaken Merman ".

There may in fact have been something of this in
the poet's mind ; yet, even were it so, we could
hardly put this reader's divination down to anything
but accident.
   To step back too far from a poem, to pay too little
attention to its actual detail, to allow thoughts and
feelings to wander off into a development of their
own may be as mistaken a method as the most
captious selection of details. But 2·7 and 2·71 will
show, if it needed showing, that the closest scrutiny
of details is compatible with the fullest, fairest and
most discriminating appraisal of the whole. Indeed,
the two inevitably go together. The sovereign
formula in all reading is that we must pass to judg-
ment of details from judgment of the whole. It is
always rash and usually disastrous to reverse the
process.
   The following description of this poet's work by
the late Sir Walter Raleigh will be of interest : ' Full

of that beautiful redundance and that varied re-iteration which are natural to all strong feeling and all spontaneous melody . . . the expression rising unsought, with incessant recurrence to the words or phrases given at first, with a delicate sense of pattern which prescribes the changes in the cadence.'

At the round earth's imagined corners blow
Your trumpets, angels, and arise, arise
From death, you numberless infinities
Of souls, and to your scattered bodies go ;
All whom the flood did, and fire shall o'erthrow,
All whom war, dearth, age, agues, tyrannies,
Despair, law, chance hath slain, and you, whose eyes
Shall behold God, and never taste death's woe.
But let them sleep, Lord, and me mourn a space ;
For, if above all these my sins abound,
'Tis late to ask abundance of Thy grace,
When we are there. Here on this lowly ground,
Teach me how to repent, for that's as good
As if Thou hadst seal'd my pardon with Thy blood.

POEM III

BETWEEN the bare apprehension of the literal sense of a passage and the full comprehension of all its meanings in every kind, a number of half-way houses intervene. To ascertain, even roughly, where failure has occurred is, in many cases, beyond our power. Innumerable cat and mouse engagements between some investigator of the acumen and pertinacity of Freud and a string of hapless ' patients ' would be needed to make plain even the outlines of the process that we so glibly call ' grasping or realising a meaning '. That the final stages are very sudden and surprising in their effects is nearly all that is known about it.

The failures to grasp the meaning which are the impressive feature of our third set of protocols are, therefore, not easy to range in order. Inability to construe may have countless causes. Distractions, preconceptions, inhibitions of all kinds have their part, and putting our finger on the obstructing item is always largely guesswork. The assumption, however, that stupidity is not a simple quality, such as weight or impenetrability were once thought to be, but an effect of complex inhibitions is a long stride in a hopeful direction. The most leaden-witted blockhead thereby becomes an object of interest.

Hazardous though this guesswork be, some of the writers supply hints which are too tempting not to be followed up.

3·1. I confess immediately that I can't make out what all the shouting is about. The poem is completely confusing. The numerous pronouns and adverbs mix up the thought, if indeed there is one definite thought throughout.

I don't like Shakespearean sonnets, I mean that form, as a rule, *so it is particularly annoying to have " good " and " blood " rime.* The first two lines are vigorous and imaginative, but the list of *oppressions of God*, Man, and Nature is a huge mental obstacle in reading this sonnet. But the confusion in thought has failed to establish, in the reader, communication, and even comprehension.

The prejudice against the alleged Shakespearean form, or rather against the couplet as a close, is hardly sufficient as an explanation, though his over-looking the form of the octave argues some strength in it. His pounce on the rhymes was at most a slight distraction. A better hint comes from his use of the word ' oppressions '. The *parti pris* that this suggests is indicated more clearly in 3·11 and may very possibly be responsible for a considerable proportion of the failures.

3·11. I can connect this stanza with nothing which has or does appeal to me. And where is " there " ? *There is or can be no condition as to whether any sin whatever will " abound " over the fearful damage* which war, dearth, chance, age and all the other tyrannies may have *inflicted upon the soul.* A man who sins repents : but *what cause has that man to repent, who is the victim of those scourges here enumerated?*

I suppose, really, I do not understand the lines, and certainly wish they had some context, some ' co-ordinates ' which might furnish an invaluable clue.

A doctrinal grudge is clearly apparent here however little luck the writer may have had in making his objection precise. And we shall probably not be wrong in tracing his misreading to his grudge, rather than the other way about. Something more than a surprising unfamiliarity with the elements of the Christian religion seems to be needed to explain the query " Where is ' there ' ? " As a speculation, no more, a paralysing influence from an anti-religious reaction seems a permissible hypothesis. That its victim was unaware of this seems to be indicated by

his desire for a context. The odd failure to recognise
the sonnet form is found again in 3.15.
The localisation of ' there ' baffles more apprecia-
tive readers.

3·12. The first four lines of the extract are impressive. The
" round earth's imagined corners " is a pretty conceit and appeals
by its apparent contradiction, while " numberless infinities "
conveys very well, the idea of the immensity of life's history.
Lines 5–8 lapse into *a matter of fact, cold-blooded, catalogue* of
the various possible ways of meeting a violent end. The sixth
line is particularly irksome. The rest of the poem is not too
coherent. The phrase " When we are there " is *extremely
mystifying*, and "*that's as good*" *hardly fits in with solemn,
religious tone of the piece.*

This perhaps tells against our hypothesis of an
anti-religious prejudice. None the less the descrip-
tion of the ' catalogue ' as ' cold-blooded ', the in-
ability to realise it, almost amounting to a refusal,
and the demand for the intimate, colloquial ' that's
as good ' to be replaced by some less actual and im-
mediate phraseology are suggestive. Among ideas
that the mind might be loath to come too near to,
that of the Judgment may well claim a place.

Some slight corroboration may perhaps be seem in
the easy patronage which another writer extends.

3·13. The sudden change from the fine tang of the first lines
to the simplicity of the last is effective, but the long strings of
monosyllables are ugly, and the fifth line is inexcusable while
the sense is not altogether clear. It is difficult to share the poet's
attitude, because although he is evidently sincere, his technique
is bad. *The lines do, however, in spite of this express the simple
faith of a very simple man.*

Contempt is a well-recognised defensive reaction.
This ' unconscious fright' hypothesis must not
be overworked however. Two extracts in which
the distaste for the doctrine present is avowed will
round the matter off. The second is more remark-
able as an astonishing example of the power of stock
responses.

3·14. A poem of this kind needs perfection. If not, enumerations as " war, dearth, age . . ." cannot but bore. Gloomy poems must express deep thoughts or give a harmonious feeling of melancholy not only a feeling of fear and discomfort else they are a failure.

3·15. Mouthfuls of words. Has no appeal whatsoever. Make a good hymn—in fact, that's the way the metre goes.
Too religious for one who doesn't believe in repenting that way.

That a stock response, elicited merely by the religious subject-matter, should be able to make a sonnet sound like a hymn is a fact that surely stretches our notions of the mind's power over matter.

A nervous reader offers a too simple excuse for his failure to grasp the meaning.

3·2. The first effect of this poem is *confusion of the mind, owing to the clamorous vigour of the first half.* The second half is quiet and effective and this effect is obtained largely by its contrast with the beginning. None the less the first half is rather oppressive, such a line as " all whom the flood did and fire shall o'erthrow " being superfluous.

A moral objection to the poet's attitude, which appears in 3·3, 3·31 and 3·32, may be allowed more occulting power.

3·3. The first line is stimulating—" the round earth's imagined corners " is associated in my mind with some great poem—does the idea come from somewhere in Paradise Lost ?" But the first 8 lines of the sonnet seem to have nothing to do with the last 6—the only connection being between the number of souls to be resurrected and the number of the writer's sins, which seems irrelevant. *It is irritating to think of the " numberless infinities of souls " being aroused only to be put to sleep again while the writer repents*—he doesn't even tell us anything about his sins to make it interesting. I noticed " whose eyes . . . shall never taste death's woe " on my third reading and when " we are there ", instead of when " I am there." More irritating every time I look at it.

3·31. There is nothing particularly poetic in the passage, it doesn't move me as poetry ought to, *it lies flat like the speaker.*

3·32. This ought to have a most terrific effect : in one sonnet we have compressed the two huge subjects of the Day of Judgment, and the Redemption of the world by Christ. But somehow the poem does not raise as much emotion as one feels it ought to have raised. I think this is because it seems to progress downwards from greater emotion to less. First one has the terror of the Judgment Day : then one has *what is really a selfish fright on the part of the writer, that he personally may be damned.*

But it is a considerable achievement to have dealt with these two subjects at all within the narrow limits of one sonnet.

Having tried unsuccessfully to write sonnets myself, I have a perhaps abnormal admiration for sonnet-writers. Had this not been so, I think I would in the end have said that this sonnet was bad.

Technical presuppositions, by destroying the movement of the verse and so precluding the emotional links from developing, certainly co-operated in producing miscomprehension and negative judgments.

3·4. Difficult to ' get '—either sound or sense—almost indistinguishable from blank verse at first reading—sonnet form unperceived till second reading.

Short, sharp, jerky syllables in

'. . . war, dearth, age, agues, tyrannies,
Despair, law, chance . . .

do not at all suit the sonnet form or the majesty which the subject calls for in its choice of a mode of expression. *Thought-sequence obscure,* and *the condensation in the fifth line of the octet is ugly both as regards rhythm and harmony.*

The sharp and jerky way in which he read these lines probably prevented him from taking in their sense. This poet is perhaps the slowest mover in English literature and here the trumpets are still blowing right down to ' taste death's woe '. The ' condensation ' complained of is, most likely, only his name for ignorance of Christian cosmology. The same ignorance helps to frustrate the next writer.

3·41. Vigorous but obscure, particularly vigorous in the first five lines and particularly obscure thereafter. Who is or are " you, whose eyes shall behold God, and never taste death's woe ". *The last two lines lack the forcefulness so desirable at the close of a sonnet.* The list in lines 6 and 7 is tedious and *the rhymes are not perfect.*

A reader unacquainted with the rules for attendance at the Day of Judgment next claims our interest.

3·42. The invocation contained in the octet seems to be rather out of relation to the sextet, which is presumably the main part of the poem. *Why invoke all those spirits more than others?* Merely because the idea of death is in the front of the man's mind. The sextet expresses an idea which is not uncommon, and does so in a rather unsatisfactory, unconvincing way. Although I don't think I like the thing, I find something striking and even puzzling about it.

Sonority in the octet and quietness in the sextet are obviously indicated ; and *obviously it slows down* and stumbles towards the end.

The same expectation that a sonnet should conform to some foreordained movement affected 3·43

3·43. The first impression I received from this passage was the thought " Rather pedestrian verse. Halting rhythm. Somehow it lets you down ". And this impression was only deepened by further consideration. *I felt that the writer had aimed at a high mark, but that the arrow had fallen short. He achieves loftiness and dignity for the first four lines, but no further.* For then, I thought, *a certain monotony creeps in.* There is an *abundance of monosyllables and of trivial words,* whose very triviality becomes evident by the failure to heighten them *in the same manner* as he has done in the opening four lines, namely by a noble rhythm and a deep, quiet music.

In the next extract this velleity is exalted to mania.

3·44. After repeated reading, I can find no other reaction except disgust, perhaps because I am very tired as I write this. *The passage seems to be a rotten sonnet written in a very temperamental kind of iambic pentameter. Not even by cruel forcing and beating the table with my fingers can I find the customary five iambic feet to the verse ;* the feet are frequently not iambic, and there are sometimes four, and even six accented syllables to the verse. In structure the passage sounds like the first labors of a school boy. Particularly displeasing are verses 5, 6, and 7. Yet the idea seems really worth while.

This is the first time that we have met the scansion enthusiast. We shall have more to do with his fellows later.

Inexperience, lack of familiarity (in spite of the reference to Milton) with any but very simple verse movements is probably behind 3·5 and 3·51.

3·5. The passage has a miltonic ring, and shows the usual miltonic devices (cf. vv. 6, 7, where we get a list of human woes strung together to give the verses a heavy slow movement). Quite an ordinary piece of versification, neither striking nor inspiring.

3·51. The first point about this sonnet, which seems most obvious is that it could have been written quite, if not more, effectively in prose. Rhythm seems to be lacking.

In contrast 3·6 provides us with a neat little object lesson.

3·6. I like *the grand Reveille* of the first 6½ lines. I appreciate *the gentle sadness* of the last 7½, and the contrast, but all the same it disappoints me, *I prefer feeling martial*. The promise and the beginning fizzles out.
I should never bother about the sense ; the sound is enough for me.

He goes very far, as far perhaps as he can get, by the purely sensuous approach. The relation of the second part to the first can only be given by the sense, and missing the sense he mistakes the feeling of the opening. 'Martial' is hardly an apt description. His neglect of the sense is perhaps not unconnected with his jejune preference.

3·7. It is impressive—but leaves no very clear impression there are no pictures in it.

The frustrated visualiser is here not a very sympathetic figure. Those who want pictures in their poems must put them in themsleves. There is nothing in this sonnet to prevent Stanley Spencer from doing with it what he pleases.

After so many grumblings three tributes from readers who seem to have understood the poem may come not amiss. That they are not so rich or glowing as in the case of some of the other poems may not amount to a slight upon this sonnet. It is in the

D

nature of some performances that they leave the spectator feeling rather helpless.

3·8. An interesting fragment. ' The round earth's imagined corners ' annoying at the first reading—but if this is a quotation from the Bible everything is all right.

Contrast good between whole of first and second part. Also a most effective change from ' all whom war, dearth, age, agues, tyrannies, etc. ; and ' you whose eyes Shall behold God, and never taste death's woe '. Here there is a mixed metaphor and it doesn't seem to matter much. The theme of the passage lifts one above such a difficulty. *There is a certain humour and a very human interest about these lines.*

The poetic part of this reader's mind probably supplied the ' who shall ' before ' never ' which un-mixes the metaphor, though his commentator part stepped in afterwards to muddle him.

3·81. Has the power of a trumpet in the first eight lines. Is an impassioned outburst, and cannot be read calmly. Note the crescendo in the sixth line ending with the shrill ' tyrannies.' In the sestet, the voice is lowered, the poet's desire for a revelation changes to a sense of humility.

3·82. If the ' sweet slipping ' movement of rhythm to express a chance mood is the characteristic excellence of No. 2 that of No. 3 is the marshalling and management of large ideas within the restrictions of poetic form. The first 5 lines sweep up in increasing intensity, to culminate in the shattering list of destructions—and then, masterly done, comes the pause, with the accent on the first word of the line—' Bút ' and *the whole thing quietens off to the level pitch of sanity and humour.* Of these four pieces, this alone has the power and assurance of the poet who knows what it is that he has to say, and its value.

There was rapture of spring in the morning
When we told our love in the wood.
For you were the spring in my heart, dear lad,
And I vowed that my life was good.

But there's winter now in the evening,
And lowering clouds overhead,
There's wailing of wind in the chimney-nook
And I vow that my life lies dead.

For the sun may shine on the meadow lands
And the dog-rose bloom in the lanes,
But I've only weeds in my garden, lad,
Wild weeds that are rank with the rains.

One solace there is for me, sweet but faint,
As it floats on the wind of the years,
A whisper that spring is the last true thing
And that triumph is born of tears.

POEM IV

I⊤ is sometimes convenient to regard a poem as a
mental prism, capable of separating the mingled
stream of its readers into a number of distinguish-
able types. Some poems—the last, for example—
merely scatter or throw back a large proportion of
the intellectual-moral light that is applied to them.
Others, of which *Poem IV* is a notable example, are
transparent ; and, since they have, as it were, a high
refractive index, they perform their analytic function
to perfection. They split up the minds which en-
counter them into groups whose differences may be
clearly discerned. And the reasons for these differ-
ences may sometimes be made out with assurance.

Here the divergent groups formed are two in
number, and, apart from some minor complexities
not at all difficult to explain, the principle of division
is shown quite clearly.

4·1. Absolute tripe.
Frightfully hackneyed in conception.
" Pretty " suits it best. On a par with the adjective " nice "
applied as a standard of character.
It's a *sham*. Sentimentality recollected in very sentimental
tranquillity. *If the girl's life indeed lay dead* she would *not* write
like that. Why, *she's thoroughly enjoying herself—more than
I am*. Not one tear in the whole piece. It's PSEUDO, it
PRETENDS, its values are worthless. False coin. Low, mimic,
stuff.

4·11. A sigh—a great sigh, despairing and tremulous. That
is what these lines seem to mean. The sigh though is put into
words and these seem to convey to us *a sense of some ineffable
sorrow*, too deep for words. Blighted hopes which seemed in
the spring so rapturous now have sunk into the hopelessness—

the utter hopelessness of the words " And I vow that my life lies— dead."

It is the very fact that *the words are so quiet and yet hopeless* that lends such a poignancy to it.   No passionate utterance but a stony blank grief.   And yet despite this in the last stanza a faint trembling hope is put forth *and this must be so for* " hope springs eternal in the human breast ".

Above all in this piece one feels a keen sense, as it were, of some *deserted ruins*, stark and bare, the wind moaning, the sky lowering and a *vivid sense of decayed splendour*.

Not too often is the adage so beautifully illustrated. One man's meat *is* another man's poison.

4·12. An invitation to a debauch which one can hardly claim credit for declining.

4·13. This is a fine poem written with deep, emotional feeling and a choice of words that is only possible for the genuine poet. The melancholy power of the whole is transformed into something greater by *the inspiring* and *courageous thought* of the last verse.

The very features which are the worst offence to one group are the poem's crowning glory to the other. The critical maxim ' When in doubt reflect whether the most glaring fault is not the prime virtue, and *vice versa* ', could hardly receive a better practical recommendation.

The antiphony continues.   Those for whom the assurance given above is insufficient to guarantee the authenticity of the protocols will certainly accuse me of over-reaching myself at this point.   But not a syllable has been added or changed.

4·14. This is such poor stuff that it hardly is worth the trouble of criticizing.   *The rhythm is a meaningless jog-trot*, which *doesn't* vary or change with any change of feeling.   The metaphors are taken from the usual hackneyed and most obvious forms of Nature, not always even appropriate, as in stanza 3.   *Sentimentality* takes the place of feeling, and *falls to the limit of bathos* in the last verse.   It has the *true cheap-magazine tone*.

But the next writer is so persuaded to the contrary that he is able to certify the absent one's affections.

4·15. There is nothing of silly sentimentalism in the lines but they show the love of one true heart for another.

4·16. This piece alone of all the four got me straight away. It is very effective indeed—obviously sincere and very pleasant to read. The theme, though somewhat obvious is one that can never be hackneyed, especially when so originally and pleasantly treated as in this case. The ending is very good and strong which always is a great point. It has *a lilt* in it which is *very pleasant when reading provided it is not overdone*.

Such exact correspondence of opposing views is strong testimony to the poem's communicative efficiency. It is indeed extraordinarily successful in ' getting there.' Sometimes when widely different views are expressed we receive the impression that, through some twist or accident in communication, different poems are being judged. But here it is evident enough that the same poem (the same primary modification of consciousness) has penetrated into these different minds. It is at a *comparatively* late stage of the response that the divergence begins.

Thanks to this, perhaps, some of the most famous critical *dicta* gain an interesting corroboration. The identity, or rather the close connection, of content with form, for example. I may quote Matthew Arnold : " The superior character of truth and seriousness, in the matter and substance of the best poetry, is inseparable from the superiority of diction and movement marking its style and manner. The two superiorities are closely related, and in steadfast proportion to one another." From both sides of the gulf this steadfast proportion between superiorities (and inferiorities) is pointed out with equal confidence.

4·2. *Really first-rate.* The technique in particular is *very good*. One notices particularly *the alliterations, e.g.* " Wild weeds that are rank with the rains." Again, the double rhyme in the last line but one is very effective : it suddenly makes the thing more cheerful. One also notices the way in which various *details are symbolical*. *The " rains " suggest tears*, to take only one example. In the last line but one, the poet is of course thinking that death is after all only the beginning of another life. But *it is, of course, by the emotion in it that one must judge a poem*. The emotion in this poem is strong and sincere.

4·21. Reminds me of Australian Bush ballads. *Has little meaning and no musical value.* A mere jingling rime, in which words are chosen carelessly. ' Life lies dead ' is nonsense. Too many unaccentuated short words ; hence slurring necessary in reading. One expects ' trala ', and repetition of last line of each verse.

In cooler, more distant praise, the conventional abstract classification of the content matches well with the routine description of the form.

4·22. Here is *a pleasant, melodious lyric*, with *love interest* and *philosophy*. The *antithetical effects* are well achieved ; the repetition of " weeds " in the third verse is an excellent touch, as is the internal riming in the third line of the fourth verse. The poem has *a swing and lilt to it* which make it delightful reading. It is *altogether well constructed* and successful.

The exercise of imaginatively realising the responses of the next two readers, pondering them, and the poem with them, until each seems the only possible response, may be recommended. A few Jekyll and Hyde transformations from the one into the other and back again, will be found instructive.

4·23. Few things are more disgusting than *cheap emotion* expressed in easy tears. No. 4 speaks of a " triumph born of tears " and apparently wishes to express a long and painful struggle. If the triumph, and the tears and the passing years are linked together only because at a first glance they seem to have a pathetic significance and a vaguely poetical and romantic effect (and surely " rapture of spring," " love in the wood," vows, lowering clouds, wailing winds, dog roses and rank weeds are *the conventional trappings and catchwords of romance*). No. 4 merits nothing but contempt. *If the writer were actuated by intense feeling* surely he was *deplorably misguided* to choose as his medium of expression *a regular fluent metre, cant phrases and obvious rhymes*. The rhymes seem to have a great influence over the sense : in line 15 " thing " means exactly nothing but it rhymes with spring so there it is. Finally *the easy antitheses*— spring and winter, roses and weeds etc. is fatal to any hope of real feeling behind the verses, and without sincerity poetry is an impossibility.

4·24. The simplicity of this poem contrasts with the empty-headedness of 2. Here ordinary words and images are used to celebrate *the most elemental passion*—love, and to express *faith in the comforting philosophy so well known* by the last line of Shelley's Ode to the West Wind " If Winter comes, can Spring be far behind ? " The metaphors are apt, and although not complicated, they carry such a train of suggestions as must appeal to the most prosaic person. The third verse contains a flood of pathos, emphasized by *an admirable contrast*, and the line " floats on the wind of years " reveals that genius for expression which is one of the most important characteristics of a great poet (as distinguished from a clever versifier).

It will be seen that what is usually described as a ' difference in taste ' may have inexhaustible implications ; whole orders of moral and intellectual perceptions and discriminations flash into view or blur out and fade as we pass from the view of one writer to that of the other. And what crudities must each writer not recognise in the other ! We should remember that these sorts of differences are in the background *always*, even *e.g.*, in 4·22.

But where are we, and where is our personality, amid such dizzying kaleidoscopic transformations of the moral world ? We may perhaps steady ourselves a little with 4·25, which is rather more objective and has opinions upon pretence, upon love, and upon vowing.

4·25. Conveys a uniformly artificial impression—verse has no adequate volume of sound to impart a strong emotion and no cadences to express a deep one, *such as is pretended to be conveyed.* Altogether too jaunty an effect, with a most annoyingly regular jig-jigging rhythm. *Sentimentality mistaken for the deeper passion of love—One does not*

   ' vow that my life lies dead '

in quite such a perfunctory way.

Opinions about the technique of the poem and opinions about its goal or final effect here hang together with a rare fidelity ; and if it were desired to prove, for example, that the way in which the *rhythm* of words is received is not independent of the emotional response which their sense excites, such evidence as this should not be overlooked. But these theoretical developments may be postponed to a later page (Part III, Chapter IV).

One dissentient upon this point demands inclusion ; but the ' subject ' here spoken of is something quite remote from the ' content,' ' matter ' or ' substance ' which we have been considering. The ' subject ' here is the content regarded abstractly and from a distance. (Part III, Chapter VI, p. 263.)

4·26. The subject is serious but the treatment childishly and forcedly simple and they don't fit in with each other. It has degenerated into mere sentimentality, the use of the word " lad " in a serious way now sounds out of place and " wild weeds rank with the rains " are all right on a rubbish heap but not in writing.

The appearance of the word ' lad ' had other consequences.

4·27. Perfect adaptation of rhythm and sound to meaning. Why is there such an appeal in the poetry of dejection ? Probably the answer is partly in the last two lines and partly in the fact that it is *an easy experience to get* and *common to all. It is rather like A. E. Housman, but better than most of his, because there is less of the morbid despairing of dejection* in it, and *none of the macabre.* It leaves no final impression of sadness, but of greatness.

The same rash inference from ' lad ' was responsible for 4·26. It is perhaps not unnatural to feel some regret that one was not present at some of the discussions alluded to.

4·28. This must be from " A Shropshire Lad " or " Last Poems " *though I cannot place it exactly.* The most pleasing to me of the four. *Excellent lyrical form*—a single idea arousing a single emotion that rises rapidly to the climax of the last two verses. Rhythm so pleasing that I have read and re-read solely for that. *Pleasing melancholy because it gives one the safe " luxury of grief " second-hand.* The singing quality and the unexpected internal rhyme of the last verse but one are decidedly effective. This verse is my particular reason for liking the lyric. It *expresses with greater skill than I have ever before found an idea which I have long held and discussed with many people.*

The attribution to Housman allowed this reader to indulge also in the ' safe ' luxury of ' correct ' praise.

To offset one of the best points made in 4·1 the opinion of 4·3 may be cited.

4·3. There is *something very real* about the atmosphere of these lines. Here is a kind of naive rural simplicity, as if the lines are actually *uttered from the heart of a country maid.* Possibly this is suggested by the metre, which is to a certain extent dactylic. It is difficult to express just how the verses obtain their effect, but these lines " find " their reader more easily than the other extracts.

The metrical suggestion does not much illumine the problem. Both points are taken further by 4·31. It is disconcerting to find him hedging, a tendency very little shown in this set of protocols.

4·31.   Tum, *túm* ti ti *Túm* titi Túm ti
              Ti *túm* ti ti *túm* titi *túm*——

This makes me feel ribald—it seems so silly—worse than a barrel-organ (which has a beauty of its own).

Surely *sorrow and loneliness are not like this?* All is correct— spring, love, woods, the lad, morning—winter, loneliness, house, no lad, evening—the desolate " garden of my heart "—and the proper sentiment of good out of evil etc. at the end.

Tears can drown triumph—*Do women feel like this?* I don't. I doubt of even a kitchenmaid's liking this.

Perhaps in another mood this would appeal to me, so simple and so sad, and yet so brave—but I cannot say.

The personal association, the mnemonic irrelevance, might be expected to threaten this poem to an especial degree. Some writers were on their guard against it :—

4·4. I have *a special personal association* with regard to this composition *which might pre-dispose me* in its *favour*. My judgement however is that it is thoroughly bad. The author seems to me to have attempted to communicate a really valuable emotion, but he has failed completely. He has however succeeded in writing words that may justly be described as both sloppy and sentimental.

The metre employed suggests doggerel and the worst kind of limerick. The *words* themselves are *badly chosen* and the *metaphors* are *conventional and unconvincing*. For example the use of the word " spring " in verse 1 and " weeds " in verse 3.

The final impression is one of Disgust.

4·41. This to me is *excellent*. I cannot tell whether from *the things with which I associate it* or from *its accurate expression* and its simplicity. Seasons and sun affect me more than anything, and *in this I can feel the spring*, the *best season of life and nature*. It has the perfect imagery so essential to a poem on nature.

Still more subtle must have been the influence of Stock Responses.

4·5. We have, obviously, here an expression of something the writer really felt. The idea that " hope springs eternal in the human breast " and is in fact the great attribute of the human spirit, is very aptly expressed by means of the simile, or rather here, metaphor of spring. *One's feelings rush out* to endorse those last two lines :

"... that spring is the last true thing
And that triumph is born of tears."

Spring has always been the favourite theme of poets whose outlook is what we ordinarily term ' Romantic'. *It is*, with all its associations, *the physical complement of poetry* to the mind of man. I am very obscure, I suppose, but *a little poem like this does do for my feelings, what spring does for flowers* and birds and fields, after winter—with all that it, too, presses upon the intelligence.

' One's feelings rush out.' So do comparisons, not only with *The Shropshire Lad*.

4·51. *Nature here used most effectively* as an " appui ", *in manner of Lamartine and of Wordsworth* (" Margaret " ?). Love is depicted *with freshness of a Burns, without his sensuousness*. Pathos of contrast between weeds in the garden (in her heart) and Nature's bloom. Epigrammatic conclusion, of importance. Comfort is born of affliction—*same lesson* in Wordsworth. Fine musical rythm. Nature beautifully and *faithfully* depicted.

And the feelings that rush out may take a course that is only partially directed by the poem.

4·52. ' One solace there is for me, sweet but faint.' ' Sweet but faint '—this seemed to me to sum up the whole atmosphere, to which I should also add the epithet ' delicate '. It is a mingling of joy and sorrow, and from this is born an emotion, at once sharper, more intense, but *sweet and faint still like the caravan bells in Hassan*. The music seems to rise and fall, like a breath of wind. Now strong and flaming, with the memory of love present, now sad and gentle with the memory of love past. And at the end it seems to rise to triumph, the very triumph that the writer was thinking of—" born of tears ".

Whether the next writer is alluding to the heroine of the poem or to the author is not made clear.

4·6. The " sweet but faint solace " floating with foolish optimism on metaphorical winds fills me with a sense of superiority and contempt. I cannot and will not give any more attention to *this effeminate weakling*.

His arrogance may contrast, finally, with the humility of 4·61.

4·61. As
    (1) I am only 19.
    (2) I have never been in love.
    (3) I do not know what a dog-rose is.
    (4) I consider that spring has no rapture.
    (5) ——the alliteration is bad and unnecessary.
    (6) ——this symbolism utterly worthless.
I will declare the whole poem to be sentimental rubbish. More detailed criticism would be foolish and futile. One reading gave me this opinion. I never hope to read it again.

Comment here again must be postponed until Part III, where the allied problems of Sentimentality and Stock Responses can be fully discussed.

What's this of death, from you who never will die ?
Think you the wrist that fashioned you in clay,
The thumb that set the hollow just that way
In your full throat and lidded the long eye
So roundly from the forehead, will let lie
Broken, forgotten, under foot some day
Your unimpeachable body, and so slay
The work he most had been remembered by ?

I tell you this : whatever of dust to dust
Goes down, whatever of ashes may return
To its essential self in its own season,
Loveliness such as yours will not be lost,
But, cast in bronze upon his very urn,
Make known him Master, and for what good reason.

POEM V

THE mere sense of this poem baffled an unusually large number of readers. Of 62 who returned protocols, 17 declare themselves bewildered; 14 appear to have fathomed it—that is to say they have followed its thought, made out what it says; 7 are doubtful cases; and 24, no less, appear not to have understood it without themselves knowing that such was the case.

These figures would suggest that the poem really is extraordinarily obscure. Yet no one who has once made out the sense will easily persuade himself that this is so. But, since, at the best, only some twenty readers construed it, and the remaining two-thirds wittingly or unwittingly failed, it seems imperative to begin by supplying a prose paraphrase which will at least bring the central issue into due prominence. Here it is:

" You should not think of death, for you will not die. It is inconceivable that God having made you so perfect will let you perish, since you are his masterpiece. Whatever may perish, your loveliness is too great to be lost, since when God dies your image will be permanently retained as a memorial of his skill as a creator." (' You ', it may be added, being a human being.)

The strain of believing that this really is the sense of a piece written with such aplomb explains the bewilderment and the failure to construe which mark so many of the protocols. What we think of it as sense is, however, not the important point here, but rather the general question of the place of the plain prose sense, or thought, in poetry.

No general rule, of course, can be laid down. Every case must be judged on its own merits, and the particular structure of the poem under judgment must be fully taken into account. There are types of poetry (Swinburne's *Before the Mirror* for example) where the argument, the interconnection of the thought, has very little to do with the proper effect of the poem, where the thought may be incoherent and confused without harm, for the very simple reason that the poet is not using the argument as an argument, and so the incoherence may be neglected. There are other types where the effect of the poem may turn upon irrationality, where the special feelings which arise from recognising incompatibility and contradiction are essential parts of the poem. (Not always mirthful feelings; they may be desperate or sublime. Compare the close of Marvell's *The Definition of Love*.) But this poem belongs to neither of these types. Since the hyperbole of this particular beauty as God's memorial is worked in twice at the two most salient places of emphasis, there can be little doubt that a full comprehension of it is necessary to the reading of the poem. This thought is really an essential part of the structure, and the poem has to accept whatever risks are implied by this fact. The core, or turning-point of the poem is in the emotional effects of this culminating thought *as realised*.

If this is so, the various struggles of the protocol-writers with the thought are instructive. First, those who knew that they did not understand may be represented.

5·1. No appeal to me. Failure of communication, as after the 20th reading *the nature of the addressee* was still obscure.

5·12. I don't understand whether the poet is addressing a *woman*, or a *statue*.

The interesting assumption that the ' unimpeachable body ' must be a woman's, not a man's, may be noted in passing. It frequently reappears.

5·13. I find the poem *unintelligible* as it stands. Is it a living woman or a statue ? *I cannot reconcile the last two lines.* A title would possibly have saved the situation. The expression is otherwise curiously excellent. The subject is viewed as by a painter or sculptor. *The thought compact and forcible,* somewhat suggestive of Browning.

How the thought, though unintelligible, can be recognised as compact and forcible is rather a mystery. Probably the writer meant that the expression sounds as though this were so, which is a true and important observation indicating that the sense here is not irrelevant to the full reading of the poem. Actually, as some readers will point out, compactness is hardly a character of this sonnet. The same willingness to accept the envelope in place of the contents is shown again and again.

5·14. *I found the poet's idea difficult—even impossible—to grasp.* Was the " wrist that fashioned " the wrist of God, or merely of a human sculptor ? It is *hard to reconcile* the " clay " and the " thumb that set the hollow ", of the first few lines, with the " cast in bronze upon his very urn " of the last lines. The sonnet, however, is finely constructed. In reading it, the voice gradually swells throughout the octave, and sinks to the close. *The thought is evidently a splendid one,* but it is *obscurely expressed,* and the sonnet fails in its object.

The thought evidently ought to be a splendid one, if it is to accord with the manner of the sonnet ; this is the reflection that dominated many judgments. The readers' pathetic distrust of their own power to construe, to penetrate through to the content, their inability to work out and grasp the splendid thought, is a point that educators will recognise as crucial.

But not all those who approved the thought without mastering it were wooed thereto by the glamour of the expression.

E

5·15. What does " cast in bronze upon his very urn " mean ?
The phrase seems unfortunate, bringing one to a sharp stop,
*seeking the meaning. A good point (for immortality), well worked
out and well put :* but is the expression very high ?   " What's
this of death " is not very felicitous, tho' perhaps a striking
opening.   " I tell you this " gives a very ' prosy ' impression.
On the other hand *the whole idea is well communicated* by the
poem, which leaves a sense of satisfaction and completeness,
perhaps mostly on account of the last two lines, *puzzling as is
the " urn " phrase* mentioned above.   I *always* feel attracted to
religious poetry, and anxious to get the best out of it.

The search for the meaning did not go very far.
It would be interesting to know what exactly ' the
whole idea ' was for this reader, and how the argu-
ment for immortality runs, and for what kind of
immortality.   Other writers will later shed some
more light upon all this.   Whatever it was, it probably
had a great deal to do with the popularity of the
poem.

But the confident air of the sonnet, by creating a
very favourable ' atmosphere of approach ', as text-
books of salesmanship say, was also influential.

5·16. *I'm sure this is a good sonnet,* but it takes a lot of getting
at.   *I like the rhythm,* and *the words please me immensely,* but in
spite of many readings I have not yet arrived at its precise
meaning.   Obviously the lady will die, physically, but whether
her loveliness is to be preserved in the minds of others or actually
in bronze is more than I can fathom.   The octave points to the
latter, but the sestet seems to confuse the issue.

Both appeals, the superficial rhythm and the ' idea ',
may be seen combined.

5·17. I am *not* quite *sure* whether the person addressed is the
most famous statue of a great sculptor, or a beautiful human
being.   The *communication* is *not* quite *clear.*
  But I like the poem very much.   *It expresses an idea, with
which I heartily agree,* but which is, *perhaps,* not new, in a very
satisfactory way.   It has some body to it.
  The form I also like.   The *words* and the *rhythm* are very *good.*
I cannot tell *quite* how it should be read.

Such shivering on the brink of understanding, such coy reluctance to plunge into the depths of ideas which, if liked so much, should surely prove more attractive, is very suspicious. In some of these surface-gazers, general or constitutional triviality and lack of enterprise may be explanation enough. But Narcissism and an intellectual timidity or inhibition based on a sense that ' things will not bear looking into and are best left alone ' are often co-operating factors.

Some of the bewildered brought objections to parts of the sense. The next writer must find *Genesis* ii. 21 very risible, but he puts his finger upon a difficulty in the poem that few commented upon, the shift from the immortality of the individual suggested by the opening to the mere eternity of beauty later on.

5·18. I don't like the general atmosphere of the poem. I really don't understand it. Is the " Master " God ?
If so *it is ludicrous to imagine him thumbing a hollow in some-body's throat.* If the " Master " is a sculptor, someday he will have to " let lie, broken, forgotten, underfoot " the unimpeachable body *even if* the " loveliness " lives. The poem—presumably an extract—seems to contradict itself and is irritating.

The failure to recognise a sonnet we have met before and shall meet again.

More curious are those many instances in which the reader is unaware that his interpretation does not exhaust the possibilities.

5·2. *Quite an ingenious way of saying that the artist has made a cast of a beautiful woman.* The opening is good—the working up to the climax, too, sustained by the questions.
The " I tell you this " almost necessary to recover one's breath—but so unnecessary otherwise. Ending very weak.
I like the way he expresses the moulding—" so roundly from the forehead ". But the wrist and thumb idea is dropped care-lessly, *although the sense is* never obscure.
Words well chosen, and rhythm carries the sense along with it.

5·21. I do not like this sonnet; it has *no deep thought* for *common sense tells us that a statue will not die.*

Read with this sense the poem did not meet with much favour, though some of the objections made to it seem hardly less arbitrary than the reading.

5·22. This gives the impression that it was written as an exercise and does not suggest genuine or deep emotion. The feeling is not strong enough to carry the reader along with it and so *he notices that the ' body ' is held up and that ' he ' is created from a wrist and thumb.* It all seems *rather a waste of courtly and artificial compliments* such as ' unimpeachable ' and ' loveliness such as yours ' *on stocks and stones,* while the second half of the last line is almost enough to damn the whole piece.

But most readers did not attempt so close a grip upon the meaning of the poem. A more general response to a traditional theme contented them.

5·3. The thought in this sonnet is noble and well expressed, *the theme being that Beauty will never die.* From beginning to end the *thought is* clear and the form is impeccable.

This was the most popular theme, but others sometimes served as well.

5·31. I like this sonnet very much. Its significance depends on the close connection which it presumes between physical and spiritual beauty, and this connection is one of the factors which make me think it is by Rossetti, since *in his ideal world of art, the connection always held.* I like the triumphant note of the second part of the poem.

These seem to express parts of ' the whole idea ' mentioned above (5·15). As we might expect other handlings of the more popular theme are recalled.

5·32. Reminds me of Keats' glorious Ode to the Nightingale, especially of the verse beginning " Thou wast not born for death,—". The thought expressed *is one which most of us feel at some time in our lives.* We feast (our eyes) on some lovely object, not necessarily animate, and groan at the idea of the dusty road to death engulfing so much loveliness and at length we burst out into remonstrance, and, if we have little time to spare, we either resign ourselves to the inevitable or console ourselves with the philosophy of John Keats.

This poem expresses, at once, *a passionate remonstrance and an inspiring hope*, in verse which, if not polished, is at least effective.

Such comparisons may have a positive or a negative effect. Sometimes the other poetry that is recalled assists the reader to make the best he can out of the poem that is before him. But equally often these recollections, rationally or irrationally, are a stumbling-block. This dual possibility recurs whenever a poem seems to (or actually does) treat a stock-subject or invite a stock-response. Two readers at least, who appear to have grappled more closely with this sonnet, are as much hindered by their recollections of Keats as the last writer was helped.

5·33. Keats expressed the message of this poem in *much simpler and yet quite as effective language* when he wrote " A thing of beauty is a joy for ever. Its loveliness increases, it will never pass into nothingness . . ." To me the poem seems *grandiloquent rather than grand.* The *obvious truth of the sentiment expressed* seems to be wrapt in unnecessary difficulties and *the meaning of the last two lines*, presuming they have a meaning, *is quite lost to me.*

5·34. The opposition of the ideas of beauty and death is not unusual but the expression in the octet is admirable. I cannot understand the last two lines of the sestet and the third line in the sestet appears to me to be clumsy. The underlying idea is valuable but is not so well expressed as in " A thing of beauty is a joy for ever " etc.

So, too, with the emotional response which follows the presentation of the theme. Very different feelings are recorded.

5·35. This poem is a good one because it is a sincere expression of the writer's feeling, and *this feeling is one of exalted worship.* Whether the belief is true or false, *we rise to something great.*

5·36. I cannot decide definitely about this poem. Its expression is simply marvellous, but the thing expressed is to me *false consolation for which I have no use.* I recognise the poem as a fine expression of a certain way of looking at things, but it is *to me an inadequate way*, and therefore I do not hesitate to put the poem aside. Perhaps it is because I feel the poet is trying to argue the point.

Yet we find other readers, less exigent intellectually, who are more responsive :

5·37. I like both the thoughts and the way they are expressed. *For a sceptic—as I—it is one of the few trains of thought that carries him towards belief in immortality.* Expressed with great conviction.

One wonders what kind of immortality this sceptic is persuaded towards, or exactly what comfort the next reader desires. Private poems due to Stock Responses are almost certainly the explanation in both cases.

5·38. Someone, fearing death, has expressed his doubts to the poet and the poet has, in consequence, written a solace. *This message of comfort sweeps away any cynical belief in " out of sight out of mind "* and states that "loveliness will not be lost ", but will be cast in bronze on an urn in Heaven, will be eternally remembered. The thought that " is it likely that God would have made you so comely and beautiful just to destroy you ? " is not a common one ; it offers comfort to those who have their doubts about the next world—death does not seem so dreadful. The last six lines which form the solace of the poem, are said with *such calm assurance* that *the troubled mind has its fears allayed,* and, as the lines seem to run more smoothly, and soothingly to the end, they cause a placidity of spirit.

It is plain that the doctrinal problem, the place and importance of beliefs in poetry, is in need of discussion. Several writers indeed either state or imply a view upon this most difficult general problem.

5·4. A sonnet expressing a sense of the permanence of beauty. Connected with a sense of the immortality behind things even human and material, and *with a sense of a definite power which creates beauty for a given purpose—a ' good reason '.* The poem is interesting from this point of view, though it is not an unfamiliar thought. It is indeed a thought *common to all poets* and expressed by all of them in some way or another. It is *both the explanation and the justification of poetry itself* as of all forms of art.

This writer's interpretation of the last words of
the sonnet—' and for what good or reason '—is rather
too bold, but his view of the beliefs supposed to give
rise to poetry is very common. It is elaborated, with
an added note of nervous asceticism, in 5·41, where
some misgivings lest doctrine should too much in-
trude are also shown.

5·41. This æsthetic conviction of immortality was most prob-
ably written by some sculptor or artist poet who could fully
appreciate the joy of creation. The poet's pleasure in physical
beauty is very sincere. The *note of sensuality* which one might
have *expected in such an admirer* is entirely absent because the
poet is thinking rather of the creator's satisfaction in contem-
plating the thing he has created than of *the emotional effect
beauty has on people*. The poet has put himself in God's place,
or rather he has considered Him as a sculptor whose name can
only be perpetuated by the creations of His hands. The *poet
has the religion of the artist who sees the beauty and glory of God
in Nature* and in this poem *what religious ideas do enter are made
very subservient* to the glorification of the person to whom the
poem is addressed.

Troubled by the same doubts as to how far
doctrine is admissible in poetry, two writers advance
the ' state of mind ' or ' mood ' solution of the diffi-
culty. If poetry only expresses a ' state of mind ' or
' mood ', the thoughts presented, it is suggested, need
not be examined on their own account. This sugges-
tion perhaps disposes of those who boggle at the
truth of the thought, but not of those whose objection
is to its intellectual or emotional incoherence.

5·42. Here is *a hopeful state of mind* expressed in verse. It is
an attractive poem. It seems rather a pity to dissociate the
opinions expressed in it from the impression made by the verse
itself. *The opinions are a little religious*—the religion that loveli-
ness cannot die. If the question must be discussed, I believe
that people's bodies must die, however perfect they may be
though loveliness in one form or another always remains in the
world. On the other hand, mind-loveliness remains as the real
thing. You must accept the truth of change in your body.
Verse form quite good. This is *not a didactic poem*—that's
why it doesn't matter very much about the discussion of the

opinions in it. I don't think it was definitely meant to teach people—but *just to express a state of mind.*

Probably any mention of anything mentioned in religion would make a passage religious for this reader.

5·43. The attraction to me of this is its extreme definiteness and conviction. It may be *the expression of a mood only.* I think it probably is, because *a man who could write this, however fervently he believed that " loveliness such as yours will not be lost " would yet scarcely hold as his real creed* that any " body " however unimpeachable would be " The work He most had been remembered by ". But its being *only the expression of a mood* this doesn't matter because for the moment the mood has complete domination : *I can find no trace of a pose assumed for the writing of the sonnet.* The sonnet form is peculiarly felicitous because a very definite form is thus used for a very definite idea. I think the impression I have received of a slightly careless technique is intentional ; so that the reader may visualise a man too eager to express his thoughts and emotions to pause over the exact words he uses.

One is tempted to inquire what it was that set this writer looking for traces of a pose. A rather suspicious disclaimer.

The general problem of doctrine in poetry will be discussed later ; it is enough here to have noted the influence of its attendant difficulties upon judgment of this poem. By way of transition to opinions about the detail of the language and handling 5·5 may be given.

5·5. I feel the *rather desperate endeavour* of the poet *to throw the reader into an attitude of belief.* To believe in her loveliness and immortality is essential to the realisation of the experience. I am no more than a spectator.

Generally, I can believe in

loveliness such as yours will never die

but specifically, the loveliness perishes.

think you the wrist
that set the hollow *just that way*

these are *tricks of style not genuine :* self-conscious, too, is " unimpeachable ". Isn't the finger too evident ?—*I tell you*

this—too heavy—that the style is not quite genuine I feel from
the continual change. Here, quite Miltonic weight of statement—
Make known him Master and for what good reason. Here,
spilling over, without much need—

in its own season—

But what really prevents my belief in the immortality is the
narrowing, specific, quite miniature picture of immortality—

cast in bronze upon an urn.

True, God's urn, but concrete and the figure merely decorative.

This reader clearly followed the thought of the
poem through to the end. The two examples of
praise that follow do not make this so apparent;
they confine themselves to questions of ' treatment '.

5·51. I like this : it is not particularly good English or a very
fine sonnet, but it *has a youthful directness about it*, *a clear
incisiveness* which makes it very attractive. It is, I think, fairly
obviously, by Rupert Brooke : it has his touch, or the touch of
his school about it. It is utterly unemotional, being more like
a description of a picture, or a bust being worked by god the
sculptor, than a sonnet to a girl he loves. It has the irregularity
common to nearly all Brooke's sonnets, whether he wrote it or
not. I like it because it has *no veiled or obscure nonsense about
it :* it is direct and striking, but oh how cold !

5·52. A strong, Browningesque vein both in substance and
rhythm. I like " your unimpeachable body ". The poem
certainly " gets across ". The last line, however, is disturbing
to the extreme. Ugly and flat and banal. But, I believe,
intentionally so. It reminds one of

' Hobbes prints blue, straight he turtle eats.
Who fished the murex up :
What porridge had John Keats ? '

The poem leaves one with a sense of strength, amounting almost
to *physical brute force ; something rugged, something clean.* ' *Of
the earth, earthy*——'.

Such studies in manner divorced from matter
rarely go further than those which show the converse
bias in the choice of approach. To consider either
treatment or content exclusively is a means of keeping
at a distance from the actual poem. Two who, on the

whole, admired the poem, did attempt to come closer, and both note in its obscurity an added relish, though on other points they contradict one another.

5·53. On first reading, without fitting together the whole grammatically, meaning and spirit is caught. Bold start : uneven, forceful rhythm ; imagery—(human, intimate, though so rapid) : absence of colour : chiefly Saxon words with bold, unrestrained Latin interpolations :—all give *clarity, vigour, cleanness, virility, etc.*
Absence of least artifice, but *natural suggestion* of sounds— " full throat .... forgotten ". *Perfect, unfaltering conviction.*
Thus matter and general effect ultimately is fine. But is whole raised or degraded by uneven quality of (*a*) rhythm, (*b*) sense ?

(*a*) Lines 1, 7, 9, 10, 14—all most difficult to render. But although marred *as verse*, it gains a conversational, intimate, forceful note.

(*b*) *Sense obscure on first reading* (8, 9-11, 14). *But if it lacks limpidity, it does, by becoming something of a nut to crack, take on a " tang "—an enticement.*

But is it artistically better or worse ? *Worse*—easier to appreciate, but rather a puzzle than a poem.

5·54. In the first part of the poem *I do not think the description of the woman's beauty sufficiently vivid* and living to make one realise the terrible tragedy of beauty " broken and forgotten " which is so simply and masterfully conveyed by the next lines. If it were not for the last two lines of the poem one would be inclined to take the poem literally and the thought of the poem would degenerate into a pathetic defiance of the laws of nature giving one nothing but a sense of unrest. The last 2 lines I think show that the poet is thinking of beauty as being a high ideal which is never lost and which is in *itself a revelation of the Divine thought.*
The poem is simple in language and *this simplicity tends to mask the thought any way in the first reading but adds to the effect when the poem is more closely studied.*

How far this closer study really carried the writer towards a comprehension of the last two lines is a point which can, I think, be fairly clearly made out. Another, who finds much in the detail to admire, also shows us the trouble that this original feature of the poem caused him.

5·55. There is *a crescendo in this sonnet made more effective by the restraint of its language.* The first lines with their long vowel sounds move slowly and melodiously. In the first four lines of the sextet the movement quickens and the passionate intensity is admirably rendered by the additional syllables and the prevalence of ' S ' sounds in it culminates in the quick monosyllables ' will not be lost.' Then follow the slower, more impressive two last lines to mark the final close.

The thought is clear enough but for the last two lines,—where *the sense of " his very urn " presumably means " that containing the ashes of the dead "—and " for what good reason " is not at first very clear.* The defect of these lines is more apparent in a poem which aims at communicating a line of action.

Throughout the moulded image and the human body are present in the thought, *the word ' slay ' giving just the trend towards the living.*

More hostile though as much at fault over the meaning is 5·56. The virtue of a ' definite division ' in a sonnet is a tenet firmly held by many. Its distribution is doubtless to be put to the credit of teaching. With a thousand other equally arbitrary and misleading snippets of critical dogma it might well be exchanged for a little more training in the construing of ordinary English. That ' for what good reason ' is almost as troublesome as the ' urn ' is a fact that should make all members of the teaching professions ponder.

5·56. This is not absolutely commonplace, though *the conceit has been a favourite one for milleniums.* The expression is Browningian, with forced words to ensure a rime, *e.g., slay, a most unsuitable word.* The metaphor at first suggests a potter (in 2nd and 3rd lines), and the abrupt introduction of " in your full throat " is disconcerting. " Unimpeachable " is tolerable, but it suggests that striving after effect which typifies *some* modern poetry.

The construction of the sonnet is excellent, as there is a definite division. The sestet is not so good as the octave, as there is obscurity in the next to last line—" Cast in bronze upon his very urn." Who does " his " refer to ? Presumably the Master, but it is not clear.

" and for what good reason " is a strikingly prosaic ending. One suspects the power of " season " earlier on.

Just as arbitrary in his conceptions of sonnet form is another writer whose capacity to construe is on much the same level.

5·57. The writer seems to be trying to write a sonnet on some lofty theme about which, no doubt, he thinks deeply. But certainly the result of his effort is not very pleasing. It seems as if he is incapable of expressing clearly his thoughts. On first reading, the various sentences seem detached and it is (at first) rather difficult to see wherein lies the connection between the various phrases ; but *after a further reading* the *meaning of the first* eight lines can be extracted. I consider that a sentence of seven lines, relieved only by commas, is rather unwieldy and clumsy for a sonnet, and the general impression of the first eight lines is that of clumsiness and disunity. The sextet is considerably worse. *Even if one supplies a mark of interrogation after the phrase* " and for what good reason " *one still has to explain the significance of the phrase.* It seems to have no connection with the rest of the sonnet.

Taking " his very urn " to be a misprint for " this very urn ", *I still fail to see the use of the urn.*

I have illustrated at some length these failures to construe because of their overwhelming practical importance. When such a very humble yet indispensable part of a reader's equipment is defective we need hardly be surprised if more difficult critical endeavours meet with ill-success. Practical remedial measures are not impossible if the need for them is once frankly recognised. And to make this need evident I have risked some monotony. However much it may be thought that there was ultimately nothing in this sonnet to construe, no meaning to arrive at—and I have admitted the strain put upon us by the contrast of its air and its actuality—none the less a reader ought to be able to tackle it. He ought to be given better defensive technique against the multifold bamboozlements of the world. He need not be as helpless as these extracts show him to be. I have not, however, nearly exhausted the material that lies before me. But we may pass on to other questions.

The sincerity of the poem—always a troublesome matter, see Part III, Chapter VII—occasioned varied pronouncements. Some attempted to judge by the rhythm.

5·6. Marked by sincerity. *The restrained yet passionate utterance of a lover.* Style full of vigour : simple yet forcible language, the very opposite of false " poetic diction ". The irregularity of the metre emphasises the sincerity and passion, *giving the impression of emotion trying to break through* the control which verse imposes : it lays a heavier stress on some words, as in line 1, and in this way gives more force and reality to the whole.

But the rhythm of most verse is so closely dependent upon the rest of the response that this excellent test may mislead. Another reader who reached the same result (and illustrates again the sonnet-form dogma above noticed) incidentally propounds a puzzling and interesting question.

5·61. This sonnet is a very fine one. The break between the octet and sestet is very pronounced. The rhythm of the octet is faster than that of the sestet and *denotes the impetuosity of the speaker and* his great admiration for the subject of the poem. The hyperboles lavished on the subject are however very conventional and *the worth of the sonnet and its genuineness depends largely on the time it was written.* It does *not* seem false *however* by the rhythm.

The mere date of a poem cannot by itself settle its genuineness, in the sense of its sincerity. All it can do is to offer presumptive evidence for or against. A poet may very well write an entirely sincere poem in the manner of a different age, but on the whole the probability is strongly against this. It is only a probability, however, though it is enough to make knowledge of a poem's date a useful aid to judgment. The final decision can only be made through a closer, fuller, contact with the poem itself. And only in this fullest contact can the rhythm test be applied. The last two writers, it will be noticed, disregard the thought, paying attention rather to the passion-broken and impetuous utterance of the poet. But these characters are far more easily mimicked than the deeper movements of thought and feeling. Compared with coherence, incoherence is a ' stunt '. To gain order and control is the poet's difficulty ; not to express agitation ; and what they praise may not be a merit.

5·7. The whole thing seems somehow laboured. There seems to be *a conscious striving after effect*, after the *striking* word and phrase. " Unimpeachable body " is a bit *too* far-fetched. There is something *would-be passionate* about the whole thing ; it does not ring quite true.

5·71. I do not think this successful, because the writer is not himself convinced in what he is expressing : he is *playing with an idea, rather than expressing a conviction*.
It is the off-hand manner of the poem which leads me to make this criticism : the absence of awe and reverence which should co-exist with religious feeling. It is especially noticeable in the first two lines of the last six, and in the word " unimpeachable " which when used in this way suggests a sneer.

These suspicions that all was not as it should be, that a flashy façade rather than a solid building was being erected before them, that a bright thought was being aired rather for its supposed originality and daring than for what it was, troubled several more readers. Only two, however, coupled these suspicions with detailed observation of the matter and manner of the poem and it is these observations which we seek in criticism.

5·8. It seems to me that these four poems have been chosen because they all play for easily touched off and full-volumed responses, and so are in danger of sentimentality and kindred vices. This one *offers cheap reassurance in what is to most men a matter of deep and intimate concern*. It opens with Browning's brisk no-nonsense-about-me directness and goes on with *a cocksure movement and hearty alliteration*. It *contains* (along with the appropriate " dust to dust ") *echoes of all the best people*. It is *full of vacuous resonances* (" its essential self in its own season ") *and the unctuously poetic*.

5·81. This is a studied orgasm from a ' Shakespeare-R. Brooke '
complex, as piece 7 from a ' Marvell-Wordsworth-Drinkwater,
etc., stark-simplicity ' complex. Hollow at first reading, resound-
ingly hollow at second. A sort of thermos vacuum, ' the very
thing ' for a dignified picnic in this sort of Two-Seater sonnet.
The ' Heroic ' Hectoring of line 1, the hearty *quasi* stoical button-
holing of the unimpeachably-equipped beloved, *the magisterial
finger-wagging* of ' I tell you this ' ! ! Via such conduits magna-
nimity may soon be laid on as an indispensable, if not obligatory,
modern convenience.

Margaret, are you grieving
Over Goldengrove unleafing ?
Ah ! as the heart grows older
It will come to such sights colder
By and by, nor spare a sigh
Tho' world of wanwood leafmeal lie ;
And yet you will weep and know why.
Now no matter, child, the name.
Sorrow's springs are the same.
Nor mouth had, no, nor mind express'd,
What heart heard of, ghost guess'd :
It is the blight man was born for,
It is Margaret you mourn for.

POEM VI

BOTH response and opinion here divide with a pleasing neatness. Furthermore, all stages of the cleavage are well shown. If some of the other protocol sets have something of the wildness and unexpectedness, the untidiness and bizarrity, of industrialised hill-country, or the variety of a rich but ill-tended garden, this set, on the other hand, has the soothing simplicity of a demonstration in elementary geology.

The incipient crack—to pursue the metaphor a little way—and the forces that provoke it appear in 6·1. This writer might, later on, be found on either side of the gulf. He is sufficiently susceptible and sufficiently impatient to have landed himself anywhere.

6·1. Has a decided *fascination* for me, but it is *an irritating rather than a satisfactory fascination.* I can't be quite sure I have grasped the meaning. One reading I really feel I do understand it, but at the next reading I am not sure that I am not completely on the wrong tack after all. Part of the fascination is the balanced alliterative rhythm and rhyme scheme, but at the same time that is part of the irritation because I find myself attending exclusively to the sound and general feel of the word-pattern regardless of the sense. Finally *I cannot make up my mind whether or not I understand it or whether or not I like it.*

Rather more pertinacity, and perhaps more intelligence, carry 6·12 over to the positive side. He shows a prudent awareness of some of the dangers of this poetic theme and a due sense of what their avoidance implies.

6·12. I have not had time to " attack " this poem as much as I should like to. It conveyed little to me on the first reading, but now I like it, and think the sentiment as good and genuine as that of No. 8 is spurious and false. I think it is a beautiful expression of a mood often expressed in poetry—that of the poet watching a child, and thinking of its future, and I think that, as *the mood is one that particularly lends itself to false sentiment*, it is a triumph for a poet to give us a new and impressive rendering of it.

Since so many readers did not succeed in applying their intelligence, a paraphrase kindly supplied by one writer may be inserted here. It will help moreover to bring out an interesting double-reading that the seventh line of the poem lends itself to.

6·13. It is difficult to understand this poem at first. After thinking about it a good deal I have come to the conclusion that this is the meaning of it—an elderly man, experienced in such matters, has found a girl grieving at the falling of leaves in autumn.

He shows that she will not longer have the same quick sensitiveness when she is old—she will no longer be able to grieve for such things (Cf. lines 2-4). Then she will weep, but this time, not for such things as the falling leaves in autumn, but because she can no longer have such feelings—the feelings of youth. (Cf. 'And yet you will weep and know why'). Even now in weeping at the transience of the things she enjoys in autumn, she is really weeping for the transience of all things. She is mourning among other things, for the fleetingness of her own youth.

The other and the preferable reading of the line is indicated in 6·2 where an admirable power of detailed analysis is displayed.

6·2. This poem shows great skill and I think it is by far the most difficult of the four. The more I read it the more I find in it ; I did not really grasp its whole meaning till I had made about three attacks on it and even now I am not sure I thoroughly understand it. *I do not think this is because it is obscure, but because it requires a special reading ;* the accenting of the seventh line is particularly important—the accent falls on ' will weep ' and ' know why '.

The way the poem is written I admire greatly. I like the simple opening and closing couplet, *the one answering the other.* The first six lines begin at a low pitch and then rise at ' Ah ! as the heart grows older ', only to fall again in the sixth line. I like the even accentuation of the sixth line. Then there is great control of vowel music, the more open vowels where the voice rises in the third and fourth lines ; the vowel ' i ' introduced in ' sights ' is made much of in the next line, and a triple rhyme made on it. There is *a breathing sigh* in ' By and by, nor spare a sigh '. I like the whole idea of the poem, and I think the last couplet is excellent, giving the poem universal application and making this specially refer to Margaret.

That the author of the poem was aware of the possible alternative readings of the seventh line is shown by an accent-mark he originally placed on ' will '.

And yet you will weep and know why.

This mark I omitted, partly to see what would happen, partly to avoid a likely temptation to irrelevant discussions. Without it, ' will ' may be read as giving the future tense, as 6·13 in fact reads it. Then the accents may fall on ' weep ' and on ' and ' ; the sense being that in the future she will know the reason for a sorrow that is now only a blind grief. When ' will ' is accentuated it ceases to be an auxiliary verb and becomes the present tense of the verb ' to will '. She persists in weeping and in demanding the reason for the falling of the leaves, and perhaps also for her grief. The rhythmical difference made by the change of sense is immense. Both the sense and the movement rejected by the poet are very good, however, and doubtless some readers will privately retain them. But because the authentic version is perhaps better still the hint given by the accent-mark ought to be retained. The swing over from one reading to another (without perhaps sufficient appreciation of the first) is remarked upon in 6·21.

6·21. I like this best of all. *What looks like preciosity—* " Golden grove unleafing " and " world of wanwood leafmeal lie "—is *really a means of compression.* I was puzzled at first reading because I took " will " in " and yet you will weep and know why " to be future. Wistfulness without sentimentality : the pang of transience well conveyed.

How much the poem conveyed to those who admitted it will appear from the next two protocols. It will be noticed that few of our chosen poems evoke praise of such quality even when most admired.

6·22. Excellent, the emotions of sorrow and forlornness lose nothing in communication ; I have never experienced them more poignantly, and could not imagine myself doing so, than in reading the poem. Rhyme words are the (intellectually and emotionally) important ones both separately and in their pairs.

Grieving ⎫
Unleafing ⎬ very strong associations.

nor mind expressed ⎫
ghost guessed ⎬

Rhythm and " sense " (scientific) inseparable. Contrast lilt of

" By and by nor spare a sigh "

with

" Tho' world of wanwood leafmeal lie."

The last two lines stick in the throat like real sorrow.

The praise here of the rhymes is worth noting, for our rhymesters, as indeed always happens whenever the least opportunity occurs, were not slow to pounce upon the opening and the close, though I am not, this time, illustrating these antics.

6·23. *Unless really soaked in, would pass unnoticed. Sounds* all way through. " Margaret " strikes note, colour and sadness. " Golden grove unleafing " full, soft. " Tho' world of wanwood leafmeal lie "—gloriously melancholy (worthy of Keats' " La Belle Dame sans Merci "). Last two lines especially rhyme. Metre : 7, 9, 11, jar unless read *most sympathetically :* they can be made to sound in perfect keeping with rest. Sound, sense, rhythm and rhyme really wonderfully interwoven. Freedom of words (wanwood leafmeal, unleafing) and the newness of the whole : with its strange simplicity, lend distinction, intimacy, spontaneity. Not the least particularising detail, therefore its appeal is universal : yet subtle strokes like " Golden grove ", " Margaret ", remove any suggestion of the " airy nothing ". Perfect melancholy, perfect artistry. It has conveyed to me a sentiment as completely as very few poems have ever done before.

This reader is mistaken in his opening remark. Many who by no means ' soaked in ' the poem, yet had plenty to say about it.

Another paraphrase at this point may make the poem seem more confusing and so assist us.

6·3. It took me a long time to find out what was being said, and *even now I am not sure that my solution is correct.* The poem . reminds me of Browning's remark of one of his poems—" When I wrote this God and I only knew what it meant, now, God only knows."

Margaret is grieving over the falling leaves, and she is told that *there are other sights colder than this, meaning death,* which when she gets older *she will not even sigh for ;* yet she will weep when she realises that all of us like leaves must die. Her mouth and her mind had neither expressed this idea of death which she felt at heart in a vague way. Man was born to die, and she is mourning for herself. The poem might have been expressed far more intelligibly without loss of any charm or impression. *A great contrast to No. 5 where death is made light of—here it is . regarded dismally.*

6·31. I read this ten times without finding any meaning in it and very little attraction. Either I am, or the writer is, more than usually idiotic, but I really am quite unable to digest this doughy, heavy, obscure, indigestible and unsustaining piece of whatever it is meant to be.

We may remind ourselves here that these are the opinions of serious and professed students of English.

6·32. The thought is worthless, and hopelessly muddled. *A nonsensical conglomeration of words.* Expressed in jerky, disconnected phrases, *without rhythm.*

Blank bewilderment and helpless inability to comprehend either the sense or the form of the poem naturally gave rise to irritation.

6·33. This is difficult to read and difficult to understand, and not worth the effort to understand it. I find it impossible to recreate the poet's experience : the poem merely annoys me when I try.

There doesn't seem to be the least vestige of a metrical scheme.
It is most difficult to scan or to read. Such lines as

> " Nor mouth had, no, nor mind expressed
> What heart heard of, ghost guesséd "

are enough to put anybody off from reading it a second time.
I certainly shouldn't have done except for this test.

Excuses were suggested :

6·34. *If this is an extract we ought to have more of it* to judge
from. If not, there is probably *some biographical information
needed.* I frankly don't understand it.

And many explanations offered :

6·35. This, to me, is a jumble of ideas, most badly expressed.
The poet is apparently sermonising in words, *in order that the
reader shall exercise his ingenuity.* The whole thing is cramped
in thought and expression. It is not surprising that a poet of
this kind considers himself born for a " blight ". It is very
annoying being told that ' the name ' in the 8th line does not
matter. It would be so delightful to know. *It might be a part
of a dialogue, in which one lunatic addresses another.* I presume
this is typically modern-born in the little philosophy which I
can gather. And in the style, the only aim of which seems to
be to baffle the reader.

6·36. What does all this mean ? Margaret *has apparently been
jilted* and is, very sensibly, *finding solace* in the autumn tints of
golden-grove. Whereat the poet tells her, by way of comfort,
that as she gets older she will get accustomed to sorrow, ' nor
spare a sigh '. " This has only been a dream. But naturally
you're feeling it a bit. Never mind, my dear. You'll get over
it. We all do ".
But I *should* like to know precisely *what* is the ' blight man
was born for '.

Tenderness for Margaret prompted further complaints :

6·37. This is the worst poem I have ever read. It is vague
and incoherent, and does not appeal to any of my senses, except
my sense of humor. The *parent or whoever it is* who is advising
Margaret *is a bitter, hard individual* who seems to be trying to
take away all the hope and happiness of the child. I don't
think that *any really kind person* would feel so little sympathy

for a child's trivial sorrow, and make her unhappy by telling
her that the worse is yet to come. As for the line

"Tho' world of wanwood leafmeal lie "

I have looked up both "wanwood" and "leafmeal" in four
dictionaries, and I cannot find their meanings. I see no excuse
for making a poem so vague.

The 'family-constellation' may have its part in
this as another personal situation may have in 6·36.
Another intrusion of something not easily to be found
in the poem is made in 6·38 and seems also to voice
some personal reverberation.

6·38. *An average reader* will probably not get anything out of
this poem—it is much too complicated and symbolical. *The
melancholy reproachful voice from a wasted life.* It is true—with
exception of the last line but one—but not sound.

The note of conscious superiority rings out clearly
in many of the protocols as the indignation swells :

6·4. This seems to me to be a remarkably bad attempt to put
into poetry *a thought that possibly the author imagined* was original.
Namely, that Margaret, though she thinks she is grieving for
Goldenbrook, is really mourning for herself. The poem appears
to me to be disconnected and rather pointless ; *the few sane
remarks in it are trite.* An extra line seems to have dropped
into the middle of the poem as it were by mistake ; thus making
three rhyming lines instead of two as in the rest of the poem.
Why the line

"And yet you will weep and know why "

is there at all I don't know.
Trite thought, somewhat incoherently and badly expressed.

The unfortunate readers bray, snort, and bleat, so
overmastering is their contempt.

6·41. This is extraordinarily bad poetry, embodying the trite
philosophy that the world is 'a vale of tears'. Winter, as so
often, reminds the speaker of the desolation and sorrows of life.
In putting his doggerel together, *the poet mixes his verbs and his
metaphors hopelessly.* The *grave air of the thing adds to the
laughableness* of it.

6·42. *Pish-posh !*

6·43. Sentamental. It is very remeniscent of Hardy in language and form, but Hardy was not in the least sentamental, he plunged in the depths for truth and felt it to be sad. I find this poem *quite unintelligable and useless.*

' Sentamentality ' was certainly invited by the poem, and the invitation was not refused. As so often happens the reader's own revulsion at his own devious excesses is counted against the poet.

6·5. The Poet has used his technical perfection *to express a common human failing* to which he is subject, in veiled language ; *he is ashamed of it* and only wishes to be understood by fellow sufferers (or cowards). That is that form of egotism which allows a person to identify himself with the changes of the seasons and to live autumn as well as see it—to read Sir Thomas Browne, Ibsen and the profounder Russian pessimists and *imagine that he is depressed.* Usually he realises that it is a form of self-satisfaction before he commits suicide for haply he may hit upon Aldous Huxley :

> " If, O my Lesbia, I should commit
> Not fornication, dear, but suicide,"

K.T.L.

The ' Obscurity — Ah ! — Browning ' association must be very widely and firmly established. It is not surprising that here it is accompanied by inability to apprehend form.

6·6. The communication of this is bad. Thoughts are packed together, half-evolved, and the sentences are consequently ruthlessly clipped. It is *a sort of combination of* A. S. M. Hutchinson *and* Browning. It is very difficult to untangle the real points. I don't think it would lose as much as it would gain by a prose paraphrase.

I like the ideas implied, except that of the last couplet, which *denies the existence of disinterestedness.* The other ideas are worth expressing better than they are here.

6·61. This is either an imitation of Browning, or Browning in one of his worst moments. The thought expressed is a fairly simple one, and there does not appear to be any reason why it should be expressed in so complicated a manner. We guess the general meaning of the sixth line. The other lines are inharmonious, and rather flat. *The* poet *adopts rather a patronising attitude towards Margaret,* in order to explain a quite elementary

truth, *i.e.* that when we weep for the past we are only weeping
for the death of ourselves. He is earnest and *evidently likes his
idea.* He *even shows some emotion* in the expression of it.

How near a reader may come to an understanding
of both aspects of a poem, only to be deprived of it
by a false expectation of what a poet should do with a
given subject appears in 6·7.

6·7. This is clearly an experiment in sound and in striving
after effect the sense suffers considerably. The style is jerky,
like convulsive sobbing, throughout : and suffers from lack of
clarity. In fact the later part of the piece is so cramped that it
takes quite a long time to make out the sense, though the meaning
is there right enough. The ingenious arrangement of *l*s and
*w*s, *m*s and *s*s seems rather a misdirection of energy, though
the result goes far to justify the attempt. This is *no mournful
and majestic dirge ;* but a very passable whimper.

Finally, a long and very subtle analysis of the
rhythm (giving perhaps a third reading to line seven,
for 6·21 may have stressed ' and ') will round the
discussion off, as in such a case justice requires.

6·8. Love at first sight. Perfect in *its sonnet-like di-partite
valvular structure ; in its ' whole ' and ' local ' rhythms ;* in its
emotion content (the poignancy with which it brings home,
from its objective Pathetic Fallacy, the subjective ' Tragedy ') ;
and *in the intellectual articulation that contrasts with its formal
economy.* A fusion, in the culmination of the last 2 lines, of
tragic disclosure with a Katharsis that unites the individual to
the universal fate.
    Thy symmetry on either side the crucial, rhythmically broken,
central line is admirably managed. Less obvious, *qua* symmetry,
is the lilt, and subtly contrasted change in it, as between the
groups of six lines on either side the lilt-breaker (l. 7). This, it
seems to me, should be read in two portions :

And yet you will weep (gap) and know why

the emphatic words ' know why ' receiving strong but long-
drawn stresses, that on know being slightly stronger on an uptake
and upward inbreathe of pitch, ' why ' being on an, equally
slight, down outbreath of pitch. *Nowhere, I think, should the
speed-tempo be* ‖ *slow as here.* If read like this the element of
slightly more argumentative disturbance differentiating the last
half from the first is more likely to be demasked and the

rhythmical rendering *invested with a certain distractedness*, which expressing itself in lines 11 and 12 (11 especially) disturbs the continuity of the rhythmic sighing which characterises all but the central line, and never so exquisitely as in 4th, 5th and 6th lines of the piece.

Particularly admirable is the relation of the first and last couplets and their manner of functionally framing the intermediate argument that draws the veil of illusion from ineluctable disillusion. They frame the remorselessly remorseful disclosure between two solicitudes—a solicitude presaging disclosure that must dispel the enchanting premise of naïvety, and a solicitude that must make what amend it can for *this exquisite vandalism*, by consolatory merging of the individual in the common fate.

(Of course I don't mistake this for overt dialogue. It is no more—and no less—than *meditated dialogue*, an imaginary conversation between young mind and old, between old and youthful ' Ego.')

Between the erect and solemn trees
I will go down upon my knees ;
    I shall not find this day
    So meet a place to pray.

Haply the beauty of this place
May work in me an answering grace,
    The stillness of the air
    Be echoed in my prayer.

The worshipping trees arise and run,
With never a swerve, towards the sun ;
    So may my soul's desire
    Turn to its central fire.

With single aim they seek the light,
And scarce a twig in all their height
    Breaks out until the head
    In glory is outspread.

How strong each pillared trunk ; the bark
That covers them, how smooth ; and hark,
    The sweet and gentle voice
    With which the leaves rejoice !

May a like strength and sweetness fill
Desire and thought and steadfast will,
    When I remember these
    Fair sacramental trees !

POEM VII

HERE, as with *Poem V*, before more essential ques-
tions can be considered, a complication must first be
untangled and set aside. It is not, this time, a mis-
understanding of the sense. Strange to say, hardly
a reader, here, either complained of obscurity or
even misread the sense, though one particular aberra-
tion, concerning the kind of trees described, in-
veigled some. The relief this lucidity afforded was
several times commented upon, and the collocation
of this set of four poems (V-VIII) may be thought to
have acted rather unfairly as a trap. But this mutual
influence between poems that are presented together
is as difficult to calculate as to avoid.

7·1. This is certainly better than V and VI for *one is able to
understand what the author means*, and coming after the first
two rather appealed to me. It certainly is clearer and more
easy to understand. The metre is regular and the whole poem
gives a general impression of quiet orderliness which is certainly
suited to the theme. The ' atmosphere ' of the poem is that of
a prayer but *it seems to be rather a prosy sort of a prayer*. After
reading it through a few more times I still do not know why
I must refrain from criticising it favourably, but although I
think it is much better than the two previous ones, I think there
seems to be something lacking.

But first the special complication must be dealt
with. Before the poem can have judgment passed
upon it, a particular set of double-action prejudices
must be got rid of. There is a doctrinal bee to be
driven out of our bonnets and it is well to realise
that our opinion of this poem need, and should, have
nothing to do with, or in any way derive from, or be

affected by, the buzzing of this bee. Whether we have it either in the right-hand side, the traditional side, of our critical bonnets, or in the left-hand, the advanced side, we should not, on any excuse, allow it to influence our decision.

Here it is as it buzzes on the right.

7·2. The whole poem pictures a man who with " desire and thoughts, and steadfast will " seeks the light ; consciously and quietly. *It does not help people struggling with incredulity. It does not give an answer to any how ? or why ?*—and that is the weak point of it.—*The form fits the contents to perfection.*

It was not the business of the poet here to help such people, or to answer such questions, so this charge may fairly be put aside. As to the final remark, it can be agreed to by people who take very different views upon the character and worth both of form and contents.

Here is the same bee buzzing on the left.

7·21. I don't like to hear people boast about praying. Alfred de Vigny held that *to pray is cowardly, and while I don't go as far as this*, I do think that it is rude to cram religious ecstasies down the throat of a sceptical age.

The violence which such prejudices can do to poetry will be remarked. Writing a modest piece of verse is hardly cramming religious ecstasies down our throats. Some of the less distracting influences of the doctrinal bee, as it buzzed in more median positions, will be noticed in the sequel.

Relevant opinion on the poem turned largely upon two points : its sincerity, whether the prime shaping motive of the poem was what it professes to be ; and its expression, whether its third verse, for example, does or does not suggest a note of factitiousness that throws doubt upon its authenticity. Both points are subtle and difficult to decide. As to the first : insincerity, in the crude and flagrant sense in which a man is insincere when he writes with his tongue in his cheek, when he consciously and deliberately tries to produce effects in his readers which don't happen for himself, is a charge which can hardly be brought on the strength of a single poem. A whole volume of verse may justify it sometimes, though conclusive evidence is hard to obtain. Here we could only be concerned with a much less damning though, from a literary point of view, a more important kind of insincerity. The flaw that insinuates itself when a writer cannot himself distinguish his own genuine promptings from those he would merely like to have, or those which he hopes will make a good poem. Such failures on his part to achieve complete imaginative integrity may show themselves in exaggeration, in strained expression, in false simplicity, or perhaps in the manner of his indebtedness to other poetry. We may confine our attention to this second point, about expression, since it concerns the evidence, if any, as to the fundamental integrity of the shaping impulse of the poem. The deeper problems of sincerity are discussed in Part III, Chapter VII.

The continuation of 7·21, clearly a biassed witness, will introduce us to the chief complaint.

7·3. Certainly a very commendable desire, this about " remembering sacramental trees ", but hardly necessary *when the trees do such remarkable things.*
Is this mysticism, humbug, or the mere raving of a fanatic ? To give the writer his due, the verse is smooth and clever, and the expression of the fifth admirable.

The same objection is stated in a more judicial manner by 7·31 who is not alone, either, in his other complaint.

7·31. I don't like the poem. The general effect of sweetness and calmness is for me quite overbalanced by two internal though outstanding blemishes. The first is *the predominating pathetic fallacies. The trees don't worship, arise, or run.* I know this sounds Johnsonian criticism but I feel it is *too blatant and insistent.* The other is I object to people going down on their knees among some trees. It would be a curious prayer that would be offered under the circumstances. Personally I don't think any words would be said ; and so why kneel ?

The problem of the ' pathetic fallacy ' we shall meet with again (cf. 10·6 and 12·4). This writer shows a clear awareness of the real difficulty about it, the question whether the attribution of feelings is used *as an argument* and overworked, a question that clearly cannot be divorced from the end to which the poem is directed.

Some of the other objections here have a more capricious air. The intrusive, accidental, visual image, for example, proved troublesome.

7·32. When I first read the third verse, *a vivid picture came into my mind* of a forward breaking away with the ball, from a loose scrum and " with never a swerve " making straight for the line. I didn't try to think of the verse in a ridiculous light but this idea occurred to me spontaneously. Do you think it could be reckoned as a fault in the poem ?

The precise image let loose cannot of course be counted against the poet ; the tendency towards the exaggerated and ludicrous might.

7·33. I could not help thinking that the poet who could leave the third verse as it stands lacks a sense of humour.

Yet some other readers found in this very expression one of the *apices* of the poem's perfection—a fact which will not now surprise us.

7·34. ' If this be not poetry what is ' ? *The thoughts behind this approach perfection ;* the expression of the sentiment is as exquisite as the sentiments themselves. " The erect and solemn trees "—" The worshipping trees arise and run with never a swerve towards the sun ", or, again, " Fair sacramental trees " . . . What a use of epithet and what a clear picture ! *A sunlit avenue always inspires me, as little else can,* with a sense of the Almighty, a feeling of smallness and insignificance. There is something holy about a tree, a feeling of superiority, *such as only some fine cathedral or Westminster Abbey can give. I find my thoughts expressed in this.*

7·35. This is a successful poem; the blend of religious experience with nature is forceful and sincere. The imagery of such a line as " The worshipping trees arise and run, with never a swerve, towards the sun " is *profound, impassioned and effective*.

7·36. I think this is a very fine poem indeed. I like the metre, and I like the atmosphere of the whole thing. It gives at once a grand picture of the forest, and the devotional feeling with which the author was imbued by the sight which he depicts. It is a fine communication of a fine feeling. *The two first lines* of the third verse perfectly express the meaning by their sudden change of rythm.

7·37. I think the dominant note of this poem is *harmony* of thought and sound and expression—and also of the atmosphere and the aspirations. This is seen in the third verse where the rhythm seems to leap forward to keep pace with the

" Arise and run, with never a swerve towards the sun."

It succeeds in giving *an impression of dignity and restfulness*; and sincerity—It pictures not only the thoughts roused by the trees but also the trees themselves.
The rhythm seems to match the march of the thought perfectly.

But what of the thought that is so perfectly matched ? Another writer is not so willing to accept ' arise and run ', though he does not show that he has considered very closely what the poet might be attempting to describe.

7·38. If the fourth verse is not literally true, the metaphor is valueless. If it is true, the trees should not be in a lyric of faith, but in a Botanic Garden.

A Menagerie, perhaps, would have been a still more suitable suggestion.
Too few of the readers attempted to connect the difficulty they felt over this line with other points in the diction and manner of the poem. A single fault, by itself, may always be merely clumsiness. To decide whether it is more than this we should have to consider with it such things as ' so meet a place ', ' Haply . . . may work in me ', ' central fire '

G

and the words ' fill ' and ' sacramental ' in the last verse. What may be just a blunder, taken by itself, becomes evidence of a tendency when it finds echoes. The direction of this tendency is sketched by several readers who respond to it with more or less hostility.

7·4. This poem seems to me disappointing ; it would have more appeal if it were differently expressed. Almost everywhere there is *a certain smugness* which makes it rather repellent. I think this lies in the choice of words—' so *meet* a place to pray ' ; the second line of the poem too is displeasing, and particularly the last verse with its moral hopes, and the last line of all where the word ' sacramental ' is rather offensive.

7·41. He is in a majestic forest, he is upon his knees and presumably hidden away between the erect and solemn trees. But nevertheless *he is much more prominent than the trees.*
The desire expressed in the last verse is laudable. But it is much *too self-conscious and far-fetched* to make me regard it as good poetry.

7·42. *Uplift.*

Here is one who makes his reasons for the same judgment superabundantly clear.

7·43. *Highly suspicious* at first and very cursory reading, after momentary marvell-ine elation, due to the verse form, and uncomfortably check'd by a *Je ne sais quoi* of *sententious egoism* combined with suspicion that a rather stark Grand Manner had been *both ùnder-studied and over-stùdied.*

2nd reading uncovered it as quite loathsome—a sin against the Holy Ghost.

Here we have the stoical sublime *to order as from the appropriate department of a literary stores*—out-Harroding Harrods, as they say—or Waring its rue with a Gillow.

Yet in spite of its horrid ' competence ', this mercenary piece phrases the image of verse 3 (1st 2 lines) so ludicrously as almost to reconcile me, in withering amusement, to its inherent factitiousness.

Verse 4 also exhibits its *facture*, wears its craft on its sleeve, in spite of itself—is discerned to be nastily " forced ", after concentration upon it has unveiled (as a general might a War Memorial) the smug sententiousness of its parable.

In Verse 5, Parable is served up cold, as at Sunday Supper—
the dose is almost domestically homiletic

[' strong trunk = father
' smooth bark = mother
and ' leaves ' the pinafored little ones—

an exquisite realisation of the *simple banale.*]

The clinically-minded critic must recognise this sort of thing
for what it is—*an infallible symptom of the anæsthetising of
spontaneity and impulse by the gas that breeds above the staid and
unspontaneous uplift spirit of a Democracy whose Literature has
been commercialised.*

Here we have the commercialisation of, say, Wordsworth's
Ode to Duty, etc. etc.—of rock-bottom by rock-bun simplicities.
In this " poem "-er piece—Wordsworth is stabbed to the *heart*
by a suburban Brutus, in, so to speak, the Senate House of
Literature.

' Assuredly ' the Contractor for this Peace-work did not find,
that day, *so meet a subject to exploit.* It was not, however, his
knees that he went down upon, but his SHANKS !

A contributory motive for such outbursts is
indicated by 7·44.

7·44. This poet is so prim that we are moved to laugh at
him, even though we feel that he would be deeply hurt if he
heard us.

Favourable opinions were not wanting, indeed
they made up a majority. The root question, as so
often, is whether these responses reflect the poem
itself, or some private poem prompted by the material
set before the reader and by his own reminiscences.

7·5. An atmosphere of peace, and deep reverence, which
transports the reader into *another world, more pure and white
than this.* With what magic is the rhythm used to bring out
first the majesty and awe that is within the speaker's soul and
then the gradually deepening solace and peace which comes over
him, as it were radiated down by the green, gaunt figures of
the trees, rising motionless up into the sky, full of worship.
Finally after peace, strength and fervent desire enter the soul,
so that the poem typifies the progress of emotion, of which the
outcome is action in accordance with the natural response to
that emotion, whatever it is. Although here, the poem stops
short of action ; but we feel that it is there, if only in the heart.

Most of the admirers were more occupied by the effect of the poem on their feelings than by the detail of the poem itself.

7·51. I like this poem because it expresses *my feelings at times when I am out-of-doors alone*. God seems much nearer, and I feel inclined to pray. I like the thought that the trees are worshipping God. In fact the poem shows us that we *can* find a religion in nature.

That more than a little of the appeal of the poem came from sources outside it is shown by the frequency with which admiration wanders off to linger upon other thoughts.

7·52. Not a forced simplicity but natural and spontaneous. The forest trees are described very beautifully showing that the poet has clearly felt the sense of stability and grandeur with which they impress one. He has well conveyed *their stillness and sense of purpose which is contrasted with the feeling that one is rather aimless and unsettled* and must pay homage to something *which lasts longer than oneself.*

Another admirer (7·56) expressly mentions the ' everlastingness ' of these trees, so that the praise of 7·53, who is unlucky in his use of ' mutual ', needs careful consideration.

7·53. Simplicity and unity seem to me the outstanding qualities of this poem. There is only one central idea : *the bond between man and nature in mutual worship :* the poet identifies his own purpose, prayer, with that of the trees ; and the natural qualities of the trees, beauty of form and strength, with traits in his own mind. Each verse is confined to this one idea, *nothing is admitted to suggest any other train of thought to the reader ;* and this seems to me a very considerable achievement.

The Cathedral image was, however, a dominant motive.

7·54. The poet has succeeded in universalizing his desire to worship. The ' erect and solemn trees ' that rush upward to the sun, *suggest the long aisle of a great cathedral*, its stillness and sanctity, and the leaves rejoicing with " sweet and gentle voice " fill it with gladness and delight in a way that trebles the evocative power of its solemnity. A very lovely poem.

7·55. *Unimportant, as the experience is capable of excitation at will by normal people, and probably therefore not very deep-seated :* cf. the frequent reference to " forest-aisles " in little books on Architecture.

This writer seems to be putting his finger on one of the most interesting problems of Stock Responses. (See Part III, Chapter V.)

7·56. Simplicity of sheer description especially noticeable after two preceding poems which are in the form of direct addresses. Perfect communication, but meaning not exhausted at first reading by any means. Describes a feeling which is inextricably interwoven with the simplicity of the actual verse form. The solemnity, grandeur, beauty—*everlastingness* of the trees can only be expressed in the simplest language. The value of the trees to the writer does not consist in their offering a meet place to pray, though *the suggestion of the cathedral-like majesty of the pillared trunks—" bare ruined choirs "—haunts the poem.* The central thought is in—" fair sacramental trees ". The spiritual value and significance of the different aspects of the trees is the main theme, and for this reason the appeal of the poem is direct to *those who find the sacrament which means most to them in Nature.* The language cannot be criticised because it is one with the poem in perfect expression

The revival of a set of feelings very ready to be revived, and the strict conformity of the poem with what many people have been taught to expect from ' nature-poetry ', undoubtedly explain much of its popularity. That it can create enthusiasm without being read is proved by the next extract.

7·57. This is *the gem of the four pieces.* It *creates the solemn peaceful reverent atmosphere of a pine wood* for us. We recollect *how often similar thoughts, occasioned by the reverent calm of the trees, have arisen in us,* as we stand awed by their grandeur and majesty. It is calm and *beautifully euphonius* in sound.

These ' how smooth ' pine-trees (with leaves) must be set beside the vision of one who, just as arbitrarily, disliked the poem. He had also a more intentional shot to aim at it.

7·58. A sense of humour spoils the last line of the 3rd verse—it reminds one (especially to-day) of " *chauffage centrale* ".
I suppose the trees are *Pines or Cypresses*.

Finally, not to leave an important minority view under-represented, we may end as we began.

7·6. There is something *superficial and conventional* in the rhythm and thought. It is all rather obvious—the reaction being ' *Yes of course quite* '. But . . .

Softly, in the dusk, a woman is singing to me ;
Taking me back down the vista of years, till I see
A child sitting under the piano, in the boom of the tingling
strings
And pressing the small, poised feet of a mother who smiles as
she sings.

In spite of myself the insidious mastery of song
Betrays me back, till the heart of me weeps to belong
To the old Sunday evenings at home, with winter outside
And hymns in the cosy parlour, the tinkling piano our guide.

So now it is vain for the singer to burst into clamour
With the great black piano appassionato. The glamour
Of childish days is upon me, my manhood is cast
Down in the flood of remembrance, I weep like a child for the
past.

POEM VIII

FEW readers will have difficulty in guessing where the division of opinion fell here. In subject, in metre, in treatment, in diction, in every *isolatable* character, the poem almost pressingly invites condemnation on the score of gross sentimentality. And the invitations were accepted. A few readers, however, on all sides of the central mob of opponents came to a different decision. We shall begin our survey at the heart of the mêlée and consider these others later.

8·1. If this, on further inspection, should prove not to be *silly, maudlin, sentimental twaddle*, I have missed the point. Such it certainly seems to me, and I loathe it. *It is a revelling in emotion for its own sake, that is nothing short of nauseating.* Moreover, it's badly done. I object to "cosy", *and* "tinkling" *used of a piano that elsewhere* "booms" *or is* "appasionato" *is just absurd.* If this be poetry, give me prose.

8·11. The general effect upon me of IV is mild. I consider it sentimental verse rather than poetry but *it doesn't strike me as being of the really nauseating type.* The emotion described might well be sincere as far as it went but to be enthusiastic over the poem I should have to be convinced that the poet's miseries were worth weeping about or casting down his manhood, and I certainly am not convinced. It seems to me to be full of "appeals to the gallery", *e.g.* "small poised feet"—anyhow they're certainly not worth weeping about, nor is a hymn in a cosy parlour, and *to a great number of people a tinkling piano is execrating.* On further consideration *I think it fails to arrive at the nauseating stage* not because of any redeeming sincerity but because it is *just too feeble to be anything so definite as nauseating.*

8·12. I think this poem is *perfectly nauseating.* The triviality of the sentiment is equalled only by the utter puerility of the versification—as in the third line of the first verse. *The poet's*

105

attitude to music is disgusting, and is perfectly summed up in his phrase about the "insidious mastery of song". *He regards it not as an art*, but as *an emotional stimulus of a very low kind*, and the hymn tunes he recalls were probably those of Messrs Sanky and Moody, and the more sentimental specimens from the Ancient and Modern Hymn Book. Sir H. Hadow once divided the main run of concert goers into two classes. Those who regarded music as a kind of audible confectionery, and those who left their intellects in the cloak room, and went in to have their souls shampooed. This man is not content with a shampoo, he is positively wallowing in a warm bath of soapy sentiment.

These will introduce us to some of the minor issues.

First, as to the sounds emitted by pianos, a point of fact that proved as disastrous to many readers as the description of the child's position.

8·13. Since I have formed my own opinion on the poem, I have experimented on one or two friends and each has started to grin when we have arrived at the phrase "a child sitting *under* a piano, in the *boom* of the *tinkling* strings". Allowing that it may possibly have been a grand and not an upright piano that the child was sitting under *we have still to satisfy ourselves that " tinkling " strings can boom*. Another rather unfortunate expression is that about the feet of the mother—poised. It is an uncommon word in poetry and naturally, as it doesn't fit in properly, it leads us away from the central idea of the poem. All these points, though small in themselves, do not allow us to get a good view of the poem as a whole.

Always, in looking over these protocols, it is illuminating to compare the type of comment with the closeness of reading evinced. So particular attention here may be invited to the fact that 8·13 has not noticed any difference between ' tingling ' and ' tinkling ', he has not even observed which word is used when. It would be superfluous to expect him to have considered whether the closeness of the child's ear to the strings might have anything to do with the character of the sounds, or whether, when the children stand up to sing, a ' tinkling ' would not

then replace ' the boom of the tingling strings.'[1]
Such a thing too as a premeditated contrast between
' the great black piano ' of the present, obviously a
grand piano, and the slighter notes of the instrument
in the ' parlour ' would escape him. 8·1 is at the
same distance from the poem, the two pianos are one
piano, any piano, for him. We shall frequently
notice the influence of this summary, ' newspaper '
type of reading in what follows.

The geometry of ' under the piano ' is almost as
distressing as the problem of the sounds to these
readers, such sticklers for ' accuracy ' do they show
themselves to be.

8·14. So many imperfections that one is prevented from judging
the poem as a whole. After the first two lines, *the vision of a
child sitting under the piano* can move nothing but laughter. It
is odd, too, that tingling strings should boom.

8·15. I don't see how a child could sit under the piano. *He
could sit under the key board but not under the piano.*

Even when with great acumen he has answered
his question, he is not satisfied. Does he hesitate to
enter the ' Underground ' at West Kensington, or
has he never taken shelter ' under a tree ' ? There
would appear to be some use after all for technical
instruction in the modes of metaphor.

We have already met one music-lover rebuking
the poet for his misuse of that art. But 8.12 is not
the only protocolist with severe standards. An
admirer will demonstrate for us how such irrelev-
ances can distort our reading.

8·2. This is the best. Its excellence lies in its securing a
feeling of ecstacy *from a sordid incident*, because it happened in
the past. Time throws a pleasantly mellow light upon *even
unpleasant* events, and it is this light which the poem expresses.

[1] A quite simple experiment will settle these points. 'Tingling'
of course, is the vibration. The vividity of the poet's memory is
remarkable.

I may add that the use of "unpoetical" words conforms admirably with the "unpoetical" character of the incident.

P.S. Please do not think, because I consider hymns sordid, that I have an inhibition : *I merely dislike bad music.* I take it that the poet didn't really enjoy the experience—otherwise he wouldn't have said "tinkle" and suchlike words. But he enjoyed recollecting the experience.

It would appear that if the child did enjoy singing hymns the poem must be condemned. Alas, there is good reason in the poem to think that he did.

Another writer is more aware of this danger, perhaps because his associations are stranger.

8·21. This poem unfortunately associates itself with jazz, and "coal black mammies" thumping the old piano down in Dixie. *This association condemns it somewhat prematurely.* After careful study, however, it appears to be worthless. Its appeal is entirely sentimental, and the subject is one of the most hackneyed. *Nearly every popular song deals with the same topic,* and the thing is not well done. "Piano" as a disyllable has an unpleasant sound. "The heart of me" is also obnoxious.

From proper attitudes to music (8·12) to correct behaviour to performers is but a step.

8·22. The second verse, which should have been the most poignant, is especially uninspiring. And *I don't think the lady singing at the piano would have been very pleased to hear her efforts described as "bursting into clamour".*

This reader, too, is a long way from having noticed what the poem is about.

With the remark about popular songs (8·21) we approach the stock-responses difficulty which more than anything else prevented this poem from being read.

8·3. *One cannot help disliking* the evocative use of such phrases as 'old Sunday evenings', 'cosy parlour', 'vista of years', etc., which are nothing but so many calls to one's loose emotion to attach itself to them.

A great number could not help themselves :

8·31. This poem suggests that some "Vain inglorious Milton" had unhappily been moved by *that mawkish sentiment with which we so often think of childhood*, to commit to verse thoughts that lie too shallow for words. These thoughts he expresses in phrases culled from *The News of the World* or others his ethereal links with literature.

That the poet might have a further use for such phrases, beyond that which his readers made of them, they failed to notice in their uneasy haste to withdraw. A haste which other things in the protocols (notably in connection with *Poem IV*) make me think suspicious.

In natural alliance with this nervousness are sundry prior demands, preconceptions as to what is proper and improper in poetry, and some personal twists and accidents.

8·32. Sentamental. The author has attached an emotion about his mother *to music which should arouse very different emotions.* Besides, *who would be a wretched, dependent child again when he can be a free person?* A particular tune might be associated with a particular person, especially if it was a lover, but that is different. I don't find this poem at all helpful nor does it express any feelings I have ever had or want to have.

That ' family-constellation ' again !

8·33. A good example of feeling without artistry. The man evidently means everything he says, but he doesn't know how to say it, and *he hasn't any idea that hymns in the cosy parlour are somehow wrong in poetry.* The picture of the time the poet is grieving for is vivid and even awakes an answering sorrow, but the expression is all wrong ; *the continual running over of the lines is irritating*, and the middle verse is very like a " Pears' Annual " sort of print.

At this point the metrical question—here a really useful test as to whether the reader has understood what the poet is, at least, attempting to do—comes to the front. For, in fact, unless the reader does contrive to master the movement of the poem he will hardly discover what its purport is. A general pre-conception that lines of verse should not run over would be a serious obstacle in this endeavour.

Though the last writer need not be accused of this, here is one who makes his views on metre quite clear.

8·4. A very vivid piece of prosy poetry—if one may call such a string of pictures poetry. I find some charm in the thoughts but *none in the verse or very little*. *Contrast the last line of each verse with Swinburne's " Thou has conquered, oh pale Galilean ; the world grows grey at they breath ".* The same metre, but what a difference of sentiment. I can't really like this.

That he should misquote his Swinburne altering its slow and weary rhythm (read : ' has grown grey from ') is just what we should expect !

All the difficulties of the stock emotional response (see Part III, Chapter VI) are paralleled in the stock reading of metre. It is as easy to import a conventional movement into the rhythm as to drag in conventional feelings. And it is just as easy to be revolted by our own importations in either case. Indeed, those who intrude the one commonly add the other.

8·41. After about 3 readings decide *I don't like this*. It makes me angry . . . I feel myself responding to it and don't like responding. I think *I feel hypnotised by the long boomy lines*. But the noise when I stop myself being hypnotised seems disproportionate to what's being said. *A lot of emotion is being stirred up* about nothing much. *The writer seems to love feeling sobby about his pure spotless childhood* and to enjoy thinking of himself *as a world-worn wretch*. There's too much about " insidiousness " and " appassionato " for me. The whole comparison between childhood's Sunday evenings and *passionate manhood etc.* is cheap by which I mean (1) It is easy ; (2) It is unfair both to childhood and manhood. I expect I am too irritated for this criticism to have value.

Re-read.
If not too lazy would throw the book into the corner.

Here ' the long boomy lines ' join hands neatly with the poet's ' pure spotless childhood '. Both the movement and the material are introduced by the reader ; they are not given in the poem, and they reflect only the reader's own private attempt at an

analogous poem constructed on the basis of a remote
and superficial awareness of this poem's apparent
subject-matter. 'Insidious' and 'appassionato', the
most evident hints that the poet is not doing, or
attempting to do, what the reader is expecting, are
dismissed without consideration. The poet 'as a
world-worn wretch' and his 'passionate manhood'
of which there is no hint, rather the reverse, in
the poem, are occupying the reader's attention
instead.

These importations are so frequent and have so
much influence upon what professes to be critical
'judgment' that they merit close attention. It would
seem that a dense medium of the reader's own poetic
product — 'much embryo, much abortion' —
surrounds him and intervenes very often to prevent
communication with the poet.

How intricate may be the co-operation between
what may be called 'detective' or 'imaginative'
intelligence and susceptibility to the suggestions of
speech-rhythms (partially concealed, of course, in
print), is again shown in 8·42.

8·42. A very dangerous metre to use unless the poetic thought
is really fine as *it is so easy to go thudding away when reading it*
without bothering to see if there is anything beautiful contained
in it. Here I think it fails because although " Sunday evenings
at home " and " tinkling pianos " are all right in themselves
they don't go in that metre. They become hackneyed in the
extreme. I don't appreciate the pictorial value any more than
the thought, diction or metre. I don't like the " boom of tingling
strings ", it isn't right and I don't like " a great black piano
appassionato ". The poem starts off well and raises one's hopes
only to be dashed beneath the piano.

The writer feels the danger of misreading the verse
form, but through not coming close enough, imagina-
tively, to 'the boom of the tingling strings' and
though not working out the contrasts in the poem,
he is victimised by his imparted rhythm in the end.
Since the poem does not turn out to be what he

expected, he does not take the trouble to find out
what it is.

The same inability to apprehend the verse-form
frustrates 8·43. He describes with fair success some
of the peculiarities of the movement, but an applica-
tion of external canons (usually fatal) to ' cast down ',
and failure to interpret the salient clue—in the move-
ment of ' the insidious mastery '—prevent him from
profiting by his observation. Perhaps if someone
had read the poem to him, giving decent prominence
to the natural speech rhythm, he would have been
converted.

8·43. The subject matter is appealing ; the picture given in
the first verse is vivid and original. *The metre, however, detracts
considerably from the* poem, and so takes from *the charm* of the
thought that the reader scarcely gives the verses a second con-
sideration.

In the first verse it is line 3 that spoils the verse which is both
harmonious *and charming* if considered without this line. But
" sitting under the piano " *upsets the whole balance of the metre,*
and gives a feeling of banality to what is otherwise an appealing
and original verse. The metre of the second verse offends less,
but " *the insidious mastery " makes it hard to read and throws the
rhythm out.* In the third verse *the pauses in the lines give an
impression of jerkiness.* The curtailing of the number of beats in
the 2nd line is not compensated for, while *the splitting-up of
" cast down " over two lines is inexcusable.*

This harping on the word ' charm ', however, is a
discouraging indication, and the final remark implies
preconceptions about metre which are not lightly
overcome.

It is significant with this poem, that the further
away any reading seems to be from the actual imagina-
tive realisation of its content the more confidently it
is dismissed. Another musical expert who has also
prepossessions in favour of metrical ' regularity ' will
strengthen the evidence on this point.

8·44. The sentimentality of this poem is perhaps the best
thing that can be said for it. For in all other respects its values

are even more negative. The diction is so forced as to appear
nothing short of ludicrous, and *the metre rivals a grasshopper in
elasticity.*

' In spite of myself the insidious mastery of song ' would
seem to me to make a fair bid for *one of the worst lines of poetry
ever written. The poet is trying to get effects the whole time.*
This is so painfully obvious. To say something out of the
common. Well, my dear sir, if ' boom of the tingling strings '
is the best you can do, *I would rather have the actual thing in
real life, much better expressed by any second-rate saxophonist.*

It is a pity that he did not attempt to discover
what effects the poet was trying to get.

While the music in the poem is under examination
yet another queer interpretation deserves admission.

8·45. Obviously a poem of homesickness—but the man who
wrote it *went to the concert* feeling homesick—' the great black
piano appassionato ' as he calls it, probably didn't really awaken
the feelings of homesickness in his mind. It merely gave him
an excuse for, and a way of putting his feelings down. But
with all this the poem doesn't express a particularly good
state of mind. Written in the heat of emotion it is simply
sloshy sentiment. The style of the poem, too, seems rather
exaggerated.

A reader who can think the woman is singing—
' softly, in the dusk '—on a concert platform has not
managed to approach very closely to the poem, and
his strictures are less binding for that reason.

It was inevitable that most of those who approved
the poem should comment upon the perils it escaped.

8·5. I have not been able to find a moment for this when I
have not been too tired to trust my judgment. *It runs an
appalling risk of sentimentality* and yet seems to have escaped all
offensiveness : a considerable achievement. It is poignant, but
not, I think, of very great value. The accent is familiar. D.H.L. ?

8·51. . . . One is made keenly aware of the strange relationship
of past and present experience—one feels the emotion the poet
experienced through his identity with and separation from his
past self. He has succeeded in conveying the acute emotion he
experienced and he has succeeded in dealing with a situation
fraught with the danger of sentimentality, without sentimentalism.
The ideas of Motherhood—the past—Sunday evenings etc. all

H

lend themselves to insincere emotion. In the second verse, it seems to me, *the poet recognises and dispels that danger.* He recognises there the difference between his man's outlook and his childish outlook and *we share his experience of being " betrayed back " by " the insidious mastery——"* I'm not sure if this explains how sentimentality is missed. I am convinced it is missed by the fact that the poem moves me more as I read it more often. An insincere emotion betrays itself by slovenly expression if one watches it closely I think.

The last remark is more a pious hope than a sound opinion. Carelessness may accompany the sincerest feelings. Perhaps the kind of carelessness will be different, but any dogmatism would be hazardous. Deft craftsmanship can easily elude this too convenient test.

8·52. The writer who introduces ' old Sunday evenings at home ' and ' hymns in the cosy parlour ' must be very sure of the sincerity of his feelings and his capability to express them if he is to avoid cheap sentimentality. Here the writer has avoided them and has succeeded in expressing the effect of music which calls back memories. *The power of music is even sufficient—though this is being very bold—to carry off the weeping.* Then there is the usual setting of the sentimental, dusk and soft singing, a little child ; one hesitates ; I think it is the ' great black piano ' that decides the day.

This writer seems less close in his reading than the last, but he illustrates the struggle the poem nearly always entailed, a struggle that did not always end in defeat.

A very few escaped this conflict and it thus becomes difficult to evaluate their acceptance.

8·6. Sentimental—fearfully so—but if sentiment must be expressed then here it is in its right setting and well done really.

Honestly I wish more people would throw off their sophistication and cynicism and be honest with themselves like the fellow in this poem !

It should be recognised that ' sentimental ' has several senses (see Part III, Chapter VI) and does not always impute low value. How near this reader came to the actual poem must, however, always remain undetermined. On the strength of ' honest with themselves like the fellow in this poem ', which seems to correspond to the analyses of 8·51, I incline to accord him the full benefit of the doubt.

More particulars of the acceptance struggle are given in 8·61.

8·61. *Although I feel almost ashamed to say so* this poem makes the biggest appeal (up to the moment of writing) of all four selections. The poem seems to be so eminently sentimental (I see no real reason why I, a grown man, should allow myself the luxury of tears) and yet the happiness of childhood does return at times in this way under the influence of music. *There seems to be a weakness in the metre in line 3 stanza 1.* I can't make it scan. And in stanza 2, ' the tinkling piano our guide ' ' guide ' I don't think a good word. Too obviously used for the sake of the rime.

This reader would have found a justification for ' guide ' if he had been able to recall, or imagine, the hymn-singing described—the children's uncertain voices rather tentatively *following* the ' tinkling ' notes of the piano. In line 3, stanza 1, a pause after ' piano ' for the realisation of the quivering thunder of the base notes would have met his difficulty with scansion.

The accusations (cf. 8·31, 8·21, 8·33) of naïvety or of exploiting conventional responses, together with the objections on the ground of inaccuracy, are well countered in 8·7.

8·7. It is difficult to pass judgment on this poem. The communication is excellent, and the experience one familiar to most people. I suppose this emotional reversion to an ordinary incident of one's childhood, and the indulgence in grief for it simply because it is past, is really sentimental. *The striking thing is, that the poet* [D. H. Lawrence ? or American ?] *knows quite well that it is so, and does not try to make capital out of the sentiment.* The simplicity and accuracy with which he records his feelings—and *the justness of the expression, not pitching the thing up at all*—somehow alters the focus ; what might have been merely sentimental becomes valuable—the strength of the underlying feeling becoming apparent through the sincerity and truthfulness of the exprsesion.

Another useful note of analysis is added in 8·71.

8·71. Associations make it difficult to judge this poem impartially. The first verse is sentimental, but pleasing ; *it is curious that the poet too feels sentimentality coming upon him—* ' *In spite of myself* '—*and he gives way to it entirely.* The last two lines of the second verse particularly show sentimentality— a shallow and languishing feeling—but yet they convey adequately the qualities of the evenings they describe ; thus we can scarcely accuse the poet of sentimentality

The poem is extremely simple, and whether it is itself weak or no, it well describes a certain psychological state of mind. The poet can convey pictures. The poem I think succeeds in doing what it sets out to do.

Whether the poem is so simple may well be doubted on the evidence now before us.

How much nearer these readers come to the poem than those who most abused it may be measured by the collocation of 8·72, where the writer is rather describing some other poem floating in his private limbo than attempting to discover what the poet is doing.

8·72. This poem is false. *One worships the past in the present, for what it is, not for what it was.* To ask for the renewal of the past is to ask for its destruction. *The poet is asking for the destruction of what is most dear to him.*

Finally 8·8 may add an observation not elsewhere made upon the peculiar quality of the emotion present.

8·8. I can't decide about this poem—it portrays something, which post-Victorians have little sympathy with, and yet there is a sense of infinite longing, and the man's weeping is the *unrestrained soul satisfying crying which we only experience in dreams.*

The rhythm emphasises the reflective strain—the words are sophisticated—the result is puzzling.

This brings us to the end of the first two groups of poems. The writers who supply the comments on the following five poems belonged to an audience of the same type gathered two years later. Only a few of the original members remained. The change greatly increases the representative character of these extracts.

A Health, a ringing health, unto the king
Of all our hearts to-day ! But what proud song
Should follow on the thought, nor do him wrong ?
Unless the sea were harp, each mirthful string
Woven of the lightning of the nights of Spring,
And Dawn the lonely listener, glad and grave
With colours of the sea-shell and the wave
In brightening eye and cheek, there is none to sing !

Drink to him, as men upon an Alpine peak
Brim one immortal cup of crimson wine,
And into it drop one pure cold crust of snow,
Then hold it up, too rapturously to speak
And drink—to the mountains, line on glittering line,
Surging away into the sunset-glow.

POEM IX

I AM privileged to print the following Note from the author of *Poem IX*, written after he had seen some of the protocols.

" The original version was written for a special occasion, which left the writer little time for revision. The final edition of the poem reads as follows :—

FOR THE EIGHTIETH BIRTHDAY OF GEORGE MEREDITH

A HEALTH, a ringing health, to the uncrowned king
 Of all our hearts to-day ! But what brave song
 Should follow on the thought, nor do him wrong ?
Unless, with bird-like body and dusky wing
Sandra return to his deep woods in Spring,
 And nightingale and sky-lark, all night long,
 Pour their new-wedded notes in a golden throng
Through her dark throat till dawn, there is none to sing !

Pledge him, as men upon an Alpine peak
 Brim one immortal cup of crimson wine,
  And into it drop one pure cold crust of snow,
Then hold it up, too rapturously to speak
And drink—to the mountains, line on glittering line,
  Surging away into the sunset-glow.

At the same time the readers of the first version showed an incapacity to take in the fact that it was not the king, but the king of the hearers' hearts on that occasion, of which the first sentence spoke. The absence of the title of the poem deprived readers of a clue ; but by no means of every clue if they had exercised a little thought. The suggestion that the ' mirthful strings ' of the harp in question were to be woven of spring lightning was, of course, an allusion to the peculiar, flickering, and dazzling character of Meredith's wit, and had no relation whatever to the cheap ideas of the readers themselves. Unfortunately, in reading poetry too many persons ' impute their own personalities ' to what they read, and often attack their own musical-comedy faults in those whom they fail to understand. This is a problem for psycho-analysis, not criticism. I hope it is unnecessary to say that ' Sandra ', in the new version does not mean a wife of Botticelli."

Two minor chases, each, unluckily, after a Wild Goose, complicate this set of protocols. The first introduces us to the Royalist Imbroglio.

9·1. Prejudice against first line. Nobody worships the King, and patriotic verse tends to be insincere.

The only other objection this writer raised was to the awkwardness of ' unto '. The rest was praise.

9·11. This poem seems to be written in the grand manner. To me it seems theatrical, full of sound but little else. *One has ceased to think of Kings in that particular way*, and in consequence the poem is without vitality.

9·111. The poem suggests *an attempt of one of the late Cavalier poets*—led to think this by *association of ' the King ' with a ' ringing health ' drunk by his defeated, though not dejected, supporters.* Impossible to fully criticise this since *no modern reader in his room can have same feeling as the writer*—writer probably half tipsy, vastly elated by the fact that he was a care-free roisterer and not a Puritan.

The assumptions behind these views upon the obsolescence of poems deserve and must receive a thorough scrutiny later.

An extraordinary number of readers were betrayed by this first line, and made no attempt to read more closely.

9·12. The similes are unsuitable. *Why, when one drinks to the King, presumably in a crowded room,* should one think of Alpine peaks and crusts of cold snow ? For these reasons I think the poem bad.

Speculation, however, awoke in some, and the Wild Goose flies high.

9·13. After reading the sonnet I do not know who ' the King ' is. Does the poet mean God, or an earthly Monarch ?

9·131. This rapturous ecstacy in the presence of natural objects is one of the most obvious forms of self complacency. *Perhaps the writer has another King for his ' mind ' ;* but that he should be content to find him in *situations which have a smack of the romantic musical comedy*—harps and glittering mountains perhaps more suggestive of the Gothic revival *shows a man who*—maybe through unconscious protest, probably through mere natural blindness—*ignores all that is interesting and vital in life in his worship of God. The expression has all the vigour of the Psalms* and is an adequate translation of the cold, hard, primary-coloured emotion.

The more popular Stock Response, as such things will, had diverse effects.

9·14. As *a staunch royalist* and one who loves to sing with all his might and main that grand old song " Here's a Health unto His Majesty " I had thought after reading the first line to enjoy this little poem. *But what a disappointment !* One could, I suppose, imagine some sense into the imagery of lines 4-8 inclusive, but the result would be a vain thing, at any rate so far as the main idea of the poem is concerned.

After the Royalist the Republican :

9·15. An altogether unpleasant effect on me : I could not persuade myself I was not reading a poem in the ' Observer '. " *King* " *associates itself in my mind with Tyranny, an impossible subject for poetry.*

Alas, poor Shelley !
One confusion not unnaturally breeds another.

9·16. It starts *with a health to the King, which is drunk later* on an Alpine peak.

Many who did not go so far as this expressed a concern which *may* be regarded as more properly a criticism of the poem :

9·17. Does the subject, the ' King ' justify the rather high-flown language ? I want to know more about this personage before I accept the poem.

Hitherto our commentators have been rather querulous. Here, unless my leg was being pulled, is the real Hero-worshipper.

9·18. Main effect is a feeling of *the size, strength and grandeur of the king.* A king comparable with a line of mountains, comparable with what that line of mountains represents to mountaineers, a king fit to be addressed by the never ending song of the sea, sung to by a ' glad and grave ' dawn with the colours of the sea-shell in her cheek. This king to be pledged in a cup, more precious than gold almost ranks with the gods. *Yet he is essentially cold and reserved, more remarked for his capability than for his humanity*, more respected than loved, more like a gaunt and " glittering " mountain than a grass covered hill basking in the sunshine. I like this poem and the effect of such lines as

> " Brim one immortal cup of crimson wine
> And into it drop one pure cold crust of snow "

is too marvellous to be described.

A fine example, towards the end, of ' reading into the poem '. Those who form an adverse view of the merits of the poem will perhaps recognise in the praise a faithful summing up of the very points they would themselves charge against it as defects.

It is noteworthy that so many readers (I have by no means emptied the basket) should have been misled by so simple a trope as ' the king of all our hearts ', and hardly less remarkable that they should have considered the identity of the actual person celebrated in the sonnet so germane to the question of its merit. This, however, is a matter to be discussed later. (See Appendix A, p. 355.)

After the Royalist Imbroglio the Drink Problem !

9·2. This poem could well have been written by a drunk devotee of Mr Rudyard Kipling. *It is incorrect* to say men drink wine on Alpine peaks, even though it be in immortal cups. No one will be sufficiently foolish to mix snow with their wine.

I regret that, as a Member of the Alpine Club, I have to declare that this critic is too positive in his assertions. The proper inference, if one must go into such matters, would seem to be either that this peak has an uncommonly easy and quick descent, or that the climbers, in view of the date, were the Signori Gugliermina.

9·21. The picture of the mountaineers rapturously holding up frozen wine seems silly to me, and I react with annoyance. *Why should they drop snow into their wine?* They would be quite cold enough already, upon an Alpine peak.

9·21. To what are these bibulous gentlemen drinking ? Firstly to a king ; then to the mountains, line on glittering line. Above all it is irritating to read a poet who doesn't even know how to drink red wine ; a pure cold crust of snow would never be put into a red wine by a connoisseur.

The writers evidently felt some difficulty in resisting the temptation to ribaldry this topic extends. But here are two entirely different objections.

9·22. Words such as ' immortal ', ' pure ', ' rapturously ', seem to fill out the line and put the drink in the far distant future. One further point—*were the cup brimmed, the ' pure cold crust of snow ' would certainly have slopped over some of the ' crimson wine ', and that were a pity and a mess !*

For the sake of completeness it is worth adding that one protocol records an " intimate personal association affecting my opinion of the poem—I am a teetotaller."

Passing now to matters more closely connected with critical opinion on the poem, two complete protocols may be set beside one another to show once again how often what most pains one reader is exactly what most pleases another.

9·3. This poem is a fake. What passes for enthusiasm in the first few lines is in reality *only a spurious form of ' heartiness '. The elaborate sea-harp simile is meaningless : the music, so catchily tuneful, that of a sublimated barrel-organ.* The rhythm not organic but superimposed from without. But it is a clever fake. The writer has evidently had much practice in versification, he has a considerable degree of skill in putting words together to form a pretty pattern. He achieves a sense of completeness and finality in the sextet *by alliteration which is almost enviably ' slick '.* If he had anything to say it is likely that he would communicate it effectively : unfortunately he has next to nothing. *His poem is a form of verbal flatulence* and belongs to a class of verse which appears with distressing regularity in the pages of such periodicals as *The Spectator* and *The London Mercury.*

9·31. *I like this—it is so exuberant and joyful*—I read it three or four times at the first attack, not because I could not make much out of it, as was the case with the third poem (*No. XI*), but because *the poet's mood was so infectious, and made me feel as hearty as he must have felt when he wrote the poem.*—I think he has achieved a stroke of genius with ' Dawn the lonely listener '—and he succeeds in impressing us with his own mood by such words as ' mirthful ', and ' rapturously '. *The metre, too, is appropriate to the mood, the verse goes with a swing, one might say.*

Here matter, mood, and movement alike come in for correspondent praise and dispraise, strong evidence that the poet has done what he wished and well suited his means to his end. Only those who objected to the aim quarrelled with the means.

9·32. The whole poem *seeks to slap you on the back with a false joie-de-vivre*, and lamentably fails.

Very many writers acclaimed this exuberance. It was certainly one of the two chief sources of the great popularity of the poem. It is admirably described in the following extract where the other source of popularity is also indicated.

9·4. A poem of *extreme enthusiasm and consequently filled with a sort of excess of expression* which seems to say ' Take me or leave me '. Personally I revelled in it. In the first half the poet gives his ideas with the help of alliteration and some telling phrases, especially his ' lightning of the nights of Spring '. In the second *he paints a truly grand picture. Colours, Alpine peaks, crimson wine,* cold crust of snow, and mountains in the background. *An admirable poetical canvas.*

Colours and pictures, the appeal to the mind's eye, to the visualiser, is a source of attraction that able advertising agents have known and used for many years.

9·41. I like the poem because of *its colour and imagery.* Lines such as ' brim one immortal cup of crimson wine ' *always appeal to my sense of colour. That is why I like Keats.*

9·42. The poet *has the right idea* and picks his words carefully with due regard to their effect ; so it is he *gives us a mind-picture of the coldness of the snow and the crystal clearness of the crimson wine which is naturally immortal.*

A question that had troubled many, though I have not represented it, is thus answered. Why immortal? Naturally so. In what sense? This writer does not venture so far, nor do any of the other writers who admire this much-praised line expatiate upon the epithet. The hostile party, however, not only quarrelled much about ' immortal ' but quibbled over ' crimson ' too. There are clearly several senses in which we may have a ' sense of colour '. Nor was this the only colour-point objected to.

9·421. There are jarring fallacies in the detail : Dawn is made to have pink eyes and green cheeks.

But the majority were content with a less meticulous examination.

9·43. I liked the modern romantic freshness, the warmth and colour.

9·44. What I like in this sonnet are *the two vividly-drawn pictures it contains*, the first reminding me in its delicate touches of a Botticelli picture, and the second glowing with warm colour and human triumph.

9·45. This is good. The lines go with a swing. The phrasing is musical and *the imagery quite original and striking*.

Others were concerned rather with its fittingness :

9·46. I was *at first partly carried away by the succession of exciting images sonorously and effectively expressed*, but was unable to respond fully to the poet's demand on my emotions. *The sight of mountains stirs me deeply, but I am quite sure they do not occasion feelings at all comparable with any feelings of enthusiasm I might have for a fellow man.* The difference is one of kind, not degree.

Since visual images were concerned it is not surprising that different imaginers saw different visions. We have already read two descriptions (9·4, 9·44). Here are others.

9·47. The second stanza suggests a Swiss Tourist Agency poster.

9·48. As to the Alpine simile, *when one has shaken off the strong emotion which naturally arises when such associations are aroused*, one is disgusted by the banality of diction and *general railway advertisement character of the poet's manner*.

The enlivening effect of the sonnet is much remarked upon.

9·5. *The mood of exhilaration is contagious*, so that without appreciating the poet's reason for the feeling I share this exhilaration so that *to this extent this poem fulfils the demand I make of poetry*. To bring me in contact with a spirit who has pondered to such effect that his work will open a window of my own spirit to *the larger purer universe* of his own.

9·51. The ' Alpine peak ' and the ' pure cold crust of snow ' convey exactly *the sense of exhilaration* produced by *the intense and enthusiastic idealism of the poet*.

9·52. It exhilarates me by its series of vivid images. The adjective I think of in connection with these images is ' chaste '.

A comment which, perhaps through association by contrast, reminds one of the American publisher who complained of the word ' chaste ' as ' always deplorably suggestive '. But certainly a too conscious quest for a larger, purer universe of intense and enthusiastic idealism does open ground for suspicion.

Keats who occurred in an earlier protocol (9·41) reappears several times :

9·6. The simile forming the last six lines of the sonnet is very fine ; *it can be held on a par* with that similar one by Keats at the end of his sonnet on " Chapman's Homer ".

9·61. The last verse is far clearer action, and *there is something in the* metre *which seems suggestive of mountains* for it brings to mind at once stout Cortés and a peak, in Darien.

A much simpler explanation seems sufficient. The word ' peak ' by itself would be quite enough.

Images other than visual played their part. The mind's ear was invited to attend.

9·7. ' Surging away into the sunset glow '. *A suitable diminuendo after the roar of the song of the sea and the lightning*.

Readers with musical interests were more critical :

9·71. The only concrete simile in the octet is the likening of the sea to a harp—surely a little extravagant.

9·72. The imagery is bad. *The sea may sound like an organ but it never had the sound of a harp.*

9·73. One wonders if the poet has correctly grasped the idea conveyed in the description of the harp,

> " each mirthful string
> Woven of the lightning of the nights of Spring ".

9·74. A far-fetched metaphor in which the sea is pictured as a harp *and each string*, besides being mirthful, *is made up of the lightning of Spring nights.* For some unknown reason *Dawn* listens to the music of this incredible instrument.

9·75. *The first definite clue to the poem's true character is the word ' woven ' (5th line). Since strings are spun or twisted, ' woven ' must have been brought in for its higher potency in releasing vague emotion.* From that point onwards the poet was obviously overwhelmed with recollected phrases and pilfered epithets.

The facts implied in this metaphor were also challenged on another ground :

9·76. Common sense suggests that if the Dawn were present the lightning of spring *nights* would be inevitably absent.

9·77. Since Dawn does not come into being till the end of night, the strings and the listener could not exist contemporaneously.

It is clear that the spirit of Dr Johnson has happily not altogether vanished from literary criticism.

Failure to recognise the sonnet form appeared again :

9·8. It seems to be part of a drama

9·81. This is essentially a piece of dramatic poetry, one which can only be properly appreciated when heard declaimed in the course of a play.

Against these may be set a more common complaint, which incidentally well illustrates some of the dangers of technical presuppositions.

9·82. I am confronted by a sonnet—a cold fact recognised before I had read a word. *I have very definite ideas of what should be the general content of a sonnet*, and of all of them, a toast is outside the list. A ringing health needs a quicker, livelier, rhythm, a faster stream of rhymes than a sonnet affords.

It will have been noticed that, for some of his readers at least (9·31, 9·45) the poet quite overcame these objections. Also :

9·83. Subject chosen is very suitable to the sonnet form ; both are dignified.

The favourable verdict of the majority has hitherto been insufficiently represented.

9·9. I like it best, *because it is a song from within me.* The words are simple, consequently the sense immediately touches my mind. ' Lightning of the nights of spring ', ' one pure cold crust of snow ' *recall ecstasies of my own.* The imperative mood moves me directly. The long swinging evenness of the thought running unbroken through many lines makes it one emotion, not a series of metaphorical attacks. *The poet has crammed in the most moving manifestations of nature, personified them, toasted the most austere of them in a rapture, and moved me beyond explaining.*

But surely this writer has himself, in the italicised passages, provided a quite satisfactory explanation.

9·91. Appeals to me because of sincerity and nobility of sentiment. The warmth of the feeling justifies the hyperbole which might so easily sound hollow, but here seems the just expression of an emotion inexpressible in words. The appeal to the imagination is as strong as that to the heart, for *nature is alluded to in its loveliest and grandest aspects.* The poem must have a lasting value because of the freedom it allows the æsthetic sense in the images called up—' the lightning of the nights of spring ', the colours of sea-shell and wave.

These, with the counterblasts in 9·22 and 9·93 will serve to indicate the point upon which opinion chiefly turned—whether the poem earned a right to exploit the associations it evoked. In other words, a problem of Stock Responses.

9·92. The poem *contains all the customary apparatus of poetical hack-work*, the conventional similes and personifications—Dawn, the sea, sunset, the Alpine peaks—all in fourteen lines !

9·93. *The main experience has nothing to do with the first line.* Health drinking may have given rise to the conviction that a song ought to be written—even a sonnet, though that is a most unlikely form in which to express a mood of anniversary high spirits—*but then that isn't the experience expressed.* What is ? Almost certainly, an adolescent reaction to the vocabulary of the romantics.

Only one writer made allusion to what may be thought a marked influence in the sonnet.

9·94. The style is Swinburne *cum* water.

The comments on this poem may show, more clearly than with any of the others, how much at a loss many readers are if required to interpret and judge figurative language. Several important questions as to the proper approach to hyperbole, and the understanding of similes which are *emotive* rather than elucidatory, arise for attention. These matters are discussed in Part III, Chapter II.

I

Climb, cloud, and pencil all the blue
   With your miraculous stockade ;
The earth will have her joy of you
   And limn your beauty till it fade.

Puzzle the cattle at the grass
   And paint your pleasure on their flanks ;
Shoot, as the ripe cornfield you pass,
   A shudder down those golden ranks.

On wall and window slant your hand
   And sidle up the garden stair ;
Cherish each flower in all the land
   With soft encroachments of cool air.

Lay your long fingers on the sea
   And shake your shadow at the sun,
Darkly reminding him that he
   Relieve you when your work is done.

Rally your wizardries, and wake
   A noonday panic cold and rude,
Till 'neath the ferns the drowsy snake
   Is conscious of his solitude.

Then as your sorcery declines
   Elaborate your pomp the more,
So shall your gorgeous new designs
   Crown your beneficence before.

Your silver hinges now revolve,
   Your snowy citadels unfold,
And, lest their pride too soon dissolve,
   Buckle them with a belt of gold.

O sprawling domes, O tottering towers,
   O frail steel tissues of the sun—
What ! Have ye numbered all your hours
   And is your empire all fordone ?

POEM X

MNEMONIC and other irrelevances, some problems of imagery, and a swarm of technical presuppositions, mainly concerning movement and diction, mark this set of protocols too, and the Stock Response is not absent. But some deeper and more disturbing problems, concerning not so much the nature of the poem as the kind of value it may possess, will be noticed to lurk frequently below the surface and to come out occasionally into explicit words.

First, let us survey the more accessible particularities of opinion.

10·1. The charm of this is twofold : *first, one can bask in the warm sunshine of a perfect September day* (such as I have not experienced in England in 1927), *and realise that America is a good country also,—England having no "golden ranks" of corn ;* secondly, the rhythm, rhyme and alliteration make one want to read it aloud a second time and then try to sing it. Did Bryant write it ? I don't know.

The mnemonic pull, with less justification and in a totally different direction, also governs 10·11. The alleged ground in the tone of the poem is not easy to make out.

10·11. The authoress (I fear it is so) should be prohibited by law from ever approaching any child whose sense and imagination are not certified normal and healthy. The poem *is the type which invades school anthologies* though it is a disreputable offspring of Shelley (misunderstood) and a woolly sentimental mind. *It endeavours to bring the young mind close to " Nature " by adopting a tone of skittish patronage.* It is such and not the Goths nor the classics that desolate Europe.

With 10·2 we pass to the image problem.

131

10·2. *I like this because clouds have a fascination for me.* Also the passage of the cloud's shadow over the fields, cottages, gardens and the sea is cleverly told. *If the test of the mental picture arising in reader's mind from poet's words is a test at all, the poem is good.* Even the necessity of looking up " Limn " in line 4 did not detract from pleasure in reading it. The words are not so happy as the picture formed : one would get tired of having the picture raised in the mind by the repetition of the words. Musically they do not satisfy. Yes, the more I read it the less I like it.

On the metrical question we shall hear other views. The imagery issue, as we have learned to expect, provoked the most extreme divergencies of opinion.

10·21. This is a very pleasant poem. *It makes heaps of pictures in the mind—some new, some recalling things one has seen before.* Stanza 3 connected itself with a certain flight of stone steps for me at once. Stanza 5 is the best of all. One *feels* the chill, when the hot sun suddenly ' goes in ', perfectly.

10·22. This poem fails utterly for me. *The words do not call up the pictures of what the poet is trying to represent.* The cloud shaking its shadows at the sun, or sidling up the stair appears merely ludicrous. *I dislike the whole idea of the cloud with a pencil in its fingers.* The poet does not give me the impression that *a little cloud in the sky* has really given him the inspiration to write ; *all is artificial and sentimental.*

If suitable images are for one reader an invaluable adjunct to his reading, erratic images for another may be a fatal bar. In general the effect of the intervention of images is to make good better and bad worse. Images in reading are perhaps best regarded as a *sign* of how the reader is getting on with the poem, they are hardly ever a means which the poet uses, the gap between the verbal image (the figure of speech, the description, simile, or metaphor) and the visual image being too great, and readers' idiosyncrasies too surprising. The littleness of the cloud in 10·22, and the pencil in its fingers are contributions of this reader's uncontrolled visualising faculty and these exercises, like the refusal to see what the poet *did* try to suggest, are prompted by a prior distaste for the poem whose source is perhaps indicated in his final remark. This seems to be the usual state of affairs when erratic imagery intervenes. It is not invariably so as 10·23 will show. A few victims of extremely lively and vivid imagery do really approach poetry (and life) through their visual imaginations, but often their other mental operations are able to correct and compensate for the freakish whimsicality this approach entails.

10·23. I could make little of this poem. *It persists in suggesting a night-marish forest scene,* with giant drooping ferns, writhing snakes and flashes of red lightning in a blue mist. *Superimposed on this, a still more weird picture of a tumbling Babylon.* There seems to be a breathless haste in the words when read mentally, but not when read aloud. There is also a rapid and chaotic jump from idea to idea which is bizarre and confusing. None the less the poem is rather fascinating.

This reader writes to me, " I visualise everything otherwise, things mean little to me ", developing by an accident of punctuation a criticism I would not be so rude as to make.

Another curiosity of imagery will ventilate a different objection :

10·24. This poem seems to me positively bad. Some of the lines are decidedly silly, like : " till 'neath the fern the drowsy snake is conscious of his solitude ". *The image is so unpleasant.* It seems the poet had a few vulgar ideas and thought he could write a poem about them.

The reader has himself to blame if his image was actually unpleasant. If all allusions to snakes are to be avoided, how lacking in taste must Milton appear. And further, the assumption that only pleasant images have a place in poetry should be hailed and challenged whenever it appears.

To pass now to quite another source of irrelevance ; critical preconceptions when they intervene as obstacles to reading are often respectable doctrine crudely applied; of this the following may appear an example:

10·3. The poem *is dead because it wants in human interest.* The poet has escaped from the world of men. His nearest approach to mankind is the 'garden stair'. The interest of the poem lies in its cinematographic reproduction in words of a phenomenon which every mortal has the joy of witnessing with his own eyes. Success lies in the magic of words which in plain black and white are capable of exciting the senses to a vivid appreciation of a series of events the poet has himself minutely observed. Turner does as much by a different medium.

It may be that ' The proper study of mankind is man'. But, if so, in poetry everything that can interest man is part of him. Every poem is a tissue of human impulses, and mention of man and his affairs is not needed to interest us. It is a little difficult to make out whether in the end this reader overcame his preconception or not.

Some other presuppositions, but of a technical order, deserve more attention. They are many and varied. First may be instanced the assumption that words *in themselves* have characters—are ugly, beautiful, delicate, light, weighty or cumbrous—apart from the way in which they are used. With it appears the parallel assumption that the ' subject ' of a poem automatically prescribes a certain selection from the dictionary.

10·4. The alliteration in the poem is very effective and gives one the idea of the cloud drifting slowly over the land and sea. *I think the author has rather spoilt it in places by using long, ugly words, such as beneficence, encroachment and elaborate.*

10·41. The poet has endeavoured to paint a word picture of a cloud. *In order to do this a poet must choose words in accordance with his picture. If the picture is going to be delicate, then must the words be light. If the picture is going to be heavy then must the words be weighty.* This poet wanted to paint a delicate picture, but he mixed delicate and cumbrous words. Such words as miraculous, encroachments, elaborate and benificence tend to blurr the picture. Having painted his picture it is a pity to break it with a harsh question

> What ! Have ye numbered all your hours
> And is your empire all fordone ?

The poet should be content that something beautiful has been shown to him.

Everything of course turns upon the fashion in which the words are put together, and it is the detailed, instant to instant, development of the poem, not the separable subject abstractly regarded, that governs the diction. The final rebuke to the poet will be considered later.

Allied objections were brought on the ground of cacophony.

10·42. Very ugly first verse. Climb, cloud—2 *hard words, consonants together.*

> *Cl*imb *cl*oud and pen*cil* all the blue
> With your mira*cul*ous sto*ck*ade.

Hard word like ' limn ' not appropriate for the beauty of cloud scenery. 2nd verse,—silly thought, awkward rhythm of second line.

' Cherish each '—awful mix-up of *ch* and *sh*. I don't quite know what the last 2 verses mean—what the steel tissue of the sun is but it doesn't seem to matter.

10·43. The whole poem is a rather ungracious and blunt address to the cloud. It strikes me as the work of an amateur or beginner. *On the whole it is ugly, chiefly because certain words are used, and placed badly. E.g.* " Climb, cloud," repeats sound *cl*. " Miraculous stockade " " his solitude " are difficult to say easily and correctly, and are ugly when said correctly because of the repetition of the s sound.

Without going so far as one reader, who heard in these last sibilants the hissing of the serpent, we may yet lay down as a general principle that no sound in poetry can be judged apart from its place and function in the poem. To apply canons of euphony from outside and bar out certain conjunctions of consonants as ugly, without regard to their exact particular effect in the precise context in which they come, is as foolish as to condemn a line in a picture without looking at the other lines which may co-operate in the design. Such arbitrary canons are popular because they are simple and because they can be applied (like the imperfect rhyme test, cf. 2·12) without entering into the poem. Fairly specious detailed justifications for all the sounds here inveighed against could be worked out, but the justification would be nearly as arbitrary as the accusation. The relations of sound-effects to the rest of the happenings in the poem are too subtle and too mingled for any analysis to have much cogency. It is sad to have to discourage so harmless a pastime, but the facts are so. Most alleged instances of onomatopœia, for example, are imaginary, are cases of the suggestion much more than of the actual imitation of sounds, and equally strong suggestion can be given in other ways. Moreover onomatopœia never by itself gave any line of verse poetic merit. All these are questions of means and to decide about most of them we have to look to the end.

Parallel reflections apply to another technical presupposition that occupied many readers :

10·44. The verse *is jangling and jerky* and is *not what one would think of associating with* the steady flowing of a fleecy cloud.

The 'fleeciness' of this cloud is possibly an accident of visual imagery. The poet said nothing about it. The demand for correspondence between subject and movement is a typical example of illegitimate technical expectations. The poet has certain effects in view. If he chooses to employ certain means, well and good. But to prescribe them is to confuse poetry with parlour games. This is true at least of English and of most European poetry. Matters appear to have been otherwise in Chinese poetry, but so was it with Chinese battles. A victory was not a victory unless it was won on a fine day.

A poet may imitate the motion of his subject by the motion of his verse. Sometimes it is a great merit that he does so, *if his purpose requires that this should be done.* It is never a defect if he does not, unless it is clear that he meant to, and that it was necessary for his purpose. Furthermore, the question whether or not a given movement of verse corresponds to any other movement, of visible things or of thoughts or of passions, is excessively delicate. It largely turns on whether the reader is willing to give it this correspondence, on the inducements the poet offers him to find it. For the rhythm of words is not independent of the way the reader chooses to take them.

10·45. *Floating, dancing movement of the poem its most striking feature.* The second verse is the most successful in the whole poem—one feels that the writer really has watched a summer cloud. Note effectiveness of the words " shudder " and " sidle ".

Compare with this :

10·46. The scheme of this poem is hardly suited to the light and airy subject which is full of motion, while *the short monotonous stanzas are essentially static.*

The same writer introduces us to another illegitimate expectation which worried many.

10·47. Unfortunately this poem immediately challenges comparison with Shelley's " The Cloud " and somewhat naturally suffers by it. We cannot imagine *this* cloud would

" . . . bind the Sun's throne with a burning zone ".

10·48. A comparison with Shelley's poem to the cloud, shows this poem in a very unfavourable light. The treatment is somewhat similar, but whereas Shelley succeeds, this author fails completely. The poem is a fantasy untouched by imagination in the Wordsworthian sense, a cold, dead piece of work with no appeal to the reader. If it arouses any interest at all, it awakens antagonism. We are inclined to question whether clouds paint patterns on the flanks of cows, for instance. The last two stanzas seem turgid and over-loaded with gorgeousness. (Cf., however, 12·7).

There are still some points about diction to be considered.

10·5. I consider this poem faulty. There is *a tendency to introduce prosaicisms* (puzzle, sidle, encroachments, elaborate) which, though doubtless deliberate, is not quite successful.

10·51. I get too much of an impression of artificiality from this to like it. The words are picturesque enough, but the way in which they are strung together seems to me forced and insincere. " Puzzle ", " encroachments ", " shoot a shudder ", " shake your shadow ", " frail steel tissue " . . . are all terms that seem to me *either out of place or else too prosaic*. It is too full of conceits to ring true.

10·53. One is continually let down by such words as limn, encroachments and benevolence.

10·54. Words with poor, commonplace and prosaic associations are used, *e.g.* stockade, gorgeous, hinges, sprawling, elaborate.

10·55. Though occasionally the poetry rises to the highest poetic pitch yet *it contains many words and phrases unsuited to verse.* It adds a prosaic nature to the cloud to term it a ' stockade '; or to say that it ' sidles ' up the garden stair. More than ' sidle ', the shadow would seem to glide swiftly over the steps. A bathetic ending to the poem is to describe the clouds as ' sprawling domes ' and ' tottering towers '. It is realistic description, no doubt, but not poetry. *A drunken man sprawls and totters.*

In the absence of any precise theory as to the nature of the prosaic and of any exact demarcation of poetic diction, the term ' prosaic ' must be regarded as equivalent only to ' unsatisfactory '. It is often only a term of abuse. All the words and phrases objected to here are selected as particularly felicitous by other writers. The prosaic flavour attributed to ' stockade ', whether through association with ' stocks and stones ', with stocks and shares or with bully beef, may indicate that *Masterman Ready* and *Treasure Island* are not as popular as they used to be.

How oddly single words may be flavoured for individual readers may be seen from 10·57, perhaps another instance of an accidental visual image.

10·57. 'Sprawling', which is *anyhow an ugly word* to bring into the climax, does not belong to the kind of cloud that has citadels and a golden belt, but to the filmy pink variety.

The chorus-girl type perhaps !

Another prepossession concerning diction we have met before :

10·58. The mixture of Latin and Anglo-Saxon words is scarcely happy in many places.

Who is responsible for disseminating this widespread piece of nonsense about the incompatibility of English words of different origin is a question that deserves to be looked into. It is too frequent not to have some active contemporary source.

After the accusation of 'prosaicism' that of 'romanticism' will be a change.

10·6. Presumably cloud obliged by climbing and pencilling, etc. Whole ' poem ' *choice example of ugliness of romantic animism* (cf. Roll on, thou deep and stormy ocean !). If the wind had changed would poet have got angry ? Puzzle the cattle—did anyone ever see cattle puzzled by a cloud. This written in study by one who might have done better by going to the country *to learn that clouds are blown by the wind, and do not climb and puzzle cattle and shoot shudders, lay long fingers and perform similar human actions at command of prigs.*

" O sprawling domes, O tottering towers "—

. O God ! O Montreal !

Possibly the vocative and the imperatives are responsible for this outburst. The poem succeeded in eliciting much vigorous abuse.

10·61. This poet tumbles over his metaphors. We confess we have never seen a cloud ' pencil ' the sky with its ' miraculous stockade ' and never shall. All is confused in the last stanza but one also. *There is no clear image, nothing to tell that the writer has grasped the significance of what he is trying to describe.* He has certainly brought no clear vision ; we seem to have heard of the ' golden ranks ' of corn before. At last he gives up trying to describe even what he has seen, and *bolsters up his verse with abstractions*—' wizardries ', ' sorcery', ' pomp ', ' beneficence '—*terms for which the rest of the poem gives no justification.* There is no rhythm. The metrical framework is just filled up according to the set pattern. The rhymes are vapid and meaningless. The poet could have gone on rhyming a hundred similar stanzas. The last stanza is ludicrous, with its ' What ! ' and its feeble question. The whole thing breaks down. ' O most lame and impotent conclusion ! '.

A few found the poem incomprehensible.

10·62. The first two lines of the poem form a good index to the characteristic of the whole. The mixture of the metaphor is significant.—Shelley in writing the Ode to the West Wind, conceived of the wind as of a person with very definite characteristics—" the uncontrollable " " destroyer and preserver ". *Our poet has no such clear conception ;* and the result is that his cloud is as a person with no character, doing all kinds of things, performing all kinds of antics. There is the touch reminiscent of Lewis Carroll in the lines—

> " shake your shadow at the sun
> Darkly reminding him that he
> Relieve you when your work is done ".

In a single stanza, one learns how the cloud puzzles the cattle, paints its pleasure on their flanks, and shoots a shudder down the golden ranks of the cornfield. There is no need to multiply instances.— The diction lacks strength as much as the poem, *and often leaves one wondering what it all means.*

10·63. This piece bores and angers me. It is *a mere string of words meaning nothing—except that they seem vaguely to talk about clouds.* Ridiculous phrases are endless—" miraculous stockade ", " the earth will . . . limn your beauty (! ? ! ? !) ", " shoot . . . a shudder ", " shake your shadow at the sun " etc., etc., etc. It must have been written by a candidate for Colney Hatch, I should imagine.

10·64. I cannot gather what made the poet wish these strange things. *If the poet wants rain, why does he dare the sun to shine in the last verse ? It's all very obscure.*

Some special obscurity does perhaps attach to the fourth verse.

10·65. ' Shake your shadow at the sun ', I dislike. I cannot imagine a cloud shaking its shadow at anything, and the word destroys the steady progress of the cloud through the rest of the poem.

The geometry in this verse proved too difficult for several.

10·66. The cloud cannot shake its shadow at the sun, since it is between them, nor does it appear dark to him.

Others supposed that the cloud itself shook and suggested that only thunder-clouds shake. But if it be the shadow of the cloud, not the cloud itself, that shakes, and if it shakes only through the motion of the sea, there seems to be nothing but sound physics in the thought of the verse.

Equally so, if another interpretation is favoured :

10·67. A cloud which, moving across the heavens, casts a shadow over the earth, causing as it were, a shudder on the areas it touches.

A certain change of tone in the poem at the sixth verse will be noted. It caused much perturbation and searching of spirit.

10·7. This poem, after raising me to *the keenest delight* for five stanzas, *suddenly gave way and let me down again with a bang.* The first part quickly met a response. Even as I enjoy the metaphysical poets, I rejoiced here in new imagery, familiar words in new connotations—the alliteration added to the sonority of the lines. I like " puzzle the cattle . . ." and the cloud shooting " a shudder down those golden ranks " of corn ; I like it slanting its hand and sidling ; its " soft encroachments " ; I like its long fingers laid on the sea and the " noonday panic cold and rude ". The words seem simple and accurate—the poem lives and means new vistas to me. Then, ah then. The sixth stanza is respectable, but " pomp ", " gorgeous designs ", and " beneficence " creep in unwelcome guests. The spirit has changed, Polonius is talking now where Professor Housman spake before. *Aping the grand style* succeeds so very infrequently, I wonder gifted poets still try and fail.

10·71. This pleased me at first by the easy quality of the metre which seemed in fact rather more suitable for addressing a cloud than Shelley's much brisker one, also the pictures were so very exact—things such as ' paint your pleasure on their flanks ' and above all ' sidle up the garden stair ' which exactly described one of the most fascinating things, to me personally, in nature, this constant pursuit of light by darkness, especially when seen in progress across an open tract of country from a mountain top. Then in the fifth verse I began to slow up. *Something new had entered the poem. I struggled through the first two lines of the sixth verse and absolutely crashed at the second couplet.* This may be due to natural stupidity, but I felt I owed the poem a grudge for misleading me as to the style at the beginning.

The possibility that this change was something deliberately intended by the poet was not meditated by these two readers. If they had considered it I think it unlikely that they would not have changed their feeling. The manner in which they describe their sense of the change gives them the air of people pushing at a door that opens inwards.

10·72. *Slight, perhaps, but charming.* An original idea worked out with the aid of original metaphors. An easy flow of language and sound construction. The " Then " of stanza 6 is perfectly timed to avoid monotony and at the same time preserve unhurried motion. It is a pity that *the last two lines tail off into an anti-climax* which looks suspiciously like a stop-gap.

These last two lines troubled many readers. All manner of conjectures were made as to their emotional tone, though no very satisfactory description was given.

10·73. The last two lines are *declamatory* and spoil the effect of the delicacy of the preceding part of the poem.

10·74. The question of the last two lines expresses *a rather perfunctory and not really earnest regret*—hardly even a sigh.

10·75. The feeling in the last verse *of half regretfulness is important* because it raises the poem out of the class of the pleasantly descriptive. It raises a question which the poet does not answer directly, except perhaps in the line " O frail steel tissue of the sun " which shows he is aware of *both ideas, that all is illusionary or that all is of value.* It is because he contrasts these 2 and raises this idea that the poem seems to me to be good.

Echoes of *The Tempest* may be influencing this reader ; and Shelley, as well as Wordsworth, inspires and imperils the next.

10·76. You feel the cloud travelling rapidly in the first five verses ; declining in the next, and finally disappearing in a glorious sunset ; *leaving the world cold and desolate behind it. The brief pleasure and joy of living is followed by darkness and death.*
But although the world totters, you feel the cloud still sailing inevitably on. *The glorious survives, man's mortal work dies.* You breathe " the still sad music of humanity ".

10·77. This poem is *the expression of a common enough feeling— transitoriness.* The whole of the first five verses is rapid move-ment—the sudden change from dark to light, cold to warmth, the contrast between " frail " and " steel " suggested throughout by this fleeting note. It is doubtful if the poet thoroughly realised the emotion of joy—of an added exhilaration in life through a knowledge of its transitoriness, which should be the natural sequence of the poem. He does not really express this in his last verse, which *in its shallow moralizing* lessens the more subtle result of the rest of the poem.

The chief difficulty seems to be to admit that the poet may have intended a real transition in feeling ; that he may have passed the point at which 10·77 would wish him to stop and have gone on to do something more.

10·78. It commences like an airy Robert Louis Stevenson rhyme for young and old, *it ends with the tone of Kipling's " Recessional ".* Thus it seems to lack unity and to express a misapplied importunate spirit. If intended to be *merely quizzical,* the clearly serious lines about " beneficence " and " pride " are out of place.

Exactly how seriously the grandiloquence of the last three verses is to be taken, is the problem. That a slightly mocking tone comes in with ' rally your wizardries ' is continued with ' sorcery', ' pomp ' and ' gorgeous new designs ' and culminates in the much disliked word ' sprawling ' was not noticed. Humour is perhaps the last thing that is expected in lyrical poetry, above all when its theme is nature. If the poet is going to smile he is required to give clear and ample notice of his intention.

.

Forty years back, when much had place
That since has perished out of mind,
I heard that voice and saw that face.

He spoke as one afoot will wind
A morning horn ere men awake ;
His note was trenchant, turning kind.

He was of those whose wit can shake
And riddle to the very core
The counterfeits that Time will break . . .

Of late, when we two met once more,
The luminous countenance and rare
Shone just as forty years before.

So that, when now all tongues declare
His shape unseen by his green hill,
I scarce believe he sits not there.

No matter. Further and further still
Through the world's vaporous vitiate air
His words wing on—as live words will.

POEM XI

AMONG the results of printing *Poems X* and *XI* on *opposite* pages of the issued sheet of four poems was the following :

11·1. This poem took me a considerable time to enjoy. At the first two readings I could make little of it—the transition from verse 8 to verse 9 rather struck me. I think it is a little sudden. The poem strikes me as imagination run riot. The poem is at first a series of little pictures, very beautiful, and not extravagant—for the poet has seized on the right words,— 'shudder', 'sidle'. Then comes a rather extravagant passage on 'silver hinges', 'snowy citadels', 'sprawling domes', etc. *Then the poet seems to turn, suddenly, to old reminiscences*—and one particular lost friend seems to occupy his thoughts solely, to the oblivion of the airy imaginations of the former stanzas of the poem. *This change is suitably marked by a change in the verse form*—four lines to three lines—ottava rime, the stanza form which, with a variation, Shelley uses for the ' West Wind ' ode.

Who shall say after this that our readers do not go out to meet our poets ?

This poem stirred comparatively few flights of enthusiasm. One good reason for this is stated in a protocol, 11·2, to which particular attention may be drawn. The demand there expressed is not often explicitly avowed yet it is frequently present and is doubtless the explanation of as much poetry-reading as it is of concert-going.

11·2. Its reflective, conversational manner *awakens a quiet mood, rather than a rapture, and since rapture is what I want of poetry, it is lacking to me.* Its allusion to ' much, perished out of mind', clothes its subject in a mysterious importance. 'Vaporous vitiate air ' offended me. Outside of the mood, *I felt no real personal connection, no personal emotion.* If they had been my words winging on, or my closest friend's—if he had alluded to my death, or let me apply it so—I should have felt it more deeply.

The writer is making a demand we shall have little difficulty in agreeing to be illegitimate when he asks for personal emotion in this fashion. Yet poetry which refuses to be so misused is rarely very popular. His desire for ' rapture ' may meet with more sympathy. But is there any good reason to require it from all poetry ? The confusion between quality and intensity of experience we have noticed before.

The complaint that the poet here has avoided any violent stirrings of emotion appears frequently :

11·21. It *arouses no emotions* in me. I understand what it says, but feel no interest in it.

This is a typical example. It is allied to two other expectations that the poet also failed to fulfil.

11·22. The reader has a feeling of knowing the man described only at second hand. *We are not made to see him.*

11·24. I feel there is something wrong with this poem. Perhaps it is that the poet plunges too quickly into his subject ; he does not pause *to create an atmosphere.*

Vivid presentation, with or without a visual appeal, and ' atmosphere ' are, of course, rightly required from some poetry. It is a natural result that they should by some readers be expected from all. But to avoid them is often precisely the poet's endeavour. To prescribe what he shall try to do is less reasonable than to hope that he will do something we should not have thought of suggesting.

The prescription that the dead man should be described led not only to disappointment. It led some to find more description than they perhaps had warrant.

11·25. He has, as he intended, given the reader *a complete understanding* of the man whom he wished to describe.

11·26. We can recognise the subject of this poem as *a man with depth of character, power of inspiration and leadership, a friend with a great and loving heart.*

To compensate for these excesses :

11·27. Portraits of strangers seldom interest me, although this has the air of being a good one.

One curiously logical enthusiast did come forward.

11·28. Evidently written by a sincere admirer—*i.e.* an idealist, for an admirer reveres the man who is carrying out his ideals. Since we are all idealists we must approve of this poem : extreme friendship between men (*i.e.* admiration) always appeals to us, since we imagine our state of life if we found someone who proves an inseparable part of whole. Bears mark of sincerity— not idle tongue-worship : sincerity can never be despised ;— another reason for approval.

It is a pity that such admirable sentiments should make such insubstantial premises ; but the conclusion that all idealists should approve of everything that other idealists do is more easy to reject than to refute.

Complaints of obscurity were, on the whole, not more frequent than might have been expected.

11·3. I think prolonged and very careful study might reveal its meaning. At present I have only an idea that there *is* one.

11·31. Bad, vague simile " as one afoot etc."—" His note was trenchant, turning kind " ?—*Language again vague and thought obscure :* " can shake and riddle etc."—Last stanza particularly ludicrous : as all the poem is inconsequential, trivial in conception and words, last verse sinks into bathos. With the language of degree of feeling of a Patmore or a Christina Rossetti, the inconsequence, the triviality and the cheerful faith of the amateur that after all the poem might be the real thing, mark it as fourth or fifth class.

11·32. The poem seems an incoherent medley of unrelated fragments. Leaves the reader with no impression of the actual character or appearance of his subject. *One learns that the old man has a voice of volume and power.*

Others learnt, or failed to learn, even stranger things.

11·33. There is *a feeling of the great, strong, silent man which means nothing at all.* The poem is summed up in the last few words :—" as live words mean ". I feel here that the poet is trying to make a strong impression and failing miserably. What are live words and whatever they are *why should they vitiate through the vaporous air ?*

Not much more successful was this more appreciative effort :

11·34. A few deft strokes of a powerful brush *painting a portrait of a powerful character on a ' counterfeit which Time would break ' if the poem were lost.* I like the poem for (1) Its life-force, (2) its appreciation of truth of ' live-words '.

Points of diction came in for much discussion, even an admirer being shocked by the last verse.

11·4. Merits of sincerity, of simplicity, of probability. Provides clear picture of subject. The line ' I scarce believe he sits not there ' *trembles on Browning's* " This is Ancona, yonder is the sea ", but *actually reaches the height of Wordsworth's* " Milton ! thou shouldst be living at this hour. England hath need of thee ". Would have done well to end here. Last stanza weak : though this more due to vocabulary and construction. " Vaporous vitiate air " damnable. " As live words will ", to finish off tribute like this, very feeble : should have ended on note of words winging on.
On the whole good, tho' apparently immature.

The comparisons adduced probably explain why the ending so frustrated this reader's expectation, though the movement of the last line gave several sorts of trouble.

11·41. The last verse is not convincing. " Vaporous vitiate " is not happy.—*Is it reasonable to expect air to be anything else but vaporous ?* The briskness, almost the skittishness, of the last line of all I find intolerable.

The answer to the question seems to be ' In some climates, yes '. Intellectual-moral climates need not be supposed to be more uniform than their physical analogues. We might agree, however, about the effect of the alleged skittishness if it existed. The rhythm of the poem seems to have been elusive :

11·411. It does not seem great, but there is something attractive about it. I must say that it is *the attraction of a jazz tune* which one can only tolerate a few times. The poem may answer a real emotion, but so do some of the horrid writings on tombstones.

11·42. This is trash. There is *no compelling subject, in fact no subject at all.* The construction is forced and at times the metaphors are absurd. The second verse is nonsense. The second line of verse four is particularly poor, *only excelled perhaps by* the second line of the last verse. *Who ever heard anything so strained, so artificial as* " The world's vaporous vitiate air ". The effort was not worth the ink it used.

Yet once more the fatal correlation may be observed :

11·421. I feel as though I were indulgent and just a bit sentimental, to say that it attains my standards *except for the one phrase* " vaporous vitiate air ".

To complete the indictment :

11·43. " He was of those . . . Time will break ", *is a long way of saying* " He hated all frauds ". Stanza 5, too, is very difficult to read aright. The poem *has not the majesty required* for an epitaph on an honoured friend.

The prior demand expressed in the last sentence seems to have as little justification as the paraphrase given in the first. Here is another paraphrase to set beside those in 11·32, and 11·34.

11·44. " All tongues declare ", is being pompous over, " it is said " just for the sake of the form of the poem. " Vaporous, vitiate air ", is ridiculous rather than impressive.

The exercise of imagining a better reason for the ' pomposity ' may be suggested.

11·45. This might well have been written by one commonplace clergyman of another commonplace clergyman. It is redeemed neither by pleasing metaphors nor deep thought, *while passion is entirely absent.* It failed after several readings to make any impression at all on me. One thing alone is striking and significant in the poem—that the complimented person would never ' wing ' ' live words '.

And to prove how rash some attempts to infer the character of a writer from his poetry may be :

11·46. It is the work of someone who, whilst acquainted with much at second hand through the experience of others, has not taken the trouble to acquire his own set of experiences as a basis for values and judgment.

Some more favourable opinions will redress the balance :

11·5. The rhythm at once suggests real emotion successfully dealt with by the technique (" *That* voice . . . *that* face '— simple, but not affectedly simple). *The similes are used not as added decoration, but to make the shades of experience clearer* (*e.g.* 2nd stanza). So too ' trenchant, turning kind ' shows *an effort at accuracy which a lesser poet would have abandoned* on account of the slight clumsiness involved.

Some of the praise has, at first sight, an air of paradox.

11·51. *Heightened by none of usual poetic diction.* Bareness varied by *occasional effectively ugly phrase.* Experience as bare as words, nothing more than statement of fact. Bareness gives impression of intensity. Poet has no time or wish to play with pretty images. Thing described too weighty to be added to or dressed up in poetic formula.

11·52. We notice first the perfect suitability of the metre and the language. There is a tranquility and gentle melancholy which we can feel by reading the poem without paying very much attention to the subject matter. When this latter element is considered, it will be found that the poem is an harmonious whole. There is *something very balanced and sane* about this poem. It seems to say just what is wanted in the best possible way. Every sentence seems fitting—*there is no expression we should quarrel with.*

11·53. This is the real thing. In contrast to Poem IX the rhythm is *in* the poem. Moreover there is a sense of *universality* about this piece which stamps it as poetry of the major order. The poet is not concerned with trivialities but with the fundamental facts of existence. His poem is in the best sense a "criticism of life". It is positive, creative, dynamic. His technique moreover is equal to the task of giving completely effective expression to his experience. *There is an economy, a lack of verbosity or any kind of ornamentation, which is utterly appropriate to the subject.* The metre also is in keeping, and the rhyme-form one of considerable subtlety. The whole poem leaves one with a sense of *complete satisfaction.*

11·54. This is a straightforward piece of work in the "middle kind of writing which . . . neither towers to the skies nor creeps along the ground" (Johnson's Life of Dryden). It is a graceful tribute, born rather of *a general feeling slowly finding voice* than of a definite emotional experience. The style, *everywhere relying on the sequence of ideas,* is appropriate (and this is the greatest praise) to an elegy on a dead friend : restrained and yet dignified, fresh without false emphasis, sincere without gush.

Finally, lest this opinion should be thought too easily attained :

11·56. I dislike it for its stilted and high-flung style, *and feel that the author might have come down from his high-horse for just a moment* in speaking of his departed friend.

The further these researches extend, the more misleading does Bishop Butler's celebrated paradox appear. 'Everything is what it is, and not another thing', may be a convenient principle to apply to things when we have caught them, but until then it is a poor guide to the investigator.

Solemn and gray, the immense clouds of even
Pass on their towering unperturbéd way
Through the vast whiteness of the rain-swept heaven,
The moving pageants of the waning day ;
Heavy with dreams, desires, prognostications,
Brooding with sullen and Titanic crests,
They surge, whose mantles' wise imaginations
Trail where Earth's mute and languorous body rests :
While below the hawthorns smile like milk splashed down
From Noon's blue pitcher over mead and hill ;
The arrased distance is so dim with flowers
It seems itself some coloured cloud made still ;
O how the clouds this dying daylight crown
With the tremendous triumph of tall towers !

POEM XII

HERE again some irrelevances have to be noticed, but in this case, as they had more influence in increasing the popularity of the poem so they may be thought to have more critical significance.

12·1. At a glance the poem reveals its grandeur and power. Not only is the description powerful but the very roll of the lines is as *the rumble of heavy clouds.* In these sonorous lines whose sound is so well suited to its sense, there is *something which sets one dreaming.*

12·11. The majestic pageantry of the clouds *is ever a favourite topic* with poets. In the other poem on clouds, the atmosphere was light; here the sky is black with rain filled clouds *of ill omen.* The poet conveys the right atmosphere. When I look at the evening sky in windy wintry moods, *I always love to think I am looking at a pageant of souls,* passing on to the throne of the Most High, to be judged and atone for misdeeds—" The moving pageants of the waning day ".

Is it unfair to be reminded of the concert-goer's explanation : " I always love to go and hear *Tristan and Isolde.* I live all my love-affairs over again " ?

Several writers contrasted the poem with No. X.

12·2. Offers a great contrast to the opposite poem. Here a certain grandeur, *and reverence in the poet* for his subject reflects itself in the verse.

A poet who permits himself to be anything but very respectful to Nature does so at his peril.

12·21. When this poet broods on the cloud patterns he sees not so much the long fingers on the sea and the shudder on the corn (*though he is conscious of them and of their beauty*) but *rather the spiritual elements* of which these are to him the symbols.

155

The reader seems here to know too much. Another symbolist, however, in part explains these certitudes.

12·22. Not merely a picture of nature but suggestive. The clouds are *symbolic of some brooding spirit :* they arouse dreams, desires, prognostications in their beholder. The atmosphere is that of the poet's mind : *while we read the poem it hypnotises us into the same mood.* We become languorous and absorbed in " the arrased distance ".

The persistence with which so many readers loaded the poem with such extra interpretations, with Stendhalian 'crystallisations', has probably two explanations. 12·23 may put us on the track of them both.

12·23. I get more ' kick ' out of this at each reading, *partly because of the rolling rhythm and sonority*, and partly because I can *feel* something I cannot understand, and I want to go on trying to understand until I get right into the poet's mind. *Like falling in love.*

This seems a valuable hint. The process is *very* like falling in love, under rather distant and formal conditions and without much intimate acquaintance.

Others, with a different result, were affected in a similar manner.

12·24. This is *elusive* at a first reading. One is led by the *general vagueness of the opening to attribute to it poetic qualities which it lacks.* Actually there is not a great deal to be said for it, it apes, rather obviously, Shelley's manner, with inconspicuous success. Nearly all the words are so well worn as to have become commonplace unless very adroitly used. When the writer attempts originality he is almost unintelligible. What, for instance, is the wise imagination of the mantel of a cloud, or the smile of spilt milk ?

12·25. I feel someone is trying to play with my emotions, and I dislike it in the same way that I dislike sobstuff in a film.

Those who most admired the poem gave as their reason, with unusual unanimity, the movement of the rhythm.

12·3. I think this very good. Its power to move is in its *rhythm which is so swelling and big and solemn* in the first part. It does not give many pictures or visual images and I do not think the sense has very much to do with the effect. It is just that, somehow, one is brought into touch with the grandeur of the clouds, which one feels as a permanent thing—not a transitory pleasure—like that the clouds give in the second poem.

12·31. The poem starts grandly : its stately roll approaches ecstasy.

12·32. Here we have lines distantly reminiscent of Shakespeare and the ' honest boldness ' of the Elizabethans. Especially in the management of the long words, which help to ' get across ' the effect of the vastness of the scene described, are we reminded of the great poets of our language. The vastness of the picture and the ideas of the poet are conveyed in *magnificent lines that strain and nearly break down* the imagination.

Before examining these *declarations* more closely let us consider some of those objections which do not seem to invalidate them.

The ' pathetic fallacy ' is again made a ground for abuse. (Cf. 7·31 and 10·6.)

12·4. The rest of the poem seems to be rubbish because :

(*a*) A cloud cannot have ' desires '.

(*b*) A mantel cannot have ' imaginations '.

(*c*) ' Imaginations ' cannot ' trail '.

(*d*) ' Milk ' does not ' smile '.

(*e*) ' Dim with flowers ' is rather weak. I always thought flowers brightened things.

(*f*) ' Tall towers ' do not ' triumph ' so far as I know. Anyhow I never saw one doing it ! Might be an interesting sight !

These complaints (except (*e*)) rest upon an assumption about language that would be fatal to poetry. All these things may happen in a poem—if there is any good reason for them happening or advantage gained. Some sympathy may be felt, however, in the present instance, with complaints (*b*), (*c*) and (*d*). Worse-founded objections with the same presupposition actually stated are combined in 12·41 with other misunderstandings.

12·41. A terrible wash of words *without any Swinburnian rhythmic music.* After half-a-dozen readings one has a faint glimmer of the meaning, only to find it not worth while. There's nothing in the shop, But Lor ! Don't 'e take the shutters down dignified. *Says the clouds sink in course of day, producing sunset. Again animistic pitfall :* heavy with dreams, desires, prognostications, Brooding with sullen and Titanic crests, they surge. *Yes but they don't. They may be heavy with H_2O vapour but that's all.* The dreams etc. are in poet's mind. Should take a course in elementary psychology. Contradiction of arrased (arras shows *clear*-cut figures) and dim with flowers. The last line a Toothful.

There is much here that will have to be discussed in Part III.

The assumption that ' subject ' automatically defines ' treatment ' dies hard. Several complained that the author's poem was not exactly that which they would have written themselves.

12·5. *Gone is the fundamental poetry of earth* and all that the author supplies us with in its place, is a " mute and languorous body "—what a joyless vision. Can anyone imagine Wordsworth receiving inspiration from such a cold cheerless sunset, duly set off by conventional clouds, with their " tremendous triumph of tall towers " ?—no. *Instead of the quiet beauty of an English evening full of the fresh smell of newly watered foliage, when the drowsy twilight creeps from the hawthorn thickets across the dusty white road and the wayfarer stops for his evening meal, we find* an extravagantly portrayed vista of a totally unsympathetic and unnatural world. If poetry is the best words in the best order— such words as prognostication seem a little out of place.

Prosodists indulge in their usual antics.

12·51. This sonnet is spoilt by its irregularity of arrangement, and by some harsh scansion. *It is only by a great effort that one can render the first line at all as an iambic pentameter.* The accent on " the " in that line is very ugly. Again in the 9th line. There are three syllables in the first foot, and two are full long ones, so that " below " becomes something like " blow ". The simile in the 9th and 10th lines must be peculiar to the writer. In any case, why should Noon splash milk more than any other part of the day ? In the 11th line we have a word which three English dictionaries fail to recognise. Does " arrased " mean the same as "erased", or "raised", or is it something to do with "scraped up" or with "arras" meaning tapestry?

"The tremendous triumph of tall towers" is not strictly applicable to clouds which are the "moving pageant" which "surge", yet trail a "mantle on the earth". Such towers would be somewhat unstable

12·52. The poem is depressing, the use of such words and phrases as "heavy as dreams", "waning", "prognostications", etc. create a gloom which to me is almost "macabre". *The language is heavy, and prosaic ;* in fact it seems almost like a piece of prose, turned into *blank verse* for the occasion.

The complaint that the language is prosaic is hardly what one would have expected, nor do the rhymes seem so unobtrusive.

Abuse that shows evidence of closer reading is not lacking.

12·6. This sonnet is plastered with highly-coloured words whose use is not strongly justifiable. The fifth line, for example, is, though mildly pleasing, vague. 'Titanic' is clap-trap. 'Mantles' wise imaginations' *is nonsense.* The simile of the hawthorns is easily the best thing in the poem ; but there is some confusion in making the milk issue from *Noon's* blue pitcher—why *Noon?* Moreover the very mention of Noon disturbs the picture of evening. 'Arrased distance' *is an affected phrase,* and 'dim with flowers' *is inaccurate.*

12·61. Licentiously verbose. Words used blindly *for their mothy aura of suggestion* rather than for their meaning.

Comparison with *Poem X* exercised an influence, negative or positive, that was perhaps unfortunate. We may conclude with two protocols which show clearly what the main division of opinion, and the choice between the two poems, turned upon.

12·7. This poem gives what the other poem on the cloud does not, the impression that the author is *deeply moved* by his own thoughts. This man can move us *to see and feel the picture he shows*—the heavy menacing clouds, the deep violent colouring, the majestic grandeur of sky and earth. The clouds become alive, "brooding with sullen and Titanic crests", "triumphant", "solemn". With long weighty words "unperturbed", "imaginations", "Prognostications", "languorous", "tremendous" ; with a sparing use of unimportant syllables the author achieves the desired impression of weight.   It is a poem that can be repeated again and again *for the mere delight of the richness of the language.* It is an exceptionally strong and colourful poem, not merely descriptive but showing in a small degree the author's attitude to life.

With this may be compared 10·48, by the same writer.   It is interesting to note that neither he nor any other admirer of *Poem XII* attempted to expound lines 9 and 10, though not a few were inclined to question them.

12·71.   This poem *elicited a hearty grin* and several re-readings. It annoyed me and I think I know why.   It instantly challenges comparison with the second poem—Nature, " clouds ", " towering ", " decline ", " waning day ", " garden ", " flowers ", " cornfields ", " mead and hill ", " crown ", and " towers ".   *This poem seems highly conceived.   It ought to be enjoyable and yet I had great difficulty in catching its mood.   When I was convinced I had it I found I was feeling quite artificial and unnatural.*   I believe it tries hard to be poetic—*the author knows his " poetic diction "* (which I count against him).

The subjects of both poems invite the reader to make up, in his own soul, a poem of his own.   Both supply material.   Any description of such scenes will easily start the poetic function going in the average reader.   When, as in *Poem XII*, the invitation is coupled with a high-sounding grandiloquent diction and a very capably handled march of verse, when, above all, the movement is familiar and ' hypnotic ', when there is nothing to force the reader to work at it, we feel safe in going ahead, the poetic function slips loose and private poems result. It was with such poems that so many readers fell in love.   I am confirmed in this opinion by noticing that none, even of the most ardent admirers of *Poem XII*, attempted any close analysis of it of the the kind which admirers of *Poem X* constantly produced.   No one seriously tried to elucidate ' whose mantles' wise imaginations trail ', to explain the force

of ' mute and languorous ' or ' dim with flowers ' ;
or to point out some appropriateness in ' the moving
pageant of the waning day ' or to appraise *moving* in
this line. The application of these words in the
poem was little considered, they were enjoyed, as it
were *in vacuo*, by readers content to loll at ease
swinging softly in the hammock of the rhythm,
satisfied to find at last something that *sounded* like
poetry and disinclined to be at pains to ascertain
whether it also read like poetry.

There remains, of course, for later discussion, the
question of the value of such swoon-reading—as
compared for example with the querulousness of
12·41.

L

In the village churchyard she lies,
Dust is in her beautiful eyes,
   No more she breathes, nor feels, nor stirs ,
At her feet and at her head
Lies a slave to attend the dead,
   But their dust is white as hers.

Was she a lady of high degree,
So much in love with the vanity
   And foolish pomp of this world of ours ;
Or was it Christian charity,
And lowliness and humility,
   The richest and rarest of all dowers ?

Who shall tell us ?   No one speaks ;
No colour shoots into those cheeks,
   Either of anger or of pride,
At the rude question we have asked ;
Nor will the mystery be unmasked
   By those who are sleeping at her side.

Hereafter ?—And do you think to look
On the terrible pages of that Book
   To find her failings, faults, and errors ?
Ah, you will then have other cares,
In your own shortcomings and despairs,
   In your own secret sins and terrors !

POEM XIII

INDIGNATION rose high in the case of this poem, and ranged wide. A glance at Appendix B will show that it was by far the most disliked of all the poems. Some special explanation seems to be required for a combined attack so varied in temper, ground and direction, yet so united in hostile intention.

As has been remarked before, a very wary eye is needed with any poetry that tends to implicate our stock responses. And this for two opposite reasons. If the easiest way to popularity is to exploit some stock response, some poem ʾalready existent, fully prepared, in the reader's mind, an appearance of appealing to such stock responses, should the reader happen to have discarded them, is a very certain way of courting failure. So that a poet who writes on what appears to be a familiar theme, in a way which, superficially, is only slightly unusual, runs a double risk. On the one hand, very many readers will not really read him at all. They will respond with the poem they suppose him to have written and then, if emancipated, recoil in horror to heap abuse on the poet's head. On the other hand, less emancipated readers, itching to release their own stock responses, may be pulled up by something in the poem which prevents them. The result will be more abuse for the hapless author.

Now to illustrate and justify these reflections. Here is a writer who finds only a stock experience in the poem. He is only mildly disappointed however:

13·1. This one seems to me a successful communication of an experience whose value is dubious, or which at most is valuable

163

only on a small scale. Plainly, I think, the communication succeeds by reason of its medium ; simple, straightforward, almost bald language, making no demand on any peculiar individual characteristic which might be a bar to general appreciation, as in the poetry of Blake, for instance. The reasons for my judgment of the experience-value are harder to formulate. I think one may be that *the experience does not go very much further than it would in the case of an " ordinary man " who was not a poet,* so that its very raison d'etre is a questionable quantity. It does, in fact, seem to me rather trite.

Here is another in the same case and only slightly less tolerant.

13·11. The theme is commonplace and the poet has failed to give it new significance by his treatment. The simplicity of the poem is that of sentimentality rather than that of profound emotion.

A third finds again only stock material and stock treatment. His description of what he finds, ' just a few commonplaces about Death the Leveller ' may make us doubt the closeness of his reading.

13·12. The poet has attempted to *describe* a quiet contemplative mood. He has not felt it. These are *just a few commonplaces about Death the Leveller* uttered with an ill-feigned naïvete which cannot pass for sincerity. The poem is like the oft-delivered sermon of a preacher who knows what he *ought* to say. Hence all its conventional tricks—" a lady of high degree ", " vanity and foolish pomp ", " Christian charity ", " failings, faults and errors "—he might have added " trespasses "—and *above all " the village churchyard ", the conventional setting* for ruminations upon death.

The same interpretation appears in other protocols :

13·13. The first three stanzas are preoccupied with the powerlessness of humans in the grip of death.

The power of the stock response to hide what is actually in the poem is remarkable here, for he adds :

13·131. It is all on the same dead level. Each stanza is divided into two parts which balance each other. But *the two parts bear precisely the same relation to each other in each stanza ; and all the six half-stanzas embody precisely the same idea.*

The opposing danger that may arise from the interference of stock responses is well illustrated in 13·2. Instead of complaining that the poem is too much, he condemns it for being too little what he expected, but in the end he combines these objections.

13·2. This poem is rubbish. The first couplet *invites comparison with*

> " I wish I were where Helen lies ;
> Night and day on me she cries ",

which shows up its crudeness. The dust in her eyes is confusing and the additional dust of the sixth line raises such a cloud that it is impossible to see through it.

Questions in poetry rarely come off and this second stanza is weak-kneed. *If only he could have substituted his questions with something like*

> " She was a phantom of delight
> When first she gleam'd upon my sight ".

It is not poetic to refer to the sensitive colouring of a maiden's cheek as shooting.

The prophecy in the last stanza is *a gross example of a pious platitude* and an insult to anyone with a conscience. If the writer had been the first to tell us to remove the ' beam ' from our own eyes before looking for a ' moat ' in another's the poem might have stimulated. But the thought has many times been better clothed.

Whether there is any emphasis on ' you ' in the first line of the last verse of the poem, and, if so, of what character, are points discussed below. But, lest it be thought that I over-estimate the part played by stock responses in these readings of the poem, let me cite another example as to which no doubt will be felt.

13·3.   Or was it Christian charity,
                 And lowliness and humility ?

Might I be permitted to ask what ' it ' refers to ? Was what Christian charity ? Also does " the richest and rarest of all dowers " refer to Christian charity, lowliness or humility ? or all three ? *If the latter then I must object, because Christian charity is a very ugly thing and neither rare nor rich* (v. *The Way of All Flesh*, Samuel Butler, *passim*).

The writer has evidently fitted himself up with a ' reach me down ' reaction from one of the most up-to-date dealers. He continues with notable confidence in his powers of divination :

13·31. Don't think I mind obscurity, because I *don't ; but I do like to get some meaning sooner or later, and this poem seems very muddled and confused.* At all events the poem is not worth much effort on the part of the reader because the underlying emotion is not of sufficient value. Nor has the poet anything to impart to us, he merely writes to hear his own voice, and any other subject would have suited him just as well.

Possibly the poem did not receive much effort in this case, but many other readers, who may have been more pertinacious, had little better success.

13·4. The sentiments expressed in this poem are by no means uncommon. The poem leaves the reader as it found him.

The first verse of the poem states the lady's present condition. The first two lines of the second verse ponders on the question as to whether she was a lady of high degree, then goes on to ask

" Or was it Christian charity ".

Was what Christian charity ? Perhaps the slaves lying at her head and feet, in that case was there need to ask the question. The charity of Christians hardly takes such a peculiar form.

These slaves proved a great difficulty.

13·41. I do not know what suggested the slaves to attend the dead ; if villagers' graves, the idea is far-fetched, if statuary on a monument to the lady, we are given no other hint of such a monument—*anyway, the metaphor is exotic* and out of place.

13·42. I don't know what the 2 slaves are symbolic of—I should like to know.

13·43. This gush of sentiment and evangelical piety is one of the worst things I have seen in the manner of Longfellow and Mrs Hemans. It has not even the merit of lucidity. *It is not customary to bury slaves by the body of their mistress in a village churchyard.* A typical mark of uninspired writers of verse is their tendency to dwell on the theme of the brevity of human life. This poem is a vague reflection on that subject, with little genuine emotion, good rhythm, or effective phrasing.

This reader was very delicate for he adds :

13·431. The number of marks of interrogation in the piece is enough to make one sick.

Apparently, for all that, they were not enough to make him inquire what it was all about. If such burials were customary, the poem, which turns entirely upon the surprising presence of the slaves, would, presumably, never have been written. Some of the conjectures advanced by those who took note of this point were not lacking in daring.

13·45. It is a satirical poem. The words which mar the poem as a poem of beauty aid it as a satire. These words persuade the reader that the poem is not to be taken seriously and *we are not shocked too forcibly by the first verse in which, I believe, we are meant to realise that two slaves were buried alive with their dead mistress*, and in the last verse the poet is able to deliver his attack on us because he has disguised his seriousness by a light, artificial manner.

Why their dust should be as 'white as hers', and whether ' those who are sleeping at her side ' are the same as those lying ' at her feet and at her head ', were further questions, and even some very careful and acute readers were in doubt whether a monument is implied.

13·46. If the lady was not known to the poet before her decease *how does he know that her eyes were beautiful?* And why bring such very big guns to bear on a piece of surely quite harmless curiosity—unnecessarily hard on himself for asking a question very innocent if rather foolish—for if Christian charity had prompted the disposition of the bodies the slaves would scarcely have been at the feet and head, but at the side. Its *extreme seriousness and queer naïveté* point, I feel, to an American origin.

13·461. Why shouldn't slaves have white dust ? And is *what* Christian charity ? The coy surprise in the third verse at the lack of a response seems uncalled for.

13·462. Careful reading reveals muddle and makes response to the poem harder.

" Dust ". We think of her dust in the earth.

" Beautiful eyes ". This makes us think of her alive. But we know nothing about her, not whether she is " of high degree " or not. But here we are asked to assume her eyes were " beautiful ", presumably because she was a woman.

" But their dust is white as hers ". This muddles one. What is the point of it ? Why *white ?* Unless it is symbolic of something, it suggests that he had actually seen the dust. But he hadn't, apparently, to judge by the rest of stanza 1.

Then " those cheeks ". But she is dust, and here we are asked to think of her flesh.

In view of all this there is reason to think either that there *was* some sort of a monument, or that she is seen sometimes as a heap of dust round a skeleton and sometimes as a beautiful corpse. This makes stanzas 1 and 3 worthless, because they build on a visual image which has no reality.

13·47. If visual images are introduced, however, we need, I shall maintain, at least two sets. This I like but find imperfect. Dust in the eye has of course the authority of Nashe,[1] but I do not feel it quite right in this more concrete work. Nor do I know quite how to account for a lady in a village churchyard with a couple of Egyptian (?) slaves. And " their dust " seems to indicate that the bodies are long since pulverised, which is all right but jars with the dust-in-eye image. But also if the lady is dust you would hardly expect to find colour " shooting " into her cheeks. " Rude question " seems just a bit comic. *But the rhythm seems to me good, and the last stanza is very good.* If this is Longfellow it shows traces of his muddle of Gothic stuff with New England meeting-house experience. Not null, though, by any means. Simply a bit clumsy.

It will perhaps be well to insert here my own interpretation of these points.

That the slaves are negro servants seems sufficient

[1] Brightness falls from the air,
Queens have died young and fair.
Dust hath closed Helen's eyes.

justification of the last line of stanza 1. Those sleep-
ing at her side are all the other inmates of the
churchyard. I take the lines

> Dust is in her beautiful eyes

and

> No colour shoots into those cheeks

to refer to her sculptured effigy, and find no difficulty
in passing from the thought of the monument to the
thought of the mortal remains at the end of the first
stanza. This reading seems to me to remove the
jars and inconsistencies felt by the two last writers.
Whether there actually exists such a monument any-
where is, of course, an entirely immaterial, though
not an uninteresting, question.

We may now turn to some of the objections
brought not against the logic or clarity of the poem
but against its tone and feeling. Here are some of
the more spirited denunciations. The influence of
the stock response danger will not be overlooked.

13·5. This poem is *a bastard of spurious rectitude and false
simplicity*—or, if you prefer, was gotten by a small Squire on
some cretinous evangelical ninny. (I hardly liked to come near
it but must confess to being a little fascinated by such an emana-
tion from Joanna Southcott's Gladstone bag).

13·51. This poem is maudlin. Artistically it is beneath
contempt. The meter is *quite unsuited to the subject*—as well as
being irregular from verse to verse : *the tripping metre of the line :*

And foolish pomp of this world of ours

jars terribly. The thought is *either bitter and coloured with the
idea of retributive justice*—as in the last verse which is most
unpleasant in tone ; *or utterly commonplace*, and cheaply senti-
mental. It was certainly *written by a neurotic or a fanatic with a
diseased mind*.

Protests against the tripping rhythm were, indeed,
not infrequent, and were associated with evidence of
moral shock.

13·52. Artistically insincere.   Contrast the solemnity of the theme *with the frivolous rhythm.*

("On the terrible pages of that Book—
Yo ho ho and a bottle of rum
With a hey and a ho and a hey nonny no").

The uncertainty whether the slaves in the first stanza were really buried with the lady or only shown on the tomb, introduces an irritation at the start.   There is a mock pre-Raphaelitish simplicity in the 2nd stanza ("lady of high degree"—"Christian charity") : "this world of ours" *is a piece of impudent sentimentality.*   Next stanza *is a fuss about nothing ; and* "rude" *a serious lapse of taste.*   It is intolerable that *this Sunday-school didacticism* (vide especially stanzas 2 and 4) should be connected with the idea of death and decay.

13·53. From the rhythm of this poem I deduce that it was written in a state of semi-somnolence by a man with St Vitus's Dance.   He was unable to keep himself awake after the end of the fourth stanza, and he wants us now to suppose that the poem ends there.   I dare say that the author writes pieces like this with quite effortless fluency ; God protect us from this kind of spontaneity ! *The author has no concrete notion of what he wishes to communicate,* or why, and assumes a false, specious kind of naïveté to make his reader think he is being passionately sincere.

A phrase like "foolish pomp of this world of ours" is both foolish and pompous.   "The richest and rarest of all dowers" is sheer gush

13·54. This is beyond all words.   If the last stanza represents the purpose and spirit of the piece—a sermon in four stanzas— one can only be thankful the sermon was not any longer.   Also the good lady's 'failings, faults, and errors' are most 'common-place, everyday and typical'.   Had the 'poet' hinted at revenge by a jealous husband for a sordid domestic intrigue between the dusty wife and her dusky slaves, the last stanza might have assumed some reality.

This expert on reality adds :

13·6. I am no prosodist, but those who are will doubtless have some choice comments to make.

They had.   Here are some of them.

13·61. The versification is worth examining.   *The first verse is presumably the criterion.   It consists of* three eight syllable lines

followed one of seven syllables, one of eight syllables and one of
seven syllables. The next verse consists of three nine syllable
lines followed by one of eight and two of nine. The third and
fourth verses seem to have no plan at all. The third verse
consists of one line of seven syllables, three of eight, one of ten
(hitherto unintroduced) and one of nine. The fourth verse
consists of one line of nine syllables, followed by one of ten,
nine, eight and two of nine. *The irregularities of the metre are
very confusing and displeasing to the ear.*

13·62. The rhythm is *very poor*. Although the arrangement
of metres chosen is one with a pleasant lilt to it, *the poet fails to
keep any regularity of rhythm.* In the first stanza, the first line
and the fifth, the last line in the second, the last of the third
and the first in the fourth only read comfortably by a difficult
elision or an accent on the wrong syllable. *For example, ' to
attend ' has to be read ' t'attend '.* The rhetorical questions are
unfortunate in this light piece. The heaviness of the dismal,
fatalistic last verse resembles a man of light build with a club
foot.

Here, however, is a different complaint :

13·63. The versification is correct, and flows with a gentle
lilt, the sense stresses coinciding with metrical ones—*not in
precisely the same pattern in every stanza but near enough to be
tiring.* The last stanza, too, (*if counted on the fingers) reveals a
derangement of metre.*

These opinions we may trace to a presupposition
which we have seen in action before. That mis-
understanding of metre which derives from the
application of external measures. But another group
of complaints against the movement of the poem
must be noticed. These show an altogether superior
understanding of rhythm and a much better applied
sensibility. But they are perhaps too evidently
motived by a violent negative reaction to the supposed
stock sanctimoniousness of the poem.

13·64 (continuing 13·5). I had come to hope, during the first
three progressive spasms that the inane zigzag of her staggering
would take her *from* me, as we passed, on a receding tack, but
the monstrous accosting lurch *towards* me of verse 4 completed,

as they say, my discomfiture, and my first instinct was to hurry off.

This ' close-up ' lurch, however, jerked to my notice not merely the ludicrous pomposity of the portent, *but that this pompous moral go-getting was spavined*, also, by a peculiar structural disjointedness, *as well as by a tendency*, as it were, *to mark a sort of muddy time*, whether *in bogged and sluggish redundance* (as in lines 3 of verses 1 and 4), or in *a sort of awe-struck loyalty to the sanctimonious clichés* in lines 3 and 6 of verse 2. These and other things, such as the peculiarly desperate staggering to the support in the last half of verse 4 of the rhymes, *here hectically pitched like camp-stools, at the last moment, to catch their tottering burden*—such phenomena tempted me, I must confess, to linger, however distastefully, with "the case". I thus observed that there was another, more typical, close to the linear spasm; in this case the patient would accompany the more normal attainment of adequate stasis by a sort of repetitive ' caw ' which I again took to be intended for rhyme. I could not, however, be certain whether such apparently nuclear utterance was the cause of a process or the excuse for it.

The justice of these strictures entirely depends I believe, upon the *sense* of the lines picked out for reproof, and our view of this is, of course, inseparable from our interpretation of the whole poem. Given the last writer's reading of the *sense* of the poem, and given his emotional response to the sense, as he takes it, then his reading of its *sound* follows. It is as subtly observed as it is surprisingly expressed. The question of the interconnection of form and content in poetry is here delicately illuminated ; and no better occasion could be imagined for insisting once more upon the meet subordination of means to ends.

To come down to detail. First as to the ' bogged and sluggish redundance ' of

No more she breathes, nor feels, nor stirs.

Another reader agrees.

13·65. ' No more she breathes ' we are told, and we are truly *most* surprised to hear that she ' nor feels nor stirs ' !

But poetry does not aim at conciseness if there is anything to be gained by expansion. The poet might reply that he was not aiming at surprise, but at its opposite, at making more obvious what is obvious already. More noticeably still with

> To find her failings, faults and errors.

The alleged redundance has the effect of turning these things into a list, a catalogue—an effect which, in view of the lines which precede it, is hardly fair ground of complaint against the poet.

As to the ' sanctimonious clichés ' of verse 2, if there are no such things here and so no ' awe-struck loyalty ' to them, the complaint against the verses as ' marking a sort of muddy time ' lapses, supposing there to be some other warrant for the slowness of movement. And perhaps there may be. This second verse is discussing the motive which prompted the strange disposal of the slaves' bodies. Was it an ignoble and mundane impulse or a more extraordinary motive ? So far from being ' a piece of impudent sentimentality ', the phrase ' this world of ours ' makes a necessary point ; and, if the great mystery ' Was *what* Christian charity ? ' is solved, the very strangeness of this possible instance justifies the epithets of the last line of this verse.

Yet other complaints concerned the word ' rude ' which is, indeed, the key to the tone of the poem.

13·7. Surely an awfully *frivolous, finicky word* in the presence of death ? It seems to be used in the sense of " What a rude man ! " not in the much less offensive sense of rough or violent.

13·71. Like a scurrilous controversialist the writer arbitrarily attributes to his imaginary interlocutor a despicable intention *and then rails at him* for it. One can see, without consulting the Book to which the writer refers, that he is a conceited, contemptible prig.

13·72. At times, also, the banality of the wording is ludicrous, reminiscent of an elderly maiden lady *shaking a mittened hand in remonstration*—' The *rude* question we have asked '.

13·73. The *winsome personal touches* (*e.g.*, ' the rude question we have asked ') strongly suggest Ella Wheeler Wilcox.

Some of these associations we can safely set aside as just the personal misfortune of the individuals they distress. We have to ask what the *tone* of the poem at this point is and what the word ' rude ' does to the tone. It was very generally assumed that since the subject of the poem is solemn the treatment must be solemn too, and many readers made it as serious as they could. Not unnaturally their results often displeased them.

13·8. *If the poem tends to check the reader from making speculations on other peoples lives then it has some value.* The poem however does not seem to do this, but *rather stimulates than quiets a man's interest in the private deeds of other people.* The reason for this is that the poet lays too little stress on the results of the enquiry. This form of stimulation to the mind *can do it no good and may do it harm.* The poem is therefore bad.

This seems perfectly to express a possible way of reading the poem. A reading whose solemnity fully merits all the adjectives that other readers found to fling against it. Sanctimonious, didactic, pompous, portentous, priggish, seem, indeed, if the poem is looked at in this light, hardly too strong. Only one reader attempted to state the issue between this view of the poem and another view by which it would escape these charges. And he so over-states his case that he discredits it.

13·9. I am in two minds as to the intention of this poem. If the mood in which it is written is serious, *if we are meant to take the situation in profound meditation closing in self-abasing remorse*, then the whole thing is clearly vicious and preposterous. The idea of an eternity spent in turning up the files of other people's sins or crouching to cry *peccavi* for our own is *either amusing or disgusting or both.* But if the last three lines are a sudden impish whirl on the complacent moral speculation of the first three stanzas the whole is *a very delightful little whimsy.* It must be the latter—" a rude question "—very impertinent indeed. And if the latter the manner is perfect with its echoing parody of similar but serious poems.

Yet on the turning-point of the word ' rude ' he seems possibly to be right. For if, to state the middle

view more fairly, the poet is not trying to be im-
pressive, to inflate the reader with swelling sentiments
and a gaseous ' moral,' but to keep the poem cool
and sober, he does so by bringing back the con-
versational, the social tone ; and the word ' rude '
would begin this process. If this interpretation of
the poem is right, ' rude ' is simply an acknowledge-
ment of the social convention, not in the least a
rebuke. Whether the buried lady were proud or
humble, this questioning of her motives in her living
presence would have had the same effect. Her
cheeks would have coloured—with resentment or
with modesty. And in both cases the questioning
would have been an impertinence, a rudeness, in
the simplest social sense. The word belongs to the
texture of the poet's meditation and is not aimed at
anyone, not even at the poet himself. It is the
admission of a fact, not an attack upon anyone, or
anything.

On this theory of the structure of the poem the
last verse would be in the same tone. Not a grim
warning, or an exhortation, but a cheerful realisation
of the situation, not in the least evangelical, not at
all like a conventional sermon, but on the contrary
extremely urbane, rather witty, and *slightly* whim-
sical. If it were said that it has more of a chuckle
in it than a groan or a threat, that might be over-
stating this view, but, even so, this would be a less
distortion than that which evoked the following :

13.91 (continuation of 13.5, 13.64). To close, as I began, *on a
suggestion of invective.* This " poem " is a storm brewed amongst
sodden Typhoo-tips, in the dregs of a cracked Woolworth
tea-cup, by an incorrigible moral charlatan, simpleton, *or* bore,—
who has become immune from self-criticism through the public
acceptance, *nem con.*, of a piously truistic diffuseness which
easily flatters and cozens the naïfly self-regarding morale of a
society in part too simple, in part intolerably smug.

We may grant that, if the demands of 13.8 represent its aim, it might be all this. But another reading is possible, one by which the poem becomes a very unusual kind of thing that it would be a pity to miss. That so few read it in this way is not surprising, for if there is any character in poetry that modern readers—who derive their ideas of it rather from the best known poems of Wordsworth, Shelley and Keats or from our contemporaries, than from Dryden, Pope or Cowper—are unprepared to encounter, it is this social, urbane, highly cultivated, self-confident, temperate and easy kind of humour.

PART THREE

ANALYSIS

' Let us go closer to the fire and see what we are saying.'
(The Bubis of Fernando Po.)

M

CHAPTER I

THE FOUR KINDS OF MEANING

From whence it happens, that they which trust to books, do as they that cast up many little summs into a greater, without considering whether those little summes were rightly cast up or not ; and at last finding the errour visible, and not mistrusting their first grounds, know not which way to cleere themselves ; but spend time in fluttering over their bookes ; as birds that entring by the chimney, and finding themselves inclosed in a chamber, flutter at the false light of a glasse window, for want of wit to consider which way they came in.

Leviathan.

AFTER so much documentation the reader will be in a mood to welcome an attempt to point some morals, to set up some guiding threads by which the labyrinth we have perambulated may be made less bewildering. Otherwise we might be left with a mere defeatist acquiescence in *quot homines tot sententiæ* as the sovereign critical principle, a hundred verdicts from a hundred readers as the sole fruit of our endeavours —a result at the very opposite pole from my hope and intention. But before it can be pointed, the moral has first to be disengaged, and the guiding threads cannot be set up without some preliminary engineering. The analyses and distinctions that follow are only those that are indispensable if the conclusions to which they lead are to be understood with reasonable precision or recommended with confidence.

The proper procedure will be to inquire more closely—now that the material has passed before us—into the ten difficulties listed towards the end of Part I, taking them one by one in the order there adopted. Reasons for this order will make themselves plain as we proceed, for these difficulties depend one upon another like a cluster of monkeys. Yet in spite of this complicated interdependence it is not very difficult to see where we must begin. The *original* difficulty of all reading, the problem of *making out the meaning*, is our obvious starting-point. The answers to those apparently simple questions : ' What is a meaning ? ' ' What are we doing when we endeavour to make it out ? ' ' *What* is it we are making out ? ' are the master-keys to all the problems of criticism. If we can make use of them the locked chambers and corridors of the theory of poetry open to us, and a new and impressive order, is discovered even in the most erratic twists of the protocols. Doubtless there are some who, by a natural dispensation, acquire the ' Open Sesame ' ! to poetry without labour, but, for the rest of us, certain general reflections we are not often encouraged to undertake can spare us time and fruitless trouble.

The all-important fact for the study of literature— or any other mode of communication—is that there are several kinds of meaning. Whether we know and intend it or not, we are all jugglers when we converse, keeping the billiard-balls in the air while we balance the cue on our nose. Whether we are active, as in speech or writing, or passive,[1] as readers or listeners, the Total Meaning we are engaged with is, almost always, a blend, a combination of several contributory meanings of different types. Language—and pre-eminently language as it is used in poetry—has not one but several tasks to perform simultaneously, and we shall misconceive most of the difficulties of criticism unless we understand this point and take note of the differences between

---

[1] Relatively, or technically, 'passive' only ; a fact that our protocols will help us not to forget. The reception (or interpretation) of a meaning is an activity, which may go astray ; in fact, there is always some degree of loss and distortion in transmission. For an account of 'understanding' see Part IV, § 13.

these functions. For our purposes here a division into four types of function, four kinds of meaning, will suffice.

It is plain that most human utterances and nearly all articulate speech can be profitably regarded from four points of view. Four aspects can be easily distinguished. Let us call them *Sense, Feeling, Tone,* and *Intention.*

1. *Sense.*

We speak *to say something*, and when we listen we expect something to be said. We use words to direct our hearers' attention upon some state of affairs, to present to them some items for consideration and to excite in them some thoughts about these items.

2. *Feeling.*[1]

But we also, as a rule, have some feelings *about these items*, about the state of affairs we are referring to. We have an attitude towards it, some special direction, bias, or accentuation of interest towards it, some personal flavour or colouring of feeling; and we use language to *express* these feelings, this nuance of interest. Equally, when we listen we pick it up, rightly or wrongly; it seems inextricably part of what we receive; and this whether the speaker be conscious himself of his feelings towards what he is talking about or not. I am, of course, here describing the normal situation, my reader will be able without difficulty to think of exceptional cases (mathematics, for example) where no feeling enters.

---

[1] Under 'Feeling' I group for convenience the whole conative-affective aspect of life—emotions, emotional attitudes, the will, desire, pleasure-unpleasure, and the rest. 'Feeling' is shorthand for any or all of this.

3. *Tone*.

Furthermore, the speaker has ordinarily *an attitude to his listener*. He chooses or arranges his words differently as his audience varies, in automatic or deliberate *recognition of his relation to them*. The tone of his utterance reflects his awareness of this relation, his sense of how he stands towards those he is addressing. Again the exceptional case of dissimulation, or instances in which the speaker unwittingly reveals an attitude he is not consciously desirous of expressing, will come to mind.

4. *Intention*.[1]

Finally, apart from what he says (Sense), his attitude to what he is talking about (Feeling), and his attitude to his listener (Tone), there is the speaker's intention, his aim, *conscious or unconscious*, the effect he is endeavouring to promote. Ordinarily he speaks for a purpose, and his purpose modifies his speech. The understanding of it is part of the whole business of apprehending his meaning. Unless we know what he is trying to do, we can hardly estimate the measure of his success. Yet the number of readers who omit such considerations might make a faint-hearted writer despair. Sometimes, of course, he will purpose no more than to state his thoughts (1), or to express his feelings about what he is thinking of, *e.g.* Hurrah! Damn! (2), or to express his attitude to his listener (3). With this last case we pass into the realm of endearments and abuse.

Frequently his intention operates through and satisfies itself in a combination of the other functions. Yet it has effects not reducible to their effects. It may govern the stress laid upon points in an argu-

---

[1] This function plainly is not on all fours with the others. See Part IV, § 16 and Appendix A, where a further discussion of these four functions is attempted.

ment for example, shape the arrangement, and even
call attention to itself in such phrases as ' for con-
trast's sake ' or ' lest it be supposed '. It controls
the ' plot ' in the largest sense of the word, and is
at work whenever the author is ' hiding his hand '.
And it has especial importance in dramatic and
semi-dramatic literature. Thus the influence of his
intention upon the language he uses is additional to,
and separable from, the other three influences, and
its effects can profitably be considered apart.

   We shall find in the protocols instances, in plenty,
of failure on the part of one or other of these
functions. Sometimes all four fail together ; a
reader garbles the sense, distorts the feeling, mistakes
the tone and disregards the intention ; and often a
partial collapse of one function entails aberrations
in the others. The possibilities of human misunder-
standing make up indeed a formidable subject for
study, but something more can be done to elucidate
it than has yet been attempted. Whatever else we
may do by the light of nature it would be folly to
maintain that we should read by it. But before
turning back to scrutinise our protocols some further
explanation of these functions will be in place.
   If we survey our uses of language as a whole, it
is clear that at times, now one now another of the
functions may become predominant. It will make
the possible situations clearer if we briefly review
certain typical forms of composition. A man writing
a scientific treatise, for example, will put the *Sense*
of what he has to say first, he will subordinate his
Feelings about his subject or about other views upon
it and be careful not to let them interfere to distort
his argument or to suggest bias. His *Tone* will be
settled for him by academic convention ; he will, if
he is wise, indicate respect for his readers and a
moderate anxiety to be understood accurately and

to win acceptance for his remarks. It will be well if his *Intention*, as it shows itself in the work, be on the whole confined to the clearest and most adequate statement of what he has to say (Function 1, Sense). But, if the circumstances warrant it, further relevant aims—an intention to reorientate opinion, to direct attention to new aspects, or to encourage or discourage certain methods of work or ways of approach —are obviously fitting. Irrelevant aims—the acceptance of the work as a thesis for a Ph.D., for example, —come in a different category.

Consider now a writer engaged upon popularising some of the results and hypotheses of science. The principles governing his language are not nearly so simple, for the furtherance of his intention will properly and inevitably interfere with the other functions.

In the first place, precise and adequate statement of the sense may have to be sacrificed, to some degree, in the interests of general intelligibility. Simplifications and distortions may be necessary if the reader is to ' follow '. Secondly, a much more lively exhibition of feelings on the part of the author towards his subject-matter is usually appropriate and desirable, in order to awaken and encourage the reader's interest. Thirdly, more variety of tone will be called for ; jokes and humorous illustrations, for example, are admissible, and perhaps a certain amount of cajolery. With this increased liberty, tact, the subjective counterpart of tone, will be urgently required. A human relation between the expert and his lay audience must be created, and the task, as many specialists have discovered, is not easy. These other functions will interfere still more with strict accuracy of statement ; and if the subject has a ' tendency ', if political, ethical or theological implications are at all prominent, the intention of the work will have further opportunities to intervene.

This leads us to the obvious instance of political speeches. What rank and precedence shall we assign to the four language functions if we analyse public utterances made in the midst of a General Election ? Function 4, the furtherance of intentions (of all grades of worthiness) is unmistakably predominant. Its instruments are Function 2, the expression of feelings about causes, policies, leaders and opponents, and Function 3, the establishment of favourable relations with the audience (' the great heart of the people '). Recognising this, ought we to be pained or surprised that Function 1, the presentation of facts (or of objects of thought to be regarded as facts are regarded), is equally subordinated ?[1] But further consideration of this situation would lead us into a topic that must be examined later, that of Sincerity, a word with several important meanings. (See Chapter VII.)

In conversation, perhaps, we get the clearest examples of these shifts of function, the normal verbal apparatus of one function being taken over by another. Intention, we have seen, may completely subjugate the others ; so, on occasion, may Feeling or Tone express themselves through Sense, translating themselves into explicit statements about feelings and attitudes towards things and people—statements sometimes belied by their very form and manner. Diplomatic formulæ are often good examples, together with much of the social language (Malinowski's ' phatic communion '),[2] the ' Thank you so very much ' es, and ' Pleased to meet you ' s,

---

[1] The ticklish point is, of course, the implication that the speaker believes in the 'facts'—not only as powerful arguments but *as facts*. 'Belief' here has to do with Function 2, and, as such examples suggest, is also a word with several senses, at least as many as attach to the somewhat analogous word 'love'. Some separation and ventilation of them, beyond that attempted in Ch. VII below, is very desirable, and I hope to explore this subject in a future work.

[2] See *The Meaning of Meaning*, Supplement I, § iv.

that help us to live amicably with one another. (But see Appendix A, Note 1.)

Under this head, too, may be put the psychological analyses, the introspective expatiations that have recently flourished so much in fiction as well as in sophisticated conversation. Does it indicate a confusion or a tenuousness in our feelings that we should now find ourselves so ready to make statements about them, to translate them into disquisitions, instead of expressing them in more direct and natural ways? Or is this phenomenon simply another result of the increased study of psychology? It would be rash to decide as yet. Certainly some psychologists lay themselves open to a charge of emptiness, of having so dealt with themselves that they have little left within them to talk about. ' Putting it into words,' if the words are those of a psychological textbook, is a process which may well be damaging to the feelings. I shall be lucky if my reader does not murmur *de te fabula* at this point.

But Feeling (and sometimes Tone) may take charge of and operate through Sense in another fashion, one more constantly relevant in poetry. (If indeed the shift just dealt with above might not be better described as Sense interfering with and dominating Feeling and Tone.)

When this happens, the statements which appear in the poetry are there for the sake of their effects upon feelings, not for their own sake. Hence to challenge their truth or to question whether they deserve serious attention *as statements claiming truth*, is to mistake their function. The point is that many, if not most, of the statements in poetry are there *as a means* to the manipulation [1] and expression of feelings and attitudes, not as contributions to any body of doctrine of any type whatever. With

---

[1] I am not assuming that the poet is conscious of any distinction between his means and his ends. (Compare foot-note on p. 190.)

narrative poetry there is little danger of any mistake arising, but with ' philosophical ' or meditative poetry there is great danger of a confusion which may have two sets of consequences.

On the one hand there are very many people who, if they read any poetry at all, try to take all its statements seriously—and find them silly. ' My soul is a ship in full sail,' for example, seems to them a very profitless kind of contribution to psychology. This may seem an absurd mistake but, alas ! it is none the less common. On the other hand there are those who succeed too well, who swallow ' Beauty is truth, truth beauty. . . .', as the quintessence of an æsthetic philosophy, not as the expression of a certain blend of feelings, and proceed into a complete stalemate of muddle-mindedness as a result of their linguistic naïvety. It is easy to see what those in the first group miss ;. the losses of the second group, though the accountancy is more complicated, are equally lamentable.

A temptation to discuss here some further intricacies of this shift of function must be resisted. An overflow into Appendix A, which may serve as a kind of technical workshop for those who agree with me ·that the matter is important enough to be examined *with pains*, will be the best solution. I am anxious to illustrate these distinctions from the protocols before tedium too heavily assails us. It will be enough here to note that this subjugation of statement to emotive purposes has innumerable modes. A poet may distort his statements ; he may make statements which have logically nothing to do with the subject under treatment ; he may, by metaphor and otherwise, present objects for thought which are logically quite irrelevant ; he may perpetrate logical nonsense, be as trivial or as silly, logically, as it is possible to be ; all in the interests of the other functions of his language—to express feeling or adjust tone or further his other intentions. If his success in these other aims justify him, no reader (of the kind at least to take his meaning as it should be taken) can validly say anything against him.

But these indirect devices for expressing feeling through logical irrelevance and nonsense, through statements not to be taken strictly, literally or seriously, though pre-eminently apparent in poetry, are not peculiar to it. A great part of what passes for criticism comes under this head. It is much harder to obtain statements about poetry, than expressions of feelings towards it and towards the author. Very many apparent statements turn out on examination to be only these disguised forms, indirect expressions, of Feeling, Tone and Intention. Dr Bradley's remark that *Poetry is a spirit*, and Dr Mackail's that it is *a continuous substance or energy whose progress is immortal* are eminent examples that I have made use of elsewhere, so curious that I need no apology for referring to them again. Remembering them, we may be more ready to apply to the protocols every instrument of interpretation we possess. May we avoid if possible in our own reading of the protocols those errors of misunderstanding which we are about to watch being committed towards the poems.

CHAPTER II

FIGURATIVE LANGUAGE

Que fait-il ici? s'y plairait-il? penserait-il y plaire?
                                                    RONSARD.

THE possibilities of misunderstanding being fourfold,
we shall have four main exits from true interpretation
to watch, and we shall have to keep an eye open, too,
upon those underground or overhead cross-connec-
tions by which a mistake in one function may lead
to erratic behaviour in another.

We cannot reasonably expect diagnosis here to be
simpler than it is with a troublesome wireless set,
or, to take an even closer parallel, than it is in a
psychological clinic. Simple cases do occur, but
they are rare. To take aberrations in apprehending
Sense first : those who misread 'a cool, green house'
in *Poem II*, the victims of 'the King of all our
hearts to-day' in *Poem IX*, the rain-maker (10·64),
and the writer (5·2) who took *Poem V* to be 'quite
an ingenious way of saying that the artist has made
a cast of a beautiful woman' (if we interpret 'cast'
charitably), are almost the simplest examples we shall
find of unqualified, immediate misunderstanding of
the sense. Even these, however, are not perfectly
simple. Grudges felt on other grounds against the
poem, misunderstandings of its feeling and tone,
certainly helped 2·2 and 2·21 to their mistakes, just
as the stock emotive power of 'King' was the strong
contributing factor, mastering for 9·111 all historical
probabilities and every indication through style.

Mere inattention, or sheer carelessness, may sometimes be the source of a misreading ; but carelessness in reading is the result of distraction, and we can hardly note too firmly that for many readers the metre and the verse-form of poetry is itself a powerful distraction. Thus 9·16, who understands that it is the King that is being toasted *on the peak*, and 5·3 and his fellows, no less than 5·2, may be regarded with the commiseration we extend to those trying to do sums in the neighbourhood of a barrel-organ or a brass band.

There is one difference however. All will agree that while delicate intellectual operations are in progress brass bands should be silent. But the band more often than not is an essential part of the poetry. It can, however, be silenced, if we wish, while we disentangle and master the sense, and afterwards its co-operation will no longer confuse us. A practical ' moral ' emerges from this which deserves more prominence than it usually receives. It is that most poetry needs several readings—in which its varied factors may fit themselves together—before it can be grasped. Readers who claim to dispense with this preliminary study, who think that all good poetry should come home to them in entirety at a first reading, hardly realise how clever they must be.

But there is a subtler point and a fine distinction to be noted. We have allowed above that a good poet—to express feeling, to adjust tone and to further his other aims [1]—may play all manner of tricks with his sense. He may dissolve its coherence altogether, if he sees fit. He does so, of course, at

---

[1] For simplicity's sake, I write as though the poet were conscious of his aims and methods. But very often, of course, he is not. He may be quite unable to explain what he is doing, and I do not intend to imply that he necessarily knows anything about it. This disclaimer, which may be repeated, will, I hope, defend me from the charge of so crude a conception of poetic composition. Poets vary immensely in their awareness both of their inner technique and of the precise result they are endeavouring to achieve.

his peril ; his other aims must be really worth while, and he must win a certain renunciation from the reader ; but the liberty is certainly his, and no close reader will doubt or deny it. This liberty is the careless reader's excuse and the bad poet's opportunity. An obscure notion is engendered in the reader that syntax is somehow less significant in poetry than in prose, and that a kind of guess-work—likely enough to be christened ' intuition '—is the proper mode of apprehending what a poet may have to say. The modicum of truth in the notion makes this danger very hard to deal with. In most poetry the sense is as important as anything else ; it is quite as subtle, and as dependent on the syntax, as in prose ; it is the poet's chief instrument to other aims when it is not itself his aim. His control of our thoughts is ordinarily his chief means to the control of our feelings, and in the immense majority of instances we miss nearly everything of value if we misread his sense.

But to say this—and here is the distinction we have to note—is not to say that we can wrench the sense free from the poem, screw it down in a prose paraphrase, and then take the doctrine of our prose passage, and the feelings this doctrine excites in us, as the burden of the poem. (See p. 216.) These twin dangers—careless, ' intuitive ' reading and prosaic, ' over-literal ' reading—are the Symplegades, the ' justling rocks ', between which too many ventures into poetry are wrecked.

Samples of both disasters are frequent enough in the protocols, though *Poem I*, for example, gave little chance to the ' intuitive ', the difference there between a ' poetic ' and a ' prosaic ' reading being hardly marked enough to appear. *Poem V*, on the other hand, only allowed intuitive readings. In 2·22, 10·22 and 10·48, however, the effect of a prosaic reading is clear ; in 6·3, intuition has all its own way, and the effect of its incursions in 11·32 and 11·33, is as striking as the triumph of the opposite tendency is in 12·41.[1]

Still keeping to the reader's traffic with the sense as little complicated as may be with other meanings, mention may perhaps be expected of *ignorance*, lack of acquaintance with the sense of unfamiliar words, the absence of the necessary intellectual contexts, defective scholarship, in short, as a source of error. Possibly through my choice of poems (*Poem III* did, however, bring out some odd examples) and perhaps through the advanced educational standing of the protocol-writers, this obstacle to understanding did not much appear. Far more serious were certain misconceptions as to how the sense of words in poetry is to be taken. (12·41 may have struck the reader as an example.) Obstacles to understanding, these, much less combated by teachers and much more troublesome than any mere deficiency of information. For, after all, dictionaries and encyclopædias stand ready to fill up most gaps in our knowledge, but an inability to seize the poetical sense of words is not so easily remedied.

Some further instances of these misconceptions will make their nature plainer. Compare the chemistry of 12·41 with the ' literalism ' of 12·4, 10·6, 8·15 and 7·38. Not many metaphors will survive for readers who make such a deadly demand for scientific precision as do these. Less acute manifestations of the same attitude to language appear frequently elsewhere, and the prevalence of this literalism, under present-day conditions of education, is greater than the cultivated reader will

---

[1] I must apologise for the manual labour such references impose. I have tried to space these bouts of leaf-turning as conveniently as may be, with long intervals of repose. The alternative of reprinting all the protocols referred to proved to have counter-disadvantages. To mention one only — the cost of the book would have been considerably increased.

imagine. How are we to explain—to those who see nothing in poetical language but a tissue of ridiculous exaggerations, childish ' fancies ', ignorant conceits and absurd symbolisations—in what way its sense is to be read ?

It would be easy to expound a grammatical theory of metaphor, hyperbole and figurative language, pointing out the suppressed ' as if ' s, ' is like ' s, and the rest of the locutions that may be introduced to turn poetry into logically respectable prose. But we should (as textbooks enough have shown us) be very little advanced towards persuading one of these hard-headed fellows that poets are worth reading. A better plan, perhaps, will be to set over against these examples of literalism some specimens of the opposing fault—5.3 and 5.32 will do as well as any others—and then consider, in the frame supplied by this contrast, some instances of a middle kind when both a legitimate demand for accuracy and precision and a recognition of the proper liberties and powers of figurative language are combined. It may then be possible to make clearer what the really interesting and difficult problems of figurative language are.

Let us therefore examine the hyperbole of the sea-harp in *Poem IX* in the light of comments 9.71 to 9.77. We shall, I hope, agree that these comments rightly point out a number of irremediable incoherences in the thought of the passage. The sense has at least four glaring flaws, if we subject it to a logical analysis. Moreover, these flaws or internal inconsistencies are unconnected with one another ; they do not derive from some one central liberty taken by the poet, but each is a separate crack in the fabric of the sense. Setting aside for a while the question of the suitability and fittingness of the figure as a whole, let us survey its internal structure, trying the while to find every justification we can.

Taking the objections in the order in which they

N

appear in the protocols, we have first the difficulty that ' the sea may sound like an organ, but it never has the sound of a harp '. I think we shall be forced to admit that the more closely we compare these sounds the less justification shall we find in their similarity. But this, by itself, is not a very heavy objection. A very slight similarity might be sufficient as a means of transition to something valuable. We ought never to forget, though we constantly do, that in poetry the means *are* justified by the end. It is when the end disappoints us that we can usefully turn to look into the means to see whether or not *the kind of use* the poet has made of them helps to explain why his end is unsatisfactory.

Next comes the objection that each string of this harp ' is made up of the lightning of Spring nights '. Here the poet has undoubtedly abrogated both fact and possibility. He has broken the coherence of his sense. But to say this, of course, settles nothing about the value of the passage. I have urged above that nonsense is admissible in poetry, if the effect justifies it. We have to consider what the effect is. The effect the poet *proposed* is clear—an exhilarating awakening of wonder and a fusion of the sea, lightning and spring, those three ' most moving manifestations of Nature ', as some of the other protocols pointed out. But an external influence so compelling that it may fairly be supposed to have overridden both thought and intention in the poet is unmistakable, and we shall not fully understand this passage unless we consider it. As 9.94 pointed out, ' the style is Swinburne-cum-water ', a sadly too appropriate admixture. Not only the diction (sea, harp, mirthful, string, woven, lightning, nights, Spring, Dawn, glad, grave . . .), and the subject-matter, but the peculiar elastic springy bound of the movement, and the exalted tone, are so much Swinburne's that they amount less to an echo than to a momentary obsession. A poet so dominated for an instant by his devotion to another, submitting himself, as it were, to an inspiration from without, may well be likely to overlook what is happening to his sense. The general problem of all responses made to indirect influences may here be considered. A reader's liking for this passage might often be affected by his acquaintance with Swinburne's descriptions and sea-metaphors. ' Who fished the murex up ? ' is a pertinent question. The point constantly recurs when we are estimating the enthusiasm of readers whose knowledge of poetry is not wide. Have they, or have they not, undergone the original influence ? It would be interesting to compare, by means of such a passage as this, a group of readers before and after they had first spent an evening over *Songs of the Springtides*, or *Atalanta in Calydon*.

But however widely they read in Swinburne I do not believe they would ever find him turning his sea into lightning—not even in the interests of Victor Hugo or Shelley. He is full of slight abrogations of sense. He is indeed a very suitable poet in whom to study the subordination, distortion and occultation of sense through the domination of verbal feeling. But the lapses of sense are very rarely so flagrant, so undisguised, that the reader, swept by on the swift and splendid roundabout of the verse, is forced to notice them. And, more often than not, when the reader thinks he has detected some nonsense, or some inconsequent distortion of sense, he will, if he examines it, be troubled to find it is he who is at fault. The celebrated opening of the Second Chorus of *Atalanta in Calydon* is a very representative example :

> Before the beginning of years
> There came to the making of man
> Time, with a gift of tears ;
> Grief, with a glass that ran.

We may think, at first, that the tears should belong
to Grief and the hour-glass to Time, and that the
emblems are exchanged only for formal reasons, or
to avoid a possible triteness ; but a little reflection
will show that several things are added by the
transposition. With the third line compare the verse
in *A Forsaken Garden*, which begins

> Heart handfast in heart

and with the fourth line compare

> We are not sure of sorrow

from *The Garden of Prosperine*. Some connection,
though it may be tenuous or extravagant, can almost
always be found in Swinburne, perhaps because of
his predilection for the abstract and the vague.
Vague thoughts articulate one with another more
readily than precise thoughts.

We have still to decide about the effect of the too
audacious physics of *Poem IX*. Do they not destroy
the imaginative reality—that is to say, the proper
power over our feelings—of both the sea and the
lightning, to say nothing of the harp and (presumably)
the harper [1] that are in the background of our con-
sciousness ? We can perhaps here extract another
moral for our general critical guidance. It might
take this form. Mixtures in metaphors (and in
other figures) may work well enough when the
ingredients that are mixed preserve 'their efficacy,
but not when such a fusion is invited that the
several parts cancel one another. That a metaphor
is mixed is nothing against it ; the mind is ambi-
dextrous enough to handle the most extraordinary
combinations if the inducement is sufficient. But
the mixture must not be of the fire and water type—
which unfortunately is exactly what we have here.

[1] It is not unfair, I think, to list this missing harper among the
blemishes of the passage, for the sea here has somehow to play itself.
Cf. Swinburne, *The Garden of Cymodoce*, Str. 8, l. 3 :
> Yea surely the sea as a harper laid hand on the shore as a lyre.

Objection number three, given in 9·75, that strings are not woven, will illustrate this moral. The ' higher potency in releasing vague emotion ', that *woven* in a proper context certainly possesses, is damped and cancelled as it blends with the sea and lightning ingredients, nor is there anything else in the passage that it can seek help from in preserving an independent existence.

The fourth objection, the time difficulty, is less serious. Personification, as we shall shortly see in connection with another passage, is a device which allows a poet to do almost anything he pleases with impunity provided, of course, as usual, he has anything worth doing in hand. The protocol writers, 9·76 and 9·77, rely too confidently upon common sense, a useful servant to the critic but not to be entrusted with much responsibility. Surely we need not fly very high in imagination, not so high as an aeroplane may fly, to see night and dawn very plainly present contemporaneously in the cosmic scene. Or, with less imaginative effort, we may reasonably urge that in Spring the usual separation of night and day may be said to lapse. But will these justifications really help the poem ? Dawn, we may still feel, has really no sufficient business in the poem. She is there as a pictorial adjunct—whether deserving of the opinion of 9·44 or of 9·421, I must leave it to the reader to decide, for the defect of syntax upon which 9·421 relies would be allowed, if the result were a sufficient compensation. But in her capacity as a listener she adds nothing. Dawn has certainly to listen to plenty of queer noises, and her presence does not necessarily glorify the song that the poet has in his mind.

This has brought us to the larger question of the suitability of the whole figure, how well it serves the intention of the sonnet ; upon which some very simple remarks may suffice. This intention is neither

recondite nor subtle—being the expression of a rather
vague and generalised enthusiasm, the creation of
an exalted feeling. Nor is any great precision
necessary in the feeling evoked. Any lofty, expansive
and ' appreciative ' feeling will do. This being so,
a certain negligence about the means employed is
not unfitting. ' *Qu'importe la boisson pourvu qu'on
ait l'ivresse* ', might be our conclusion but for one
consideration. The enjoyment and understanding
of the best poetry requires a sensitiveness and dis-
crimination with words, a nicety, imaginativeness
and deftness in taking their sense which will prevent
Poem IX, in its original form, from receiving the ap-
proval of the most attentive readers. To set aside this
fine capacity too often may be a damaging indulgence.

We have been watching a group of readers, with,
on the whole, a well-balanced tendency to literalism,
making their points against a passage of figurative
language whose liberties and inconsistencies were
of a kind that might excuse the dislike which
less well-balanced literalists sometimes feel for all
the figurative language of poetry. Let us turn
now to another group of exhibits, where rationality
is rather more in danger of tripping itself up. Can
the metaphors of the first two lines of *Poem X*, and
those of the last two verses, defend themselves from
the attacks of 10·61 and 10·62 ? Is their literalism
of the kind exemplified in the chemistry of 12·41
(which would be fatal to nearly all poetry) ; or is it
the legitimate variety, aimed at the abuse, not at the
use, of figurative language ? And if the latter, is it
rightly aimed, does the poem deserve it, or have we
here only instances of misreading ?

First we may reconsider 10·6, with a view to
agreeing, if we can, that the objection there lodged
would really condemn a great deal of good poetry, if
it could be sustained. It is a general objection to
Personification and, as such, worth examining irre-

spective of the merits of *Poem X*. ' Animism ', as this writer calls it, the projection of human activity into inanimate objects of thought, has been expressly pointed to by innumerable critics as one of the most frequent resources of poetry. Coleridge, for example, declared that ' images ' (by which he meant figurative language) ' become a proof of original genius . . . when a human and intellectual life is transferred to them from the poet's own spirit '. And he instanced it as ' that particular excellence . . . in which Shakespeare even in his earliest, as in his latest, works surpasses all other poets. It is by this, that he still gives a dignity and a passion to the objects which he presents. Unaided by any previous excitement, they burst upon us at once in life and power.' (*Biographia Literaria*, Ch. XV). There are indeed very good reasons why poetry should personify. The structure of language and the pronouns, verbs and adjectives that come most naturally to us, constantly invite us to personify. And, to go deeper, our attitudes, feelings, and ways of thought about inanimate things are moulded upon and grow out of our ways of thinking and feeling about one another. Our minds have developed with other human beings always in the foreground of our consciousness ; we are shaped, mentally, by and through our dealings with other people. It is so in the history of the race and in the individual biography.[1] No wonder then if what we

---

[1] Compare Wordsworth on the effects of the tie between the infant Babe and his Mother.

> For him, in one dear Presence, there exists
> A virtue which irradiates and exalts
> Objects through widest intercourse of sense
> No outcast he, bewildered and depressed
> Along his infant veins are interfused
> The gravitation and the filial bond
> Of nature that connect him with the world.

The Prelude, Bk. II.

One result is that for some seven years all objects are regarded more as though they were alive than otherwise. The concept of 'the inanimate' develops late. Cf. Piaget, *The Language and Thought of the Child*.

have to say about inanimate objects constantly presents itself in a form only appropriate, if strict sense is our sole consideration, to persons and human relations.

Often, of course, there is no necessity for personification so far as sense is concerned, and we use it only to express feelings towards whatever we are speaking about (Function 2). But sometimes personification allows us to say compendiously and clearly what would be extraordinarily difficult to say without it. *Poem X* in its third verse provides a good example :

> On wall and window *slant* your hand
> And *sidle* up the garden stair.

Both ' slant ' and ' sidle ' were occasion for divided opinions, as the protocols show ; those readers who took their sense accurately being pleased. To get this sense into a prose paraphrase with the personification cut out is not an easy matter. In fact the task almost calls for geometrical diagrams and illustrative sketches. But the bending of the cloud shadow as it passes from the surface of the earth to the upright plane of ' wall and window ' is given at once by ' slant your hand'. The changed angle of incidence thus noted adds a solidness and particularity to the effect described, and since vividness is a large part of the intention of the poem at this point, the means employed should not be overlooked. Of course, if ' hand ' be read to mean a part of the cloud itself and not as the extremity of a limb of the cloud's shadow, the image becomes merely silly, and some of the condemnations in the protocols are explained if not excused.

So, too, with ' sidle '; it gives the accidental, oblique quality of the movement of the shadow, and gives it in a single word by means of a single particularising scene. Condensation and economy are so often necessary in poetry—*in order that emotional impulses shall not dissipate themselves*—that all means to it are worth study. Personification, for the reasons suggested above, is perhaps the most important of them.

But there are degrees of personification ; it can range from a mere momentary loan of a single human attribute or impulse to the projection of a complete spiritual being. Nothing recoils more heavily upon a poet than a too ample unjustified projection. As with some other over-facile means of creating an immediate effect, it destroys the poetic sanction, and seems to empty the poet in the measure that the poem is overloaded. In *Poem XII* the dreams, the desires, the prognostications, the brooding and the wise imaginations of the clouds' mantles may seem in the end to have just this defect. Yet to decide whether a personification is or is not ' overdone ' is a matter of very delicate reading. In 10·62, however, we have a complaint that the personification is not carried far enough and a useful peg for some further critical ' morals '.

In the first place, what another poet (here Shelley) did in another poem is never in itself a good ground for deciding that this poet by doing differently has done wrong. This over-simple form of ' comparative criticism ' is far too common ; in fact we hardly ever see any other kind. Shelley's intent and this poet's intent differ, the means they use inevitably differ too. It is hardly possible to find instances so closely parallel that divergence of *method* will prove one poem better or worse than another. We have always to undertake a more subtle inquiry into the ends sought or attained. It would be an excellent thing if this type of critical argument could be labelled and recognised as fallacious. It is really only one of the more pretentious forms of recipe-hunting. This is not to say that comparisons are not invaluable in criticism, but we must know what it is we are comparing and how the relevant conditions are also to be compared.

To come closer to this example, 10·62 has not asked himself whether so shifting and various a thing as this cloud can be given a definite character, whether a changeful tricksiness is not all the personality it can bear. A ' clear conception ' of the personality of the cloud would have hopelessly overburdened the poem. The poet indeed has been careful of this very danger. When after five verses of ' antics ', chiefly concerned with the cloud-shadows, he turns to the cloud itself in its afternoon dissolution, he cuts the personification down, mixing his metaphors to reflect its incoherence, and finally, ' O frail steel tissue of the sun ', depersonifying it altogether in mockery of its total loss of character. This recognition that the personification was originally an extravagance makes the poem definitely one of Fancy rather than Imagination—to use the Wordsworthian division—but it rather increases than diminishes the descriptive effects gained by the device. And its peculiar felicity in exactly expressing a certain shade of feeling towards the cloud deserves to be remarked.

Probably 10·62 expected some different feeling to be expressed. But 10·61, who also quarrels with the opening metaphor, seems to miss the descriptive sense of the poem for some other reason. In view of the effect of ' miraculous stockade ', no less than of ' limn ', ' puzzle ', ' paint ', ' shoot ' and ' sidle ' upon other readers, one is tempted to suspect some incapacity of visual memory.[1] Or perhaps he was one of those who supposed that a cloud rather than its shadow was being described. ' Pencil ', if we take it to mean ' produce the effects of pencilling ' (such are the exigences of paraphrasing) hardly mixes the metaphor in any serious fashion. Its

---

[1] Not of visualisation, however. See Ch. V and Appendix A.

suggestion both of the hard, clear outline of the cloud's edge and of the shadowy variations in the lighting of its inner recesses, is not in the least cancelled by ' climb ' or by the sky-scraper hoist of ' miraculous stockade '. Incidentally, would it be capricious to meet the many objections to the sounds in these words (10·42 and 10·43) with the remark that they reflect the astonishment that a realisation of the height of some clouds does evoke ? ' Miraculous stockade ' seems, at least, to have clear advantages over ' the tremendous triumph of tall towers ' in point of economy and vividness. ' Puzzle ' has accuracy also on its side against these cavillers. Anyone who watches the restless shift of cattle as the shadow suddenly darkens their world for them will endorse the poet's observation. But if the cows never noticed any change of light the word would still be justified through its evocative effect upon men. Similarly with ' paint ' and ' shoot '; they work as a rapid and fresh notation of not very unfamiliar effects, and there is no reason to suppose that those readers for whom they are successful are in any way damaging or relaxing their sensibility.

With this we come back to the point at which we left *Poem IX*. We can sum up this discussion of some instances of figurative language as follows : All respectable poetry invites close reading. It encourages attention to its literal sense up to the point, to be detected by the reader's discretion, at which liberty can serve the aim of the poem better than fidelity to fact or strict coherence among fictions. It asks the reader to remember that its aims are varied and not always what he unreflectingly expects. He has to refrain from applying his own external standards. The chemist must not require that the poet write like a chemist, nor the moralist, nor the man of affairs, nor the logician, nor the professor, that he write as they would. The whole trouble of literalism is that the reader forgets that the aim [1] of the poem comes first, and is the sole justification of its means. We may quarrel, frequently we must, with the aim of the poem, but we have first to ascertain what it is. We cannot legitimately judge its means by external standards [2] (such as accuracy of fact or logical coherence) which may have no relevance to its success in doing what it set out to do, or, if we like, in becoming what in the end it has become.

[1] I hope to be understood to mean by this the whole state of mind, the mental condition, which in another sense *is* the poem. Roughly the collection of impulses which shaped the poem originally, to which it gave expression, and to which, in an ideally susceptible reader it would again give rise. Qualifications to this definition would, of course, be needed, if strict precision were needed, but here this may suffice. I do not mean by its 'aim' any sociological, æsthetic, commercial or propagandist intentions or hopes of the poet.

[2] This was Ruskin's calamitous though noble mistake. See his remarks on the Pathetic Fallacy (*Modern Painters*, Vol. III, pt. 4). He is unjust, for example, to Pope, because he does not see tha poetry may have other aims besides clear thinking and strong feeling.

CHAPTER III

SENSE AND FEELING

My belief is that there every one is under the sway of preferences deeply rooted within, into the hands of which he unwittingly plays as he pursues his speculation. When there are such good grounds for distrust, only a tepid feeling of indulgence is possible towards the results of one's own mental labours. But I hasten to add that such self-criticism does not render obligatory any special tolerance of divergent opinions. One may inexorably reject theories that are contradicted by the very first steps in the analysis of observation, and yet at the same time be aware that those one holds oneself have only a tentative validity. FREUD, *Beyond the Pleasure Principle.*

So far we have been concerned with some of the snares that waylay the apprehension and judgment of the *sense* of poetry, treated more or less in isolation from its other kinds of meaning. But the *interferences* with one another of these various meanings give rise to more formidable difficulties. A mistake as to the general intention of a passage can obviously twist its sense for us, and its tone and feeling, almost out of recognition. If we supposed, for example, that *Poem I* should be read, not as a passage from an Epic, but as a piece of dramatic verse put in the mouth either of a prosing bore, or of a juvenile enthusiast, our apprehension of its tone and feeling would obviously be changed, and our judgment of it, though still perhaps adverse, would be based upon different considerations. The different intentions attributed to *Poem II* by readers who take it to express on the one hand ' a deep passion for real life ' (2·61) and on the other ' an atmosphere of quietness and uninterrupted peace ' (2·71) reflect themselves in the different descriptions they give of its tone (' breathless tumultuous music ', ' delicate movement with clear, fine tone,[1] gravity and steadiness '). More plainly the rather one-sided debates about the intentions of *Poems VIII* and *XIII* reveal how much this major aspect, as it were, influences the minor aspects, through which the major aspect, one would suppose, must be apprehended. The rapidity with which many readers leap to a conviction as to a poem's general intention, and the ease with which this assumption can distort their whole reading, is one of the most interesting features in the protocols. And its moral is perhaps as important as any that can be drawn. With most good poetry more than one look is needed before we can be sure of the intention, and sometimes everything else in the poem must become clear to us before this.

Tone, as a distinct character in a poem, is less easy to discuss than the others, and its importance may easily be overlooked. Yet poetry, which has no other very remarkable qualities, may sometimes take very high rank simply because the poet's attitude to his listeners—in view of what he has to say—is so perfect. Gray and Dryden are notable examples. Gray's *Elegy*, indeed, might stand as a supreme instance to show how powerful an exquisitely adjusted tone may be. It would be difficult to maintain that the thought in this poem is either striking or original,[2] or that its feeling is exceptional. It embodies a sequence of reflections and attitudes that under similar conditions arise readily in any contemplative mind. Their character as common-

---

[1] 'Tone' in a quite different sense here, of course; but these descriptions of the qualities of the verse sounds do enable us to infer differences in the way the reader feels that he is being addressed.

[2] The originality of the thoughts and that of the expression are to be distinguished here. 'The four stanzas beginning, *Yet e'en these bones*, are to me, original: I have never seen the notions in any other place; yet he that reads them here persuades himself that he has always felt them.' Dr Johnson may be right in this, but I find it hard not to believe that the notions in these four stanzas have not been familiar to many who neither knew the *Elegy* nor received them from those who did.

places, needless to say, does not make them any less important, and the *Elegy* may usefully remind us that boldness and originality are not necessities for great poetry. But these thoughts and feelings, in part because of their significance and their nearness to us, are peculiarly difficult to express without faults of tone. If we are forced to express them we can hardly escape pitching them in a key which ' overdoes ' them, or we take refuge in an elliptic mode of utterance—hinting them rather than rendering them to avoid offence either to others or to ourselves. Gray, however, without overstressing any point, composes a long address, perfectly accommodating his familiar feelings towards the subject and his awareness of the inevitable triteness of the only possible reflections, to the discriminating attention of his audience. And this is the source of his triumph, which we may misunderstand if we treat it simply as a question of ' style '. Indeed, many of the secrets of ' style ' could, I believe, be shown to be matters of tone, of the perfect recognition of the writer's relation to the reader in view of what is being said and their joint feelings about it.

Much popular verse, of the type with which the name of Wilcox is nowadays somewhat unfairly associated, fails more in this respect than in any other. It ' overdoes ' what it attempts, and so insults the reader. And such overstressing is often a very delicate indication of the rank of the author. When a commonplace, either of thought or feeling, is delivered with an air appropriate to a fresh discovery or a revelation, we can properly grow suspicious. For by the tone in which a great writer handles these familiar things we can tell whether they have their due place in the whole fabric of his thought and feeling and whether, therefore, he has the right to our attention. Good manners, fundamentally, are a reflection of our sense of proportion, and faults of tone are much more than mere superficial blemishes. They may indicate a very deep disorder.

The importance of tone appears clearly if we reflect how comparatively easy it is to acquire acceptable doctrines and how difficult to avoid mistakes in tone.

We must distinguish, however, between what may be called fundamental manners and the code that rules in any given period. Good manners for the eighteenth century may be atrocious by twentieth-century standards, or *vice versa*, and not only in literary matters. There are more than a few verses in *The Rape of the Lock*, for example, which would be thought in very poor taste if they were written to-day. But the codes that rule wit are peculiarly variable. Of all literary products jokes are the most apt to become ' flat ' and tasteless with the passage of time.

Eighteenth-century verse writers, on the whole, rarely forget the reader. They paid him, indeed, rather too much deference, a result of the social character of the period. In comparison, Swinburne and Shelley often show atrocious manners as poets[1]; they please themselves and continually neglect the reader. Not that good tone requires that the reader be remembered always, much less that he be constantly flattered. But the occasions on which he is ignored must be exciting enough to excuse the poet's rapt oblivion. Faults of tone, especially over-insistence and condescension, can ruin poetry which might otherwise have had value, though usually, as I have suggested, they betoken fatal disabilities in the poet. They may, however, be due to clumsiness only. The poet has to find some equivalent for the

---

[1] Unless we suppose that we are not so much being addressed as invited to stand by the poet's side and harangue the multitude with him. Tone in Swinburne frequently lapses altogether ; he has neither good nor bad manners, but simply none. This, perhaps, aristocratic trait in part excuses his long-windedness for example.

gestures and intonations which in ordinary speech so often look after this whole matter, and this translation may at times ask for special discernment and tolerance in the reader. It will have been noticed that the reception of *Poems V* and *VII* was very largely determined by the readers' estimation of their tone (5·5, 5·8, 5·81, 7·4, 7·43, 7·6). But in judging such questions we must remember, though it is not at all easy to do so, that tone is not independent of the other kinds of meaning. We can allow a poet to address us as though we were somewhat his inferiors if what he has to say convinces us of his right to do so. But when what he offers us is within our own compass, we may be excused if we grow resentful. The subtleties possible here can easily be imagined, and some effects that may seem very mysterious until we look into them from this point of view can then be explained. Questions of tone arise, of course, whether the reader is ostensibly addressed in the second person or not. The reader can be as grossly insulted in a third-person narrative or in an Elegy, by underrating his sensitiveness or intelligence for example, as by any direct rudeness.

But the most curious and puzzling cases of mutual dependence between different kinds of meaning occur with sense and feeling. They are, as a rule, interlinked and combined very closely, and the exact dissection of the one from the other is sometimes an impossible and always an extremely delicate and perilous operation. But the effort to separate these forms of meaning is instructive, and can help us both to see why misunderstandings of all kinds are so frequent, and to devise educational methods that will make them less common.

Let us set one complication aside at once. The *sound* of a word has plainly much to do with the feeling it evokes, above all when it occurs in the

o

organised context of a passage of verse. Let us postpone—so far as we can—all consideration of this whole *sensuous* aspect of words (including their character as products of the speech-organs and their associated dance-movement) until the following Chapter, where the difficulties of the apprehension of poetic form must be tackled. In practice, of course, the sound is very important, as one of the causes (together with the word's history, its semantics, its usual applications and contexts and its special context in the poem) of the feeling it carries. But here let us confine our attention to the relations between sense and feeling and to the ways in which the feeling may be, in various degrees, dependent on the sense. And let us be careful to remember that we are concerned, firstly, with the feeling actually aroused by the word in the poem, not with feelings the word might have in other contexts, or the feeling it generally has, or the feeling it ' ought to have ', though these may with advantage be remembered, for a word's feeling is often determined in part by its sense in other contexts.[1]

Even the evident complexities of this subject are prodigious, and it must be left for some treatise of the future on the Emotive Functions of Language to display in full their tedium, their beauty, and their supreme significance.[2] Here three main situations can alone be discussed, three types of the interrelation of sense and feeling.

Type I.—This is the most obvious case where the feeling is generated by and governed by the sense.

---

[1] On the semantic aspects of this, Owen Barfield, *History in English Words*, may be profitably consulted. His *Poetic Diction* is less satisfactory, owing to an unfortunate attempt to construct a philosophical account of meaning — an account which blurs the distinction between thought and feeling and reduces the many-sided subject of Meaning to a matter of one aspect only, namely, semantics.

[2] If we reflect, for example, upon the emotive formulæ in the liturgies of various religions, we shall not underrate the importance of this topic.

The feeling evoked is the result of apprehending the sense. As examples, ' miraculous ' and ' sorcery ' may serve (*Poem X*). Given the apprehension of their sense, the feeling follows, and as a rule the two, sense and feeling, seem to form an indissoluble whole.

Type II.—Here there is an equally close tie, but fixed the other way round. For the word first expresses a feeling, and such sense as it conveys is derived from the feeling. ' Gorgeous ' (*Poem X*) is an excellent example ; its sense is ' being of a kind to excite such and such feelings '. The description of the feelings would have to be long and include mention of a tendency to contempt, grudging admiration, and a certain richness and fullness and, perhaps, satiation. ' Gorgeous ', it will be noticed, is a representative ' æsthetic ' or ' projectile ' adjective.[1] It registers a ' projection ' of feeling, and may be considered along with ' beautiful ', ' pleasant ' and ' good ' in some of their uses.

Type III.—Here sense and feeling are less closely knit : their alliance comes about through their context. ' Sprawling ' may be taken as an example. Its sense (in *Poem X*) may be indicated as an absence of symmetry, regularity, poise, and coherence, and a stretched and loose disposition of parts. I have been careful here to use only neutral (or nearly neutral) words, in order not to import the feeling in my paraphrase of the sense. The feeling of ' sprawling ' here is a mixture of good-humoured mockery and affected commiseration. And this feeling arises from the sense of the word only through the influence of the rest of the poem. It does not derive at all inevitably from the sense of the word considered by itself. One test by which we can distinguish Type III from Type I is by noticing that

[1] See Appendix A, Note 3. Like most projectile adjectives it is applied to very different things by different people.

very special circumstances would be needed to make
'miraculous' evoke quite another set of feelings,
whereas no great change need be imagined for
'sprawling' to excite feelings either of contempt or
of easeful relaxation. As 10·55 puts it, 'A drunken
man sprawls and totters', and 10·57 has some other
association, though what it is, is open to conjecture.

The looser relation described in Type III is of
course the usual condition in poetry. Its separation
from Type I[1] is a matter only of degree, for no
word carries a fixed feeling quite irrespective of its
context. But the distinction between words whose
feeling tends to dominate their context and words of
a more malleable nature is useful, for upon it most
mistakes in apprehending feeling turn. The last
two lines of Donne's Sonnet (3·12, 3·31, 3·41), the
last verse but one of *Poem VII* (7·4, 7·43, 7·53),
'boom', 'poised', and 'tinkling' in *Poem VIII*
(8·1, 8·11, 8·13), 'immortal' in *Poem IX* (9·41, 9·42)
'vaporous vitiate air' in *Poem XI* (11·2, 11·4, 11·421),
and 'rude' in *Poem XIII* (13·7, 13·73), provide
some examples upon which to test the distinction.
Is the pull exerted by the context (and in these
cases the whole of the rest of the poem is the con-
text) sufficient to overcome what may be described
as the normal separate feeling of the questionable
word? Can this pull bring it in, as an item either
in accordance or in due contrast to the rest? Or
does the word resist, stay outside, or wrench the
rest of the poem into crudity or confusion? To
triumph over the resistances of words may some-
times be considered the measure of a poet's power
(Shakespeare being the obvious example), but more

---

[1] These types of situation are not mutually exclusive. The same
word may give rise simultaneously to situations of Types I and II.
We are often unable to say which of the two, sense or feeling, is the
dominant partner, both views being possible. The dilemma may be
a tribute to our insight rather than a sign of its deficiency, for both
views may be true.

often it is the measure of his discretion, and a reader who is aware of the complexity and delicacy of the reconciliations of diverse feelings that poetry effects will walk as carefully.

The influence of the rest of the poem upon the single word or phrase is exerted in two ways—directly between feelings and indirectly through sense. The feelings already occupying the mind limit the possibilities of the new word ; they may tinge it, they may bring out one of its possible feelings with an added tang of contrast. Words, as we all recognise, are as ambiguous in their feeling as in their sense ; but, though we can track down their equivocations of sense to some extent, we are comparatively helpless with their ambiguities of feeling. We only know that words are chameleon-like in their feeling, governed in an irregular fashion by their surroundings. In this ' psychical relativity ' words may be compared with colours, but of the laws governing the effects of collocation and admixture hardly anything is known.

It is more interesting, therefore, to consider the other way in which the feeling of a phrase or word is controlled by the context—through the transactions between parts of the sense in the whole passage. On this much more can be said, for here the whole apparatus of our verbal and logical intelligence can be brought to bear. When a phrase strikes us as particularly happy, or particularly unfortunate, we can usually contrive, by examining the fabric of the sense into which it fits, to find rational grounds for our approval or dislike. And we often seem to see clearly why the emotional effect should be just what it is. But there is an odd fact to be noted which may make us hesitate. The phrase commonly is accepted or rejected, and its feeling merged, for good or ill, into the poem long before the discursive intelligence has performed its task of working out the cross-implications, affiliations and discrepancies of senses which later on may seem the explanation of its success or failure.

Three conjectures may be offered to account for an instantaneity which has led many critics to undervalue the work of intellectual analysis in the reading of poetry. It may be that the apprehension of a network of logical relations between ideas is one thing and that the analysis and clear formulation of them is quite another, and that the first may often be easy and instantaneous when the second is difficult and laborious. This seems likely, and many parallel cases can be found. A cricketer, for example, can judge a ball without in the least being able to describe its flight, or say how or why he meets it as he does. Secondly, if, as seems possible, some degree of 'dissociation' occurs in the reading of poetry, we may actually, while under the influence of the poem, apprehend more than we are able to recall when we come to reflect upon it out of the 'trance' afterwards. This conjecture, however, seems extravagant. Thirdly, the compression of poetic language tends to obstruct the discursive intelligence that works by spreading ideas out and separating their parts. But this very concentration may assist immediate, instantaneous, apprehension. Nowhere but in poetry, unless in mathematics, do we meet with ideas so closely packed together, so tightly woven. (See further Appendix A, Note 5.)

An instance may assist us to keep in touch with the observable facts while considering this obscure but important matter. The point is worth some trouble, for it is cardinal to any account of how poetry is read and why misunderstandings both of sense and feeling are so common and so difficult to avoid. The second line of the last verse of *Poem X* will serve our purpose :—

O frail steel tissue of the sun——

It will be agreed that the sense here is intricate, and

that when it is analysed out it shows a rational correspondence with the feeling which those readers who accept the line as one of the felicities of the poem may be supposed to have experienced. Let me give a fairly detailed analysis, first asking any reader who approves of the line to consider how much logical structure the sense seems to him to have *as he reads* (not when he reflects). How far does this logical structure which appears to him while reading seem the source of the feeling of the words ? Does it not rather remain in a vague background, more a possibility than an actuality ?

' Tissue ', to begin with the noun, has a double sense ; firstly, ' cloth of steel ' in extension from ' cloth of gold ' or ' cloth of silver ', the cold, metallic, inorganic quality of the fabric being perhaps important ; secondly, ' thin, soft, semi-transparent ' as with tissue-paper. ' Steel ' is also present as a sense-metaphor of Aristotle's second kind, when the transference is from *species* to *genus*, steel a particular kind of strong material being used to stand for any material strong enough to hold together, as it appears, the immensity of the cloud-structure. The colour suggestion of ' steel ' is also relevant. ' Frail ' echoes the semi-transparency of ' tissue ', the diaphanousness, and the impending dissolution too. ' Of the sun ' it may be added runs parallel to ' of the silk worm ', *i.e.*, produced by the sun. I give such an elaborate explanation partly because of the many readers (10·42) who had difficulty in making out this line.

It is safe, perhaps, to affirm that few readers will become clearly aware of more than a small part of these fibrillar articulations and correspondences of the sense until they deliberately question the line and think it over. Yet it can be accepted (and, I must add, rejected) with certainty and conviction on the strength of what seems the merest glimpse of its sense. Moreover, a definite and relevant feeling can be aroused at once. In fact, a feeling that is quite pertinent seems often to precede any clear grasping of the sense. And most readers will admit that, *as a rule*, the full sense, analysed and clearly articulated, never comes to their consciousness ; yet they may get the feeling perfectly. The reception of *Poems I* and *V* was largely determined by whether the readers responded first to sense or to feeling. (Compare 1·17 and 1·3 ; and 5·81, 5·38 and 5·53. Also 7·43.) Still more does all this apply to *tone*.

I am far from wishing to quarrel with this summary kind of reading when it is practised by highly competent readers. A mere glimpse, to the right kind of eye, may be amply sufficient, but the dangers to those who are less quick and sensitive are obvious. Dangers both of a false understanding of the sense and of a distorted development of feeling. The corrective, in ideal perfection, is equally obvious —exercise in analysis and cultivation of the habit of regarding poetry as capable of explanation. But in practice the corrective has its own dangers. It has not been enough recognised in schools that making a paraphrase or gloss for any poem worth reading is a delicate exercise. Recalling some of the atrocities which teachers sometimes permit themselves, one is tempted to believe that the remedy might be worse than the disease. The risk of supposing that the feelings which the logical expansion of a poetic phrase excites must be those which the phrase was created to convey is very great. We easily substitute a bad piece of prose for the poem— a peculiarly damaging form of attack upon poetry. (See p. 191.) Furthermore, we must recognise that a single paraphrase will rarely indicate more than a single partial aspect of a poem. We often need one form of paraphrase to elucidate its sense and quite another to suggest its feeling. Since the only cure that can be suggested for the general unintelligibility of poetry that the protocols exhibit is some more enlightened use of interpretation exercises in our schools, it is worth while to consider what means are available for developing this power of apprehending both sense and feeling in teachers and pupils alike. It may be remarked that this is not a matter which concerns poetry only, though incapacity, obtuseness and failure in discrimination most appear through poetry, the most concentrated and delicate form of human utterance.

If we compare our powers of analysing sense and feeling we shall recognise at once that feeling, in contrast with sense, is a will-o'-the-wisp. We have a marvellous apparatus of inter-engaging and overlapping symbols for handling and elucidating sense, a logical machine of great sensitiveness and power, equipped with automatic safety devices and danger signals in the form of contradictions. Logical language has even reached such a high state of development that it can now be used to improve and extend itself, and may in time be made self-running and even fool-proof. For handling feeling we have nothing at all comparable. We have to rely upon introspection, a few clumsy descriptive names for emotions, some scores of æsthetic adjectives and the indirect resources of poetry, resources at the disposal of a few men only, and for them only in exceptional hours. Introspection has become a by-word, even where intellectual and sensory products and processes are concerned, but it is even more untrustworthy when applied to feelings. For a feeling even more than an idea or an image tends to vanish as we turn our introspective attention upon it. We have to catch it by the tip of its tail as it decamps. Furthermore, even when we are partially successful in catching it, we do not yet know how to analyse it. Analysis is a matter of separating out its attributes, and no one knows yet what attributes a feeling may have, what their system of interconnections is, or which are important, which trivial.

This, it may be hoped, matters less than might be supposed. For if we had to wait until psychology had conquered *this* territory we might reasonably despair. But we shall find encouragement if we look more closely into the methods by which we do actually—in spite of the backwardness of psychology —contrive to discriminate between feelings, and it is not impossible that by so doing we may be able to give psychology a leg up.

We do somehow manage to discuss our feelings, sometimes with remarkable facility and success. We say things about them sometimes that seem to be subtle and recondite, and yet true. We do this in spite of our feebleness in introspection and our ignorance of the general nature of feelings. How do we come to be so knowledgeable and clever ? Psychologists have never, I think, resolutely faced this question of how we know so much about ourselves that does not find any way at present into their text-books. Put shortly, the answer seems to be that this knowledge is lying dormant in the dictionary. Language has become its repository, a record, a reflection, as it were, of human nature.

No one who uses a dictionary—for other than orthographic purposes—can have escaped the shock of discovering how very far ahead of us our words often are. How subtly they already record distinctions towards which we are still groping. And many young philologists and grammarians must have indulged dreams of bringing some of this wisdom into the ordered system of science. If we could read this reflection of our minds aright, we might learn nearly as much about ourselves as we shall ever wish to know ; we should certainly increase enormously our power of handling our knowledge. Many of the distinctions words convey have been arrived at and recorded by methods no single mind could apply, complex, methods that are, as yet, not well understood. But our understanding of them is improving—psychology has notably helped here— and our power of interpreting the psychological records embodied in words is increasing and capable of immense increase in the future. Among the means to this end a combination or co-operation of psychology and literary analysis, or criticism, seems the most hopeful. Neither alone can do much, both together may go far. There is a possibility that something parallel to the recent advances in physics might be achieved if we could combine them. As geology, in the early stages of inquiry into radio-activity, came in to supply evidence that experiments could not elicit, so the records, hidden not in rocks but in words, and accessible only to literary pene-tration, may combine[1] with groping psychological analysis to produce results as yet unprofitable to conjecture.

From these high speculations let us come back nearer to the problem of sense and feeling. How actually do we enquire into the feeling a word (or phrase) carries ? How we inquire into its sense is not so difficult to make out. We utter the word or phrase and note the thoughts it arouses, being careful to keep them in the context of the other thoughts aroused by the whole passage. We then attempt, by a well recognised and elaborate technique, to construct a definition, choosing from among several methods to suit our purpose and the situation. If we still have any difficulty in distinguishing the precise sense, we can put definite questions, we can substitute other words—which the dictionary will supply—that in part arouse the same thoughts. We

---

[1] This inquiry will not be so much a matter of semantics (though semantics obviously provide invaluable information) as of a com-parative study of the resources (direct and indirect) available in different languages and periods for psychological purposes.

note the samenesses and differences and plot the
position of the thought we wish to define with regard
to these other thoughts.

In these and other ways we exploit the syntactical
suppleness of language and its overlapping vocabulary
to disentangle sense, but if we consider how far the
same resources are available for disentangling feeling
we find a difference. There is, it is true, a depart-
ment of language, a certain selection of the dictionary,
which can be applied in the same fashion. There
are the names of the emotions and of the emotional
attitudes—*anger, fear, joy, sorrow* . . . ; *hope, sur-
prise, discouragement, dread*. . . . And the derivative [1]
adjectives, verbs and adverbs, *enthusiastic, passionate,
tender* . . . ; *startle, delight, distress* . . . ; *mourn-
fully, eagerly, gaily*. . . . Moreover, we have the
special apparatus of the æsthetic or ' projectile '
adjectives. We express our feeling by describing
the object which excites it as *splendid, glorious, ugly,
horrid, lovely, pretty* . . . words which really indicate
not so much the nature of the object as the character
of our feeling towards it.[2] Thus we obtain an
indirect notation for our feelings by projecting them
rather than describing them. But we use this
notation in a very unsystematic fashion, though a very
curious and interesting order may be sometimes
glimpsed behind it. Some of these words, for
example, may be used together, while others bar one
another out. A thing may be both grand and
sublime, it can be glorious and beautiful, or gorgeous
and ugly ; but it can hardly be both pretty and
beautiful, it can certainly not be pretty and sublime.
These accordances and incompatibilities reflect the
organisation of our feelings, the relations that hold
between them. But our power to take advantage of
this linguistic reflection of our emotional constitution

---

[1] Logically, not grammatically, derivative, of course.
[2] See Appendix A, Note 3.

is at present very limited—perhaps because so little
work has been done upon this subject. And it is
when we attempt to describe the difference between
the feelings which *pretty* and *beautiful* express,
for example, that we discover how unsatisfactory
are the verbal resources expressly allocated to this
purpose.

There is, it is true, a certain apparatus of qualifying
words and phrases that we use rather speculatively
and uncertainly to describe feelings. We can say
of a feeling that it is *elevated* or *gross*, or *tenuous*, or
calm, or *grave*, or *expansive*. Most of these are
clearly metaphorical expressions, words whose sense
has not normally anything to do with feeling, trans-
ferred and applied to feeling on account of some
glimpsed or supposed character in the feeling
analogous to a character in the object the word
usually describes. Sometimes the analogy is close—
fleeting, massive, intense, constricting—and our slight
knowledge of the physiology of emotions may also
help us here. But often the resemblance or analogy
is remote and will not bear pressing. It is hard to
be certain what is being said when a feeling is
described as *profound*, or *vital*. Perhaps very little
indeed, may be being said. And often, if we look
closely, the metaphor turns out to be not a prose or
sense metaphor at all but an *emotive* metaphor. The
difference between these is worth some reflection.[1]

A metaphor is a shift, a carrying over of a word
from its normal use to a new use. In a sense
metaphor the shift of the word is occasioned and
justified by a similarity or analogy *between the object*
it is usually applied to and the new object. In an
emotive metaphor the shift occurs through some
similarity *between the feelings* the new situation and
the normal situation arouse. The same word may,

---

[1] Some further explanations of this distinction will be found in
Principles, p. 240, and in *The Meaning of Meaning*, Ch. VI.

in different contexts, be either a sense or an emotive metaphor. If you call a man a swine, for example, it may be because his features resemble those of a pig, but it may be because you have towards him something of the feeling you conventionally have towards pigs, or because you propose, if possible, to excite those feelings. Both metaphorical shifts may be combined simultaneously, and they often are. But in studying our methods of describing feelings they have to be distinguished. Consider, for example, *profound*, one of the commonest terms by which we attempt to describe emotions. When we use it we may be doing either of two things, or both together. We may be simply inviting from our reader the awed respectful feelings he usually has towards other things that are said to be profound—deep lakes, vast chasms in the earth, night, human error, the wisdom of sages, and so forth. Often we can obtain this respect for our feeling without requiring the reader to consider the feeling itself in any fashion, and in fact while discouraging investigation. This is the simplest type of emotive metaphor. Or we may be asking him to recognise that our feeling has in some (undefined) way something of the character of other profound things—that it is not easily explored, for example, that it may contain all kinds of things, or that it is easy to get lost in it. This is the sense metaphor. Usually the two are combined, without analysis of either. It is not a very encouraging sign of our general intelligence, or of our emotional discrimination, that this word has been found invaluable by many popular critics and preachers. I must take some credit for charity in not citing a collection of examples that lies upon my table.

Most descriptions of feelings, and nearly all subtle descriptions, are metaphorical and of the combined type. The power to analyse explicitly the ground of the transference is not widely possessed in any

high degree, and it is less exercised both in school-
training and in general discussion than might be
wished. A better understanding of metaphor is one
of the aims which an imposed curriculum of literary
studies might well set before itself. But a writer
may use a metaphor and a reader take both its sense
and feeling correctly without either writer or reader
being capable of explaining how it works. Such
explanations are a special branch of the critic's
business. Conversely, however acute and pene-
trating a reader may be, it does not follow that he
will be able to create good metaphorical language
himself. It is one thing to be able to analyse
resemblances and analogies when they have first
been seized and recorded by someone else ; it is
quite another thing to effect the discovery and
integration oneself.

This brings us obviously back to the poet, one of
whose gifts, ordinarily, is just this command of
original metaphor. From the technical point of
view indeed the poet's task is constantly (though not
only) that of finding ways and means of controlling
feeling through metaphor. He has to be expert, if
not in describing feeling, in presenting it, and
presenting and describing are here rather near
together. Even in the case of *profound*, dissected
above, there was a third possibility. The word
may instigate in the reader an echo, a shadow-
semblance of the emotion it describes. He may find
a sympathetic pulse awaken in his bosom, and feel
serious, self-conscious and responsible, at grips with
Destiny. If so, the word may in part have presented
the feeling as well as described it. Any lively, close,
realistic thought of an emotion is so apt to revive it
that most descriptions that are at all concrete or
intimate, that do succeed in ' putting it before one ',
also reinstate it.

Of the two kinds of paraphrasing which, we

suggested, might be made more use of in our schools —the one to exhibit the sense of a poem, the other to portray its feeling—the first requires only an intelligent use of the dictionary, logical acumen, a command of syntax, and pertinacity. The second demands qualities of sensitiveness and imagination, the power to use remote experience and to create metaphors, gifts which may seem to belong by birthright to the poet alone. It may seem strange to suggest that these gifts could be developed by school training, but remembering the original endowment of average children and comparing it with the obtuseness of the sample adult, the proposal (if we can guard against some of the dangers hinted at above), may not in the end prove to be so unduly optimistic. It was partly to show the need and to suggest the possibility of improved methods in education that my documentation in Part II was extended to such length.

CHAPTER IV

POETIC FORM

Beauty and melody have not the arithmetical password, and so are barred out. This teaches us that what exact science looks for is not entities of some particular category, but entities with a metrical aspect. . . . It would be no use for beauty, say, to fake up a few numerical attributes in the hope of thereby gaining admission into the portals of science and carrying on an æsthetic crusade within. It would find that the numerical aspects were duly admitted, but æsthetic significance of them left outside.

A. S. EDDINGTON, *The Nature of the Physical World.*

THAT the art of responding to the form of poetry is not less difficult than the art of grasping its content—its sense and feeling—will be evident to anyone who has glanced through Part II. And since half perhaps of the feeling that poetry carries comes through its form (and through the interaction of form and content) the need for better educational methods, here also, will be admitted. The condition of blank incapacity displayed in 1·161, 3·15, 3·51, in half the comments on *Poem VI*, in 10·61, 11·41, 12·52 and 13·61, to mention but a few salient examples; the desperate efforts to apply the fruits of the traditional classical training shown in 3·44, 6·33, 12·51 and 13·62; and the occurrence of such divergences as those between 1·14 and 1·141, 2·2 and 2·61, 4·27 and 4·31, or 9·3 and 9·31, all tell the same story. A large proportion of even a picked public neither understand the kind of importance that attaches to the movement of words in verse, nor have any just ideas of how to seize this movement or judge it.

It may be objected that just ideas upon a point

admittedly so difficult as the nature of rhythm are
not easy to attain, that what matters is sensitiveness,
and that this is a special endowment. But, once
again, too many young children show an aptitude
for the reading of poetry and a capacity to seize its
rhythm, for us to admit that so many adults need
be so obtuse. Mistaken ideas, and crude uncon-
sidered assumptions certainly play their part. It
may be that the best way to learn how verse should
be spoken is to listen to a good speaker ; but a few
reasonable ideas upon the matter can certainly
assist, and without them we remain unnecessarily
at the mercy of any authoritative mangler of verses
we may encounter.

Let us begin with the assumption that the protocols
show to be most damaging, the notion that _regularity
is the merit of verse_. (13·62 and 3·44 will make the
force of this notion clear to us). It derives very
largely from the cruder by-products of Classical
Education. Unless very well taught, Latin verse
composition is a bad instrument by which to train
a mind in the appreciation of rhythm. A few very
brilliant or very rebellious boys escape, but the rest
receive the impression (often indelible) that good
verses are simply those that fit a certain framework
of rules, and that this framework is the measure of
their rhythmical virtue. Applied to English verse
the notion meets with a check in the fact that no
set of rules has been found (or, at least, agreed upon),
but the efforts of the rival schools of prosodists seem
all directed towards establishing some set of rules,
and the general impression that metrical excellence
lies in regularity is encouraged, and readers who
have not heard of more refined ideas naturally retain
this simple notion. ' Irregular ', as we know from
other contexts, is a word that carries several shades
of disapprobation.

But the patent fact that the best verses are frequently irregular, that almost as often as not they fail to conform, however many ' licences ', 'substitutions ' and ' equivalences ' are introduced into the rules of scansion to bring them into line, has forced upon many prosodists an improved idea of metre. Instead of strict conformity with a pattern, an arrangement of departures from and returns to the pattern has come to be regarded as the secret of poetic rhythm. The ear, it has been thought, grows tired of strict regularity but delights in recognising behind the variations the standard that still governs them.

This conception, though an improvement, is still too superficial. I have put it in a language which reveals its weakness, for the apprehension of poetic rhythm is only partly an affair of the ear. The defect of the view is that it regards poetic rhythm as a character of the sound of the words apart from their effects in the mind of the reader. The rhythm is supposed to belong to them and to be the cause of these effects. But the difference between good rhythm and bad is not simply a difference between certain sequences of sounds ; it goes deeper, and to understand it we have to take note of the meanings of the words as well.

This point, which is of some practical importance, appears clearly if we imagine ourselves reciting verses into the ear of an instrument designed to record (by curves drawn on squared paper) all the physical characters of the sequences of sounds emitted, their strength, pitch, durations, and any other features we choose to examine. (This is not a fantastic suggestion, for such instruments can be arranged and begin to be part of the furniture of good phonetic laboratories.) The shape of our curves will give us a transcription of all the physical rhythms [1] of the

---

[1] I use the word 'rhythm' here in the very wide sense of a repetitive configuration, *i.e.*, a group of groups such that the several

verses. Now the view objected to would lead us to
conclude that verses which are good poetry would show
some peculiarity [1] in their curves, that verses which
are bad poetry could not show. Put in this manner,
it will be agreed, I hope, that the conclusion is most
unplausible. But if we say, as many have said, that
poetic rhythm is a quality of the sound, the sensuous
form, of words, there is no means of escaping it.

Yet it is perfectly true that many great passages of
poetry do *seem to possess*, merely as sounds, a peculiar
undeniable virtue. And it is sometimes suggested
that a sensitive listener, knowing no Italian, who
listens to Dante, well read, would be able to dis-
tinguish the verses of the *Divina Comedia* from those
of some skilful but negligible imitator. Their
superiority in sound, it is said, would reveal them.
The experiment might be interesting, but it has an
obvious flaw which makes it inconclusive. The
reader must be presumed to understand what he is
reading, and it is likely that what the sensitive listener
would really discern would be signs, in the reader's
voice and manner, of the differences due to this
understanding. For whether a speaker is really
interested or not in what he is saying, and in what
fashion, is a point we can be quick to detect.

How, then, are we to explain this apparent
superiority in the sound of good poetry if we admit
that on the recording drum its curves might be

constituent groups are similar to one another, though not necessarily
exactly similar. Elsewhere (in *Principles of Literary Criticism*,
Ch. XVII) I have used the word in a quite different sense, namely, for
that dependence of part upon part within a whole which derives from
expectation and foresight. This last is not, perhaps, the most natural
use of the word, but this dependence is, I think, what many people
who discuss, for example, the rhythm of prose, rhythm in pictures, or
rhythm in golf, have in mind ; if so, the use is justified. The sense
here used, on the other hand, allows us to speak of the movements of
the planets as being rhythmical apart from any mind which observes
them.

[1] Not, of course, a simple, direct similarity of rhythm ; but some
order or regularity, some relevant peculiar property.

indistinguishable from those of rubbish. The answer is that the rhythm which we admire, which we seem to detect actually *in* the sounds, and which we seem to respond to, is something which we only *ascribe* to them and is, actually, a rhythm of the mental activity through which we apprehend not only the sound of the words but their sense and feeling.[1] The mysterious glory which seems to inhere in the sound of certain lines is a projection [2] of the thought and emotion they evoke, and the peculiar satisfaction they seem to give *to the ear* is a reflection of the adjustment *of our feelings* which has been momentarily achieved. Those who find this a hard saying may be invited to consider anew the reception of *Poem IV*, pp. 55-58 above.

Such an explanation has this incidental advantage, that it accounts for the passionate admiration sometimes accorded to stray lines that seem of a mediocre manufacture. The reader (1·31) who compares the exhortations in *Poem I* to 'wonderful music' serves us excellently as an example (1·145, 1·21 and 1·3 may also be re-examined). The phenomenon is paralleled in all human affairs into which feeling enters, and this is no occasion to expatiate upon it.

But the theory of poetic rhythm as something 'projected', *ascribed* to verses rather than inherent in them, must not lead us to *under*-estimate the part played by the actual sounds. They are a very important contributing factor though they do not carry the whole responsibility for the rhythm. They are the skeleton upon which the reader casts flesh

---

[1] See Appendix A, Note 4.

[2] Projected in the sense that our pleasure is projected when we describe someone as 'pleasant' (to be distinguished from 'pleasing') or ugly (to be distinguished from 'causing a loathing'). See Appendix A, Note 3. A clear indication that this projection occurs in apprehending rhythm is the fact that we can give several alternative rhythms to a simple series of stimuli, such as a metronome-beat or the ticking of a clock. Many other facts of experiment and observation might be brought to support this conclusion.

and clothing. And if the skeleton is too much out of joint, or if it is the skeleton of a whippet, when sense and feeling demand that of a cat, no goodwill on the part of the reader and no depth of realisation of sense and feeling will overcome the disability. To see this we have only to change the rhythm of any convenient passage of good verse, while preserving its vocabulary and, so far as possible, its syntax.

> Whether nobler it is in the mind to suffer
> The arrows and slings of Fortune outrageous.

The effect is that of comic-opera patter. The sense fights in vain to master the form, and its failure gives it an inevitable air of frivolity.

Metrical form, therefore, that is to say the rhythm inherent in the sequence of the actual sounds in verse, the rhythm that appears in the records of the kymograph, is very important. It can easily make what might be a good poem into a bad one. But it cannot be judged apart from the sense and feeling of the words out of which it is composed nor apart from the precise order in which that whole of sense and feeling builds itself up. The movement or plot of the word-by-word development of the poem, as a structure of the intellect and emotions, is always, in good poetry, in the closest possible relation to the movement of the metre, not only giving it its tempo, but even distorting it—sometimes violently. Readers who take up a poem as though it were a bicycle, spot its metre, and pedal off on it regardless of where it is going, will naturally, if it is a good poem, get into trouble. For only a due awareness of its sense and feeling will bring its departures from the pattern metre into a coherent, satisfying whole.

The notion that verses must conform to metrical patterns was described earlier in this chapter as the most damaging enemy to good reading. It is a double-edged notion, blindly destructive on both sides. It leads, on the one hand, to mechanical reading, to a ' cruel forcing ' (3·44) of syllables into a mould which they were never meant to fit, and to a ruthless lopping away of vocables (cf. 8·44, 12·51, 13·62), treatment that is fatal to the movement of the verse. On the other hand it leads to bitter complaints against irregularity and a refusal to enter into poems which do not accord smoothly with the chosen pattern (8·43).

Against these unnecessary mistakes it cannot be too much insisted that there is no obligation upon verses to conform to any standard. The pattern is only a convenience, though an invaluable one; it indicates the *general* movement of the rhythm ; it gives a model, a central line, from which variations in the movement take their direction and gain an added significance ; it gives both poet and reader a firm support, a fixed point of orientation in the indefinitely vast world of possible rhythms ; it has other virtues of a psychological order ; but it has no compulsory powers, and there is no good reason whatever to accord it them.

After the conformity notion, its close cousin, the notion that poetic rhythm is independent of sense, is the most hurtful. It is easy, however, to show how much the rhythm we *ascribe* to words (and even their inherent rhythm as sounds) is influenced by our apprehension of their meanings. Prepare a few phrases with their sounds and inherent rhythms as closely alike as possible but with different meanings. Then compare for example :—

Deep into a gloomy grot

with

Peep into a roomy cot.

The ascribed rhythm, the movement of the words, trivial though it be in both cases, is different, though almost every prosodist would have to scan them in the same fashion, and the kymograph would, I think, for most readers, show few important differences.[1]

Going a step further, if the meaning of the words is irrelevant to the form of the verse, and if this independent form possesses æsthetic virtue, as not a few have maintained (3·6 will do as a specimen) it should be possible to take some recognised master-piece of poetic rhythm and compose, with nonsense syllables, a double or dummy which at least comes recognisably near to possessing the same virtue.

> J. Drootan-Sussting Benn
> Mill-down Leduren N.
>   Telamba-taras oderwainto weiring
> Awersey zet bidreen
> Ownd istellester sween
>   Lithabian tweet ablissood owdswown stiering
> Apleven aswetsen sestinal
> Yintomen I adaits afurf I gallas Ball.

If the reader has any difficulty in scanning these verses, reference to Milton, *On the Morning of Christ's Nativity*, xv, will prove of assistance, and the attempt to divine the movement of the original before looking it up will at least show how much the sense, syntax, and feeling of verse may serve as an introduction to its form. But the illustration will also support a subtler argument against anyone who affirms that the mere sound of verse has *independently* any considerable æsthetic virtue. For he will *either* have to say that this verse is valuable (when he may be implored to take up his pen at once and enrich the world with many more such verses, for nothing could be easier), *or* he will have to say that it is the differences *in sound* between this purified dummy and the original which deprive the dummy of poetic merit. In which case he will have to account for

---

[1] I am aware that all such experiments are invalidated by the fact that *some* difference in vowel and consonantal sounds is introduced, and so the balance of the inherent rhythm is to some degree disturbed, but though not persuasive, these experiments seem to me instructive.

the curious fact that just those transformations which
redeem it as sound, should also give it the sense and
feeling we find in Milton. A staggering coincidence,
unless the meaning were highly relevant to the effect
of the form.

Such arguments (which might be elaborated) do
not tend to diminish the power of the sound (the
inherent rhythm) *when it works in conjunction with
sense and feeling.* The reception of *Poem VI* (and
especially 6·32, 6·33) proves both the subtlety and
the importance of this collaboration. The twofold
contrasts of 4·23 and 4·24 and 4·25 also admirably
display the point. The mistake of neglecting sound
altogether must rank next after the Regularity and
Independence myths as a source of bad reading. In
fact the close co-operation of the form with the
meaning—modifying it and being modified by it
in ways that though subtle are, in general, perfectly
intelligible—is the chief secret of Style in poetry.
But so much mystery and obscurity has been raised
around this relation by talk about the *identity* of
Form and Content, or about the extirpation of the
Matter in the Form, that we are in danger of forgetting
how natural and inevitable their co-operation must be.

By bad reading I suggest that we should mean
not so much reading that would offend our sus-
ceptibilities if we were listening,[1] as reading that
prevents the reader himself from entering into the
poem. The sounds most people make when they read
aloud probably seem very different to their audience
and to them. The phenomena of ' projection ' are
noticeable here. We invest our rendering with the

[1] Very unfortunately most of the gramophone records yet available
must be described as exceedingly bad in both senses. They would
justify in a sensitive child a permanent aversion from poetry. And
less sensitive children may pick up habits of 'sentimentalisation',
'emotionality' and exaggeration, very difficult to cure. Some of
Mr Drinkwater's records, however, point in a better direction and
deserve honourable mention.

qualities we wish it to have—unless some critical eye is cocked upon us—and two readings of the same poem that sound very different may not, to the readers themselves, be after all so unlike. The rhythms they *ascribe* to the poem may be more similar than the rhythms they actually succeed in giving it. Thus though private reading aloud is much to be recommended [1] as an aid in working out the form of a poem, it is doubtful whether public-reading (in the classroom for example) should be encouraged. Nothing more easily defeats the whole aim of poetry than to hear it incompetently mouthed or to struggle oneself to read out a poem in public before it has given up most of its secrets. For to read poetry well is extremely difficult. One piece of advice which has proved its usefulness may perhaps be offered : to remember that we are more likely to read too fast than to read too slow. Certainly, if the rhythm of a poem is not yet clear to us, a *very slow* private reading gives a better chance for the necessary interaction of form and meaning to develop than any number of rapid perusals. This simple neurological fact, if it could be generally recognised and respected, would probably more than anything else help to make poetry understood.

[1] Partly because movements of the organs of speech (with muscular and tactile images of them) enter into the ascribed *sound* of words almost as much as auditory sensations and images themselves.

CHAPTER V

IRRELEVANT ASSOCIATIONS AND STOCK RESPONSES

O now when the Bardo of the Dream-State upon me is dawning !
Abandoning the inordinate corpse-like sleeping of the sleep of
    stupidity,
May the consciousness undistractedly be kept in its natural state ;
Grasping the true nature of dreams, may I train myself in the clear
    Light of Miraculous Transformation :
Acting not like the brutes in slothfulness,
May the blending of the practising of the sleep state and actual
    experience be highly valued by me.
Tibetan Prayer.[1]

FROM the first two of our ten critical difficulties
(p. 14) we must pass to a group of more particular,
less general, obstacles to just discernment. As to
erratic imagery—whether visual imagery or imagery
of the other senses—when the extreme variety of
human beings in the kinds of imagery they enjoy,
and the use they make of it, has been realised, little
need be added to what has already been said *a propos*
of *Poem X* (10·2–10·24) and elsewhere. (Cf. 13·462,
12·7, 11·22 ; 9·4–9·48, 9·91, 7·32, 3·7. Also Ap-
pendix A, Note 5.) With some readers imagery of
all kinds rightly plays an immensely important part
in their reading. But they should not be surprised
that for equally good readers—not of the visualising
or image-producing type—images hardly appear, and
if they appear have no special significance. It may
seem to the visualisers that the poet works through
imagery, but this impression is an accident of their
mental constitution, and people of a different
constitution have other ways of reaching the same
results.

[1] See W. Y. Evans Wentz, *The Tibetan Book of the Dead*, p. 202.

Visualisers, however, are exposed to a special danger. The vivid and precise images which arise before us, owe much of their character and detail to sources which are quite outside the poet's control. To use them as an important thread in the texture of the poem's meaning, or to judge the poem by them, is a very risky proceeding. In so far as the meaning of the poem has actually embodied itself for us in our imagery, and is really reflected therein, we are justified, of course. And I would not deny that many readers may find their imagery a most sensitive and useful index to the meaning. But the merit of the poem is not in the imagery. To put the error in its cruder form : a poem which calls up a ' beautiful picture ' is not thereby proved to be a good poem.

The detail, especially, of most readers' imagery is likely to be irrelevant, to depend upon circumstances only by accident connected with the meaning of the poem ; the *general character* of the imagery and its feeling may be more significant. We ought to be very wary in discussing such a point, for the threads of relevant connection which the poem may touch, as it enters now into one, now into another of the vast reservoirs of experience in different readers' minds, are too various, complex and subtle for any external observer to trace. In this sense there is far more in any poem than any one reader can discover. A quality in an image which seems to one reader quite beside the point may be an essential item to another. Those whose experience comes to them chiefly through their eyes may rightly attach extreme importance to nuances in their imagery. None the less, in less sensitive and more chaotic visualisers, imagery is a frequent occasion for irrelevance.

We shall understand the situation better if we consider some other instances of irrelevance, for the problem of the intrusion of what is not germane to the meaning is a general one. Examples in plenty will have been noticed in the protocols, and we may resurvey a few of them with advantage. The simplest case is where some particular memory of the reader's personal biography is recalled, and his response to the poem becomes largely a response to this reminiscence. The ' tinkling piano ' association of 8·11 belongs here. It is not hard to imagine the sounds which the poem recalled to this reader's mind, nor (if we read ' execrating ' as a portmanteaux-word for ' excruciating ' and ' execrable ') difficult to sympathise with him. But his association fails to illustrate the poem as evidently as the odder associations of 8·21. More doubt may be felt about the thunder-storm association of 12·1. It must surely be this, for clouds, however ' heavy ', will not otherwise be heard to ' rumble '. But there is, it may be thought, something oppressive and thundery about the feeling of *Poem XII*. The cathedral associations of *Poem VII*, on the other hand, were clearly relevant (7·54–7·56), and may be sharply contrasted with the pine-wood phantasy of 7·57.

Slightly more complicated are these instances where it is a train of thought, not a memory, that intrudes. The home-sickness of 10·1, the opinions on the musical qualities of hymns (8·2) and on the proper use of music (8·12, 8·32), the historical background of 9·111 and the politics of 9·15, betray themselves as having nothing to do with the matter, but it is not so easy to decide about the War Memorial (7·43) or Joanna Southcott's gladstone-bag (13·5). The associated train of ideas may be merely an *ignis fatuus*, or a flash of inspiration. Everything depends upon how essential the bond of thought or feeling may be that links it with the poem. We have to ask whether it really springs from the meaning[1] or whether it is

---

[1] I may remind the reader that, here and elsewhere when I use the word ' meaning ', all the four kinds of meaning discussed in Chapter I are referred to.

an accidental by-product of a reading which does not realise the meaning; whether the train of association has at least started right and is rooted in something essential, and whether or not accidents of the individual reader's mood or history or temperament have twisted it.

A special case which well illustrates the general situation occurs when what is thought of is some other poem. If it is another poem by the same author the association is likely to be relevant; but if the title, the subject, or some similarity of a single phrase is responsible, the dangers of aberration are obvious. Something has already been said about them in connection with the introduction of Keats into the discussion of *Poem V* (5·32, 5·34), and the effect of Shelley on *Poem X* (10·47, 10·48, 10·62, also Ch. II, p. 201). Only the very closest and most sensitive reading will show whether two poems really have anything that matters in common, and such superficial resemblances as may be picked up in cursory reading prove nothing unless we can trace them deeper. The great services that comparisons so often render come from the assistance they can give to closer reading, and the greatest possible difference may be as useful as the closest similarity in shaking our minds out of the routine of expectation. But direct comparisons based upon the supposition that poems can be classified—by their themes, or metres, for example—and that poems in the same class (cloud poems, immortal-beauty poems, graveyard poems, sonnets, and so forth . . .) must be alike, can only serve to exhibit stupid reading. As with other associations, the quality of the link (the depth of its grounds in the inner nature and structure of the associated things) is the measure of its relevance.

Often, of course, an association with another poem will be no more than a means by which a reader defines, for himself or for others, the kind of feeling the poem evokes in him. This is perhaps what is happening in 1·193 and in 11·4. Such comparisons do not so much influence the reader's judgment of the poem as reflect it, but with most of the associations we are concerned with here, the association becomes clearly a contributing factor to the poem.

The most flagrant cases of irrelevance come from the intrusion into the poem of the hobby-horse or the obsession. The unlucky lover (6·36), the victim of parental advice (6·37), and the victim of circumstances (6·38) provide hardly less clear examples than the symbolist (12·11), the indignant moralist (8·41), or the educational reformer (10·11). What stray reminiscence prompted this last is a point that should be not uninteresting to teachers.

The personal situation of the reader inevitably (and within limits rightly) affects his reading, and many more are drawn to poetry in quest of some reflection of their latest emotional crisis than would admit it if faced with such a frank declaration as that in 11·2. Though it has been fashionable—in deference to sundry confused doctrines of ' pure art ' and ' impersonal æsthetic emotions '—to deplore such a state of affairs, there is really no occasion. For a comparison of the feelings active in a poem with some personal feeling still present in the reader's lively recollection does give a standard, a test for reality. The dangers are that the recollected feelings may overwhelm and distort the poem and that the reader may forget that the evocation of somewhat similar feelings is probably only a part of the poem's endeavour. It exists perhaps to *control and order* such feelings and to bring them into relation with other things, not merely to arouse them. But a touchstone for reality is so valuable, and factitious or conventional feelings so common, that these dangers are worth risking.

Thus memories, whether of emotional crises or of scenes visited or incidents observed, are not to be hastily excluded as mere personal intrusions. That they are personal is nothing against them—all experience is personal—the only conditions are that they must be genuine and relevant, and must respect the liberty and autonomy of the poem. Genuine memories, for example, of ' the most moving manifestations of nature ' and ' its loveliest and grandest aspects ' (9·9 and 9·91), if they were compared with what the poem contained, would have influenced the opinions there expressed of *Poem IX*. It is the absence of such memories that allows a word like ' glittering ' to pass unchallenged in the last line but one of the poem. At a moment when accuracy and verisimilitude in description are important, appears a word completely false to the appearances that are being described. Mountains that are ' surging away into *the sunset glow* ' do not glitter ; they cannot, unless the sun (or moon) is fairly high in the heavens. But ' glittering ' is a stock epithet for icy mountains. With this we are brought to the important, neglected and curious topic of Stock Responses.

So much that passes for poetry is written, and so much reading of even the most original poetry is governed, by these fixed conventionalised reactions that their natural history will repay investigation. Their intervention, moreover, in all forms of human activity—in business, in personal relationships, in public affairs, in Courts of Justice—will be recognised, and any light which the study of poetry may throw upon their causes, their services, their disadvantages, and on the ways in which they may be overcome, should be generally welcome.

A stock response, like a stock line in shoes or hats, may be a convenience. Being ready-made, it is available with less trouble than if it had to be specially made out of raw or partially prepared materials.

And unless an awkward misfit is going to occur, we may agree that stock responses are much better than no responses at all. Indeed, an extensive repertory of stock responses is a necessity. Few minds could prosper if they had to work out an original, ' made to measure ' response to meet every situation that arose—their supplies of mental energy would be too soon exhausted and the wear and tear on their nervous systems would be too great. Clearly there is an enormous field of conventional activity over which acquired, stereotyped, habitual responses properly rule, and the only question that needs to be examined as to *these* responses is whether they are the best that practical exigencies—the range of probable situations that may arise, the necessity of quick availability and so forth—will allow. But equally clearly there are in most lives fields of activity in which stock responses, if they intervene, are disadvantageous and even dangerous, because they may get in the way of, and prevent, a response more appropriate to the situation. These unnecessary misfits may be remarked at almost every stage of the reading of poetry, but they are especially noticeable when emotional responses are in question. Let us survey a few examples to show the range of incidence of this disorder before attempting to analyse its causes. We may then inquire whether it is inevitable, to what extent and by what means it might be avoided.

At the humbler end of the scale, those readers who were barred out from *Poem II* through their stock response to ' cool, green house ', and those betrayed by the monarch in *Poem IX*, show the mechanism of the mistake very clearly. The ordinary meaning, the automatic, habitual interpretation, steps in too quickly for the context of the rest of the poem to make its peculiarities effective. Similarly, when it is a larger body of ideas that intrudes—the religious and anti-religious prejudices of 7·2 and 7·21, the

Q

political leanings of 9·14 and 9·15, the R.S.P.C.C.
zeal of 10·11, all tell the same story, but they show
something further. An ' idea ', as we are using the
term here, is not a merely passive item of conscious-
ness, dragged up by the pull of blind forces at the
mercy of routine laws of association. It is rather an
active system of feelings and tendencies which may
be pictured as always straining to appear and ready
to seize any opportunity of disporting itself. We
shall not understand the phenomena of stock
responses unless we regard them as energy systems
which have the right of entry, unless some other
system of greater energy can bar them out or perhaps
drain their energy away from them. Fundamentally,
though this is an unfair way of putting it, when any
person misreads a poem it is because, *as he is at that
moment*, he wants to. The interpretation he puts
upon the words is the most agile and the most active
among several interpretations that are within the
possibilities of his mind. Every interpretation is
motivated by some interest, and the idea that appears
is the sign of these interests that are its unseen masters.
When the interest is unusual in kind and its distorting
effect large and evident, as in 10·11, we readily
admit that this is so. With stock responses—where
the dominating interest is excessively ordinary and
no distortion may result—we are more likely to
overlook this ' energetic ' aspect of ideas, but to
remember it is the key to the whole matter.

The principle that it is the most ' attractive '
reading which is adopted is often disguised, and may
seem to be contradicted, for example, when a reader
says that he would like to read a poem in a certain
way and regrets that he cannot. But there a major
interest—his desire to read faithfully—has over-
reached and controlled a more local interest. It is
to be feared that this major interest is too often
dormant, and the need for its watchful control too

little realised. In its place an initial prepossession, the desire to *find* grounds for approval (or condemnation)—a desire arising well ahead of any adequate justification—frequently takes charge of the whole process.

A stock rhythm can be imported quite as easily as a stock idea, as we have seen (8·41); and if we could listen to the readings of the protocol writers it is probable that we should notice this often, but whether distortions equal to that in 3·15 are common may be doubted.

In the cases so far cited the stock response intervenes to distort a passage whose more adequate reading develops otherwise. To the same group belong 5·37, 5·38 and 5·4 (where more traditional notions than those really present in the poem are responsible for the effects recorded), 8·3–8·33 (where the poet is modifying conventional feelings, but his readers refuse to let him change them), and 13·1–13·4 (where several different stock sentiments replace the poem and bring discredit upon it). But the stock response can interfere in other ways. In 12·5 it is the *difference* between the poem and the stock poem the reader has in his mind that is the objection. Similarly in 10·44 and 11·43, deviation—in the one case from a stock image of a cloud, in the other from a stock notion of an epitaph—is the ground of complaint. This type of adverse criticism, objection brought to a poem for not being quite a different poem, without regard paid to what it is *as itself*, ought to be less common. Poets are often guilty of it towards one another, but they have some excuse, since absorption in one kind of aim may well make a man blind to other aims. Intelligent critics, however, who realise that no poem can be judged by standards external to itself, have no excuse. Yet few original poems have escaped general abuse for not being more like other poems—which proves how hard the task of being intelligent and a critic is.

But a much more subtle situation involving stock responses remains to be discussed. Here—instead of distorting the poem or of setting up an irrelevant external standard—the stock response actually is in the poem. *Poems I, IV, VII* and *IX*, with some differences in level and degree, I believe illustrate this condition of affairs. The most correct reading of them, the reading which most accords with the impulses that gave them being, is in each case, unless I am mistaken, such that every item and every strand of meaning, every cadence and every least movement of the form is fatally and irrevocably familiar to anyone with any acquaintance with English poetry. Furthermore this familiarity is *not* of the kind which passages of great poetry ever acquire, however often we may read them or however much we have them by heart. We may be weary to death of ' To be or not to be . . . ', but we still know that if we were to attend to it again it could surprise us once more. The familiarity of these poems belongs to them as we first read them, it is not an acquired familiarity but native. And it implies, I think, that the mental movements out of which they are composed have long been parts of our intellectual and emotional repertory and that these movements are few and simple and arranged in an obvious order. In other words the familiarity is a sign of their facility as stock responses.

There is a contributory reason for taking this view. The more we examine the detail of these poems the more we shall notice, I believe, their extreme impersonality—the absence of any personal individual character either in their movement as verse or in their phrasing. The only touches of character that anyone can point to are the echoes of other poets. Each of them might well have been written by a committee. This characterlessness appears very plainly if we compare[1] them with Donne's Sonnet, where there are hardly seven words together anywhere which have not a peculiar personal twist. Such impersonality, like the familiarity, is a sign that they are composed of stock responses. In addition it will be recalled that these poems (with the exception of the first line of *Poem IX*) were rather oddly immune from serious misunderstanding. With this point in view I included all the examples of misreading that occurred.

Such stock poems are frequently very popular. They come home to a majority of readers with a minimum of trouble, for no new outlook, no new direction of feeling, is required. On the other hand, as we have seen, readers who have become more exigent often grow very indignant, the degree of their indignation being sometimes a measure, it may appear, of the distance they have themselves moved from the stock response and the recency of the development. But such cynical reflections are not always in place here, for these responses must evidently be judged by two partially independent sets of considerations—their appropriateness to the situations to which they reply, and the degree in which they hinder more appropriate responses from developing. There are clearly stock responses which are in both ways admirable—they are right as far as they go, reasonably adequate to their situations, and they assist rather than prevent further, more refined, developments. On the other hand, no one with the necessary experience will doubt that inappropriate stock responses are common and that they are powerful enemies to poetry. Some of the *differences in origin* between good and bad responses are therefore worth tracing.

---

[1] Such a comparison is not an introduction of an external standard : it is merely a means of bringing out more clearly a feature of the poems which might escape us.

If we consider how responses in general are formed, we shall see that the chief cause of ill-appropriate, stereotyped reactions is *withdrawal from experience.* This can come about in many ways. Physically, as when a London child grows up without ever seeing the country or the sea ; morally, as when a particularly heavy parent deprives a child of all the adventurous expansive side of life ; through convention and inculcation, as when a child, being too easily persuaded what to think and to feel, develops parasitically ; intellectually, as when insufficient experience is theoretically elaborated into a system that hides the real world from us.

These last two cases are the more interesting for our purpose here, though the effects of sheer ignorance and of such moral disasters as produce timidity are not to be overlooked. But more often, perhaps, it is a too loose and easy growth in our responses that leads to premature fixation. Ideas, handed to us by others or produced from within, are a beguiling substitute for actual experience in evoking and developing our responses. An idea— of soldiers for example—can stay the same through innumerable repetitions ; our experience of actual soldiers may distressingly vary. The idea, as a rule, presents one aspect ; the actual things may present many. We can call up our idea by the mere use of a word. And even in the presence of the Army it is by no means certain that what we perceive will not be as much our idea as the soldiers themselves. Since a response becomes firmer through exercise, it is clear that those among our responses that are early hitched to an idea, rather than to the actual particularities of the object, gain a great advantage in their struggle for survival. It behoves us, therefore, to consider very carefully what kinds of things these ideas are, how we come by them and to what extent they can be trusted.

An idea, in the sense we are using here, is a representation[1] but it is both very much less and very much more than a mental replica or copy of the thing it represents. It is less, because even the most elaborate idea falls short of the complexity of its object, is a sketch that is incomplete and probably distorts. It is more than a replica because besides representing the object it represents (in a different sense) our interest in the object. We can all observe that our idea of an acquaintance, for example, is a compromise. It reflects in part his actual qualities, some of them ; but it also reflects our feelings towards him, our tendencies to act in one way or another towards him, and these, as we well know, are governed not by his real qualities only—as though we were impartial deities—but by our needs, desires, habits and the rest. The example is typical. Pure ideas, that reflect only features of the object, are to be found only in some of the sciences—where centuries of careful testing have reduced the effects of our partiality to a minimum. All our ordinary ideas about objects that matter to us, that are, as we say, *interesting*, are coloured by our emotional and practical relations to them. We can hardly help thinking that our nation, for example, is, on the whole, the best. Naturally enough, we are usually blind to this subjective colouring and our quickness to detect bias in other people rarely makes us ponder long upon our own. This is one of the reasons for thinking that Part II may be useful, for to imagine that a mirror stands between us and other people is certainly the most reliable means of studying ourselves.

[1] Whether the mental representative is an image—more or less like the object represented—or a word, or some other more mysterious kind of event in the mind, we need not discuss here. As a rule it is probably this latter. The author's opinions upon these matters will be found in *The Meaning of Meaning* and, more summarily, in *Principles of Literary Criticism*. See also Appendix A, Note 5.

We come by our ideas in three main fashions : by direct interaction with the things they represent, that is, by experience ; by suggestion from other people ; and by our own intellectual elaboration. Suggestion and elaboration have their evident dangers, but are indispensable means of increasing our range of ideas. It is necessary in practice to acquire ideas a great deal faster than we can possibly gain the corresponding experience, and suggestibility and elaboration though we must make them responsible for our stock responses, are after all the capacities that divide us from the brutes. Suggestion, working primarily through language, hands down to us both a good and an evil heritage. Nine-tenths, at the least, of the ideas and the annexed emotional responses that are passed on—by the cinema, the press, friends and relatives, teachers, the clergy . . .—to an average child of this century are—judged by the standards of poetry—crude and vague rather than subtle or appropriate. But the very processes by which they are transmitted explain the result. Those who hand them on received them from their fellows. And there is always a loss in transmission which becomes more serious in proportion as what is transmitted is new, delicate and subtle, or departs in any way from what is expected. Ideas and responses which cost too much labour both at the distributing end and at the reception end—both for writer and reader—are not practicable, as every journalist knows. The economics of the profession do not permit their transmission ; and in any case it would be absurd to ask a million tired readers to sit down and work. It is hard enough to get thirty tired children to sit up, behave and look bright.

A very simple application of the theory of communication shows, then, that any very widespread diffusion of ideas and responses tends towards standardisation, towards a levelling down. But, as we have already agreed, any responses that work, even badly, are better than none. Once the basic level has been reached, a slow climb back may be possible. That at least is a hope that may be reasonably entertained. Meanwhile the threat to poetry in this state of affairs must be recognised. As our chief means by which subtle ideas and responses may be communicated, poetry may have a part to play in the climb back. It is, at least, the most important repository of our standards.

We have still to consider the other influence which encourages in the individual the fixation of inappropriate responses—*speculative elaboration divorced from experience*. Thinking—in the sense of a thorough attempt to compare all the aspects of an object or situation, to analyse its parts, to reconcile one with another all its various implications, to order it in one coherent intellectual fabric with everything else we know about everything connected with it—is an arduous and not immediately profitable occupation. Accordingly, outside the scientific professions and endowed institutions and even within them, it is much less practised than we conventionally suppose.

What we usually describe as thinking is a much more attractive mental exercise ; it consists in following out a train of ideas, a process which affords us most of the pleasures of thinking, in the stricter sense, without its pains and bewilderments. Such trains of associations may, and in the minds of men of genius often do, lead to new and valuable ideas. But—accidents apart—the condition for this happy result is a wide available background of relevant experience. The valuable idea is, in fact, the meeting-point, the link between separate parts of this field of experience. It unites aspects of existence that ordinarily remain unconnected, and in this lies its value. The secret of genius is perhaps nothing else than this greater availability of all experience coupled with larger stores of experience to draw upon. The man of genius seems to take in more every minute than his duller companion, and what he has received seems to be more readily at his disposal when he needs it. This obvious description of Shakespeare seems to apply in lesser degree to other good poets.

The man of less endowment (I am incidentally describing many bad poets) attempting a similar achievement with less experience and with what experience he has less available,[1] is likely to arrive at merely arbitrary results. Lacking the control of a many-sided, still active, past experience, his *momentary* tendencies, desires, and impulses shape and settle his conclusions for him, and it is more likely to be the *attractiveness* of the idea (in the light of some particular desire) than its *relevance* that causes it to be adopted. It might be thought that the test of subsequent experience would lead such a man to abandon or correct the inappropriate ideas and responses he arrives at in this arbitrary fashion. So it does in many practical matters. We all know enthusiasts who constantly have their unreal hopes and projects dashed to the ground. But attitudes and responses of the kinds with which poetry is likely to be concerned unfortunately escape this corrective test. The erratic individual cannot himself see that his responses are inappropriate, though others might tell him. When he misreads a poem, no practical consequences arise to teach him his folly; and, similarly, if he mismanages his emotional relations with his fellow-beings he can readily persuade himself that *they* are at fault. I have been describing a type of reader—familiar to every teacher concerned with poetry—whose interpretations have

---

[1] If we ask why one man's past experience should be less available to him than another man's, and so less useful to him in guiding his desires and thoughts, the answer must be given in terms of inhibitions. See Chapter VI.

a quality of wilful silliness which matches well the obstinacy and conceit that are the primary traits of the character. Often considerable mental agility is shown, enough to support an affectation of 'brilliance', but in time a striking monotony, a repetition of the same forms of response is equally apparent. Though fundamentally some disorder of the self-regarding sentiment [1]—a belated Narcissism, perhaps—must be at the root of these afflicting phenomena, their approximate cause is certainly withdrawal from experience through the day-dream habit. And since milder forms of this condition seem a very frequent cause of erratic reading (cf. 2·2, 6·4, 6·5, 7·38, 8·4, 8·45, 9·111, 10·11, 10·6, 11·33, 12·41, 13·51) it seemed worth while to attempt a rough analysis. But on the whole the characterological aspects of the protocols will have to be neglected.

Enough perhaps as to some of the causes of stock inappropriate responses, whether of the standardised, or the personal-whimsy, type. The only corrective in all cases must be a closer contact with reality, either directly, through experience of actual things, or mediately through other minds which are in closer contact. If good poetry owes its value in a large measure to the closeness of its contact with reality, it may thereby become a powerful weapon for breaking up unreal ideas and responses. Bad poetry certainly can be their very helpful guardian and ally.

---

[1] Cf. the opening lines of Part II of Pope's *Essay on Criticism*.

Of all the causes which conspire to blind
Man's erring judgment, and misguide the mind,
What the weak head with strongest bias rules;
Is pride, the never-failing vice of fools.
Whatever nature has in worth denied
She gives in large recruits of needful pride !
For as in bodies, thus in souls, we find
What wants in blood or spirits, swell'd with wind. . .
Trust not yourself; but, your defects to know,
Make use of every friend—and every foe.

The last couplet may perhaps be taken to indicate one piece of profit that may be drawn from study of the protocols.

But even the best poetry, if we read into it just what we happen to have already in our minds, and do not use it as a means for reorganising ourselves, does less good than harm.

Most good poetry, of course, resists this kind of misusage, but often the emotional and intellectual habits of the readers are too strong for the poet. Moreover, the official doctrine of the eighteenth century that

> True wit is nature to advantage dress'd,
> What oft was thought, but ne'er so well express'd.

is still firmly entrenched in many minds. The notion that all that a poet can do is to put strikingly, or nicely, or elaborately, or *euphoniously*, ideas and feelings that we already possess, is so serious and frequent an obstacle to good reading, that I need not apologise for quoting from a letter I received from one of the protocol writers at about this stage in my discussion :

'Although interested in the remarks you made yesterday, I could not help feeling that your talk about " Stock Responses " was somewhat obscure and misleading. . . . The truth of the matter is, I think, that *every poem* calls up stock responses, but bad poetry is poetry which touches us superficially and leads us to take the response for granted. Thus in reading Gray's *Elegy* we are prepared to have certain feelings about life and death stirred up within us. Nor are we disappointed, for we find at the end of the poem that we have genuinely been moved *as we expected*, and the stock response to Churchyard scenery has been drawn out of us, as it were, and given a chance to expatiate. But in *Poem XIII* on your sheet, the process is different. We expect[1] the

[1] Compare Seami Motokiyo on one of the 'secrets' of the Nō 'The "flower" consists in forcing on the audience an emotion which they do not expect.' Waley, *The Nō Plays of Japan*, p. 47.

stock responses to thoughts on Death to be drawn out, but in reality they are not, since the poet does not touch us deeply enough to do so. However we take the drawing-out of these responses for granted, and it is not until we read the poem through a second or third time that we find we have been deceived '.

My correspondent's account does peculiarly fit the *Elegy* of which Dr Johnson well wrote : ' The *Churchyard* abounds with images which find a mirror in every mind, and with sentiments to which every bosom returns an echo ', though it is doubtful whether ' mirror ' is a word which the lexicographer would, on reflection, have here retained. The *Elegy* is perhaps the best example in English of a good poem built upon a foundation of stock responses. These responses are of the kind which we granted—indeed insisted—above, may be admirable, perfectly appropriate as far as they go and no hindrance to responses which may go further. But these stock responses do not exhaust[1] the *Elegy*; though its extreme familiarity may blind us to the peculiarities of tone and sequence of feeling that it contains— the qualities in the poem that belong to Gray, not to the common stock from which it develops. And we have only to open Hardy's poems at almost any page to discover that besides ' the stock response to Churchyard scenery ' there are many other possible responses. Furthermore, as with other good poems so even with the *Elegy*, the interpretations of good readers will vary appreciably with their varied minds. No one can say, ' There is only this and this in the poem and nothing more '. There is everything

[1] All that beauty, all that wealth e'er gave
Awaits alike the inevitable hour.

Between the stock response to these lines which may be rendered by ' How sad !' and the response of Gautama Buddha, there is evidently room for many other responses, some of a stock pattern and some not.

there which a reader who starts right and keeps in
a balanced contact with reality can find. But minds
too much subjugated to their own fixed stock
responses will find nothing new, will only enact once
more pieces from their existing repertory. Better
this than nothing perhaps. The shock of dis-
covering how alive with new aspects everything
whatever is when contact with reality is restored is
anæsthetising to minds that have lost their capacity
to reorganise themselves ; it stupefies and bewilders.
Nearly all good poetry is disconcerting, for a moment
at least, when we first see it for what it is. Some
dear habit has to be abandoned if we are to follow it.
Going forwards we are likely to find that other
habitual responses, not directly concerned, seem less
satisfactory. In the turmoil of disturbed routines
that may ensue, the mind's hold on actuality is tested.
Great poetry, indeed, is not so safe a toy as the con-
ventional view supposes. But these indirect effects
of the overthrow of even a few stock attitudes and
ideas is the hope of those who think humanity may
venture to improve itself. And the belief that—on
the whole and accidents apart—finer, subtler, more
appropriate responses are more efficient, economical,
and advantageous than crude ones, is the best ground
for a moderate optimism that the world-picture
presents.

CHAPTER VI

SENTIMENTALITY AND INHIBITION

May the tears of sympathy crystallise as they fall and be worn as pearls in the bosom of our affections.

Nineteenth Century Commercial Travellers' Toast.

AMONG the politer terms of abuse there are few so effective as ' sentimental '. Not very long ago the word ' silly ' was fairly useful for this purpose. The most intelligent would wince, the less intelligent would become angry, and the stupid would grow indignant if they, or views dear to their hearts, were so described—the three shades of feeling corresponding perhaps to a suspicion, a fear, and an absolute certainty as to there *not* being something in it. But since Bergsonism began its insidious dry-rot-like invasion of contemporary intellectualism the word ' silly ' has lost some of its sting. Nowadays the accusation of sentimentality is more annoying than any slur cast upon our capacity as thinkers, for our moral capital is invested in our feelings rather than in our thoughts.

The very fact that it is so annoying suggests that ' sentimental '—though often it *may* mean something precise and capable of definition—may be also, like an insulting gesture, the vehicle of another kind of utterance ; that it is sometimes not so much the instrument of a statement as an expression of contempt. Such an expression cannot, of course, be defined as though it were a scientific term. Given the occasion and the speakers we can describe the feelings the word excites and the attitudes from which it springs. But there we have to leave the matter. And ' sentimental rubbish ' is doubtless more often than not a mere phrase of abuse. Compare the phrase ' damn nonsense '. The logician or the expert in definitions would waste his time trying to assign a precise scope to the adjective in either case.

But ' sentimental ' may be more than a piece of abuse, an emotive gesture. It may be a description, may stand for a vague idea, or for any one of several precise ideas ; and two of these are extremely important. So important that there is no need to be surprised if ' sentimental ' is one of the most overworked words in the whole vocabulary of literary criticism. Its frequency, its twofold use, as an insult and as a description, its fogginess in the second capacity and its social significance in the first are all sufficiently evidenced in the protocols. *Poems IV* and *VIII* and, to a lesser degree, *Poems II* and *XIII* provide us with our most instructive examples. But before examining these in detail we must attempt some definitions and elucidations.

Setting aside the abusive use of ' sentimental ' as a mere gesture indicating little more than dislike, let us reflect first upon the vaguer senses of the word. We often use it to say only that there is something wrong in the feelings involved by the thing, whatever it is, which we call sentimental. And we do not attempt to specify what is wrong. Using a vague thought like this has been happily compared by Bertrand Russell to aiming at a target with a lump of putty. The putty spreads out, and we have a good chance of bespattering the bull's-eye with some of it. But it will spread over the rings too. A precise thought is more like a bullet. We can perhaps hit with it just what we want to hit and nothing else, but we are much more likely to miss altogether. Vague thoughts are best sometimes ; they economise labour and are easier to follow, they have their obvious uses in poetry ; but for this purpose we need more precise ones.

The first of these is easy to state. A person may be said to be sentimental when his emotions are too easily stirred, too light on the trigger. As we all know to our cost the trigger adjustment for the feelings varies with all manner of odd circumstances. Drugs, the weather, ' the brave music of a *distant drum* ', fatigue, illness—these and many other extraneous factors can make our emotions too facile. The lover of the bottle in his maudlin stage is a famous sentimentalist. Certain rhythms—as in the case of the brass band above mentioned—and sounds of a certain quality, perhaps through their associations—the trumpet and the nightingale, for example—all these readily facilitate emotional orgies. So do certain conditions of mass suggestion. Reunions, processions ; we often have to blush for our sentimentality when we escape from the crowd. Most remarkable of all, perhaps, are some effects of illness. I reluctantly recall that the last time I had influenza a very stupid novel filled my eyes with tears again and again until I could not see the pages. Influenza is thought by many to be a disorder of the autonomic nervous system, and if this be so, there would be nothing surprising in this effect. All our emotional susceptibilities may be more or less affected, but the results are most marked with those which we can luxuriate in, those which do not obviously endanger our self-esteem.

This last factor is one in which individuals vary amazingly. Some people regard indulgence in the soft and tender emotions as always creditable, and they wallow in them so greedily that one is forced to regard them as emotionally starved. Others are apt to think about these emotions as Alexander Bain, the once celebrated author of *The Emotions and the Will*, thought about kissing (he called it osculation).

R

" The occasion ", he said, " should be adequate and the actuality rare ".

But what is this adequate occasion and what makes it adequate ?

Postponing consideration of this awkward problem, let us first trace these differences in emotional susceptibility, in the touchiness of the feelings, a little further. They are very noticeable as between infancy, maturity, and old age. The child often appears singularly unfeeling, so does the over-experienced adult.

> No more, no more, O never more on me
> The freshness of the heart will fall like dew,
> Which out of all the lovely things we see
> Extracts emotions beautiful and new—

as Byron wrote. The point expressed in the last word will also have to be considered later. In between the infant and the adult come the adolescents, who, as is well known, are regarded both by their juniors and their seniors as sentimentalists *in excelsis*. The girl of twelve is apt to think her seventeen-year-old sister very ' sloppy '. As we shall see, there may be several reasons for this phenomenon. In old age, sometimes, but not always, a return of heightened emotional susceptibility takes place. ' Sentimental ' here applies to persons. It means that they are too susceptible, the flood-gates of their emotions too easily raised.

This then gives us a precise, though very general, sense for ' sentimental ', a *quantitative* sense. A response is sentimental if it is too great for the occasion. We cannot, obviously, judge that any response is sentimental in this sense unless we take careful account of the situation.

Another sense, of which this is not true, is that in which ' sentimental ' is equivalent to ' crude '. A crude emotion, as opposed to a refined emotion, can be set off by all manner of situations, whereas

a refined emotion is one that can only be aroused by
a narrow range of situations. Refined emotions are
like sensitive instruments ; they reflect slight changes
in the situations which call them forth. The
distinction is parallel in several ways to the dis-
tinction made above between vague and precise
thoughts. Though refined responses are capable of
much more appropriateness than crude ones, they
are much more likely to go astray, as super-subtle
folk often show us. On the other hand, though crude
emotions are less likely to go altogether wrong, they
are less likely to go entirely right, if we judge them
by high standards of rightness. Neither crudeness
nor refinement need imply anything about the
intensity of the emotion—they are *qualitative* not
quantitative characters. A crude emotion need not
be intense, nor a refined one feeble. It is true,
however, that the most violent emotions are usually
crude. Terror and rage, as we all know, are apt,
once they are aroused, to spread and apply them-
selves to anything. And while intensity is under
discussion one further point may be noted. Violence
of emotion, though much popular criticism seems to
assume so, does not necessarily imply value. Poems
which are very ' moving ' may be negligible or bad.
It is the quality rather than the violence which
matters. As Wordsworth wrote,

> The Gods approve
> The depth, and not the tumult, of the soul.

We may suspect that to-day the demand for violence
reflects some poverty, through inhibition, in the
everyday emotional life. In Elizabethan times a
perhaps not analogous demand could not, however,
admit of this explanation.

One more sense of ' sentimental ' requires definition
before we can turn to consider when accusations of
sentimentality are justified and when they are not.

This sense derives from the psychologists' use of the word 'sentiment'. A sentiment in his terminology is not an experience in the way that an emotion, a pain, the sight of something, an image, and a thought, are experiences. It is not a momentary thing but a more or less permanent arrangement in the mind : a group of tendencies towards certain thoughts and emotions organised around a central object. Love, for example, is a sentiment, if by love we mean, not a particular experience lasting certain minutes or hours, but a set of tendencies to behave in certain ways, to think certain thoughts, to feel certain emotions, in connection with a person. Sentiments can be very complex; love includes a tendency to feel resentful towards anyone who annoys the loved person, and so on. A sentiment, in brief, is a persisting, organised system of dispositions.

Sentiments, in this sense, are formed in us through our past experience in connection with the central object. They are the result of our past interest in the object. For this reason they are apt to persist even when our present interest in the object is changed. For example, a schoolmaster that we discover in later life to have been always a quite unimportant and negligible person may still retain something of his power to overawe us. Again the object itself may change, yet our sentiment towards it—not as it was but as it is—may so much remain the same that it becomes inappropriate. For example, we may go on living in a certain house although increase in motor traffic has made life there almost insupportable. Conversely, though the object is just what it was, our sentiment towards it may completely change—through a strange and little understood influence from other sentiments of later growth. The best example is the pathetic and terrible change that can too often be observed in the sentiments entertained towards the War by men who suffered from it and hated it to the extremist degree while it was raging. After only ten years they sometimes seem to feel that after all it was ' not so bad ', and a Brigadier-General recently told a gathering of Comrades of the Great War that they ' must agree that it was the happiest time of their lives '. A familiar parallel example is the illusion so many middle-aged men entertain that they enjoyed their school-days, when in fact they were then acutely wretched.

I shall use these two forms of distortion to define a third sense of ' sentimental ' as follows : A response is sentimental when, either through the over-persistence of tendencies or through the interaction of sentiments, it is inappropriate to the situation that calls it forth. It becomes inappropriate, as a rule, either by confining itself to one aspect only of the many that the situation can present, or by substituting for it a factitious, illusory situation that may, in extreme cases, have hardly anything in common with it. We can study these extreme cases in dreams and in asylums.

Let us now apply these three definitions to some of the accusations of sentimentality contained in the protocols. With the first two senses however—the quantitative sense and the crudeness sense—an obvious ambiguity remains that must first be disposed of. When we apply the word to a human product, a poem for example, we may mean either of two things which we hardly ever distinguish, or we may mean both. If we would more often distinguish them we should avoid many mistakes and some needless injustice.

We may mean—to take Sense One—that the poem was the product of a mind which was too easily stirred to emotion, that it came about through facile feelings, that the *author* was himself sentimental. Or we may mean that *we* should be too easily moved, we should ourselves be sentimental, if we allowed our own emotions a vigorous outing. Sometimes doubt-less, both these assertions are true, but often we are only entitled to make the second. (Compare what has been said about sincerity in connection with *Poem VII*, p. 95, and *Poem VIII*, p. 114.)

Now let us consider *Poem IV* with this distinction in mind. We must, of course, not read the verses as a piece of imaginative sociology such as Zola dreamed of. It is not an attempt by a novelist to render *realistically* the stock thoughts and feelings and the diction of a girl without poetic ability, expressing herself in verse. (But cf. 4·1, 4·3.) We have to take it, in the usual way that lyrical, emotional verse is taken, as a semi-dramatic utterance not *inviting* ironical contemplation—to be judged on its merits as poetry.

This problem of approach is especially relevant here. ' Sentimentality recollected in very senti-mental tranquillity ' (4·1) with the rest of the protocol as a gloss, seems to accuse the author (perhaps identified, improperly, with the heroine of the poem) of over-production of emotion (Sense One) and suggests further a cause for this excess :[1] namely, preoccupation with the emotion for its own sake rather than with the situation occasioning it. New emotions—as Byron hints in the verse quoted above— easily divert attention to themselves. Very few people, for example, fall in love for the first time without becoming enthralled by their emotions merely as a novel experience. They become absorbed in them often to the exclusion of genuine interest in the loved object. Similarly those who are dis-covering for the first time that poetry can cause them emotion do often, for this very reason, pay little attention to the poetry. Writers too, who find

---

[1] Not, of course, an excess in the feeling ascribed to the girl, but an excess of the author's sympathetic emotion or of our sympathetic motion.

that they can imagine feelings and express them in words, may readily become fascinated by this occupation, as a kind of game, and lose sight of the real sanctions of the feelings in experience. We may easily work the feelings up for their own sake, forgetting intermittently what the feelings are like in our eagerness to hang them on to the forms of expression which occur to us. Seeing a chance to make a violent emotional effect, we forget whether this is the effect we desire.

Both the accusation and the suggestion as to the source of the excess feeling seem justified here. The antitheses, so much praised (4.22, 4.24) and so much disliked (4.23, 4.31), the rhymes, and the mechanical structure, do seem to indicate that facilities and conveniences of expression have led feeling, rather than that feeling has dictated expression. As to the excess of feeling over its justification in the actual situation presented by the poem, we must beware of a misconception which though obviously a mistake is none the less insidious.

If we separate out the subject or theme of the poem, *A girl bewailing her lost or absent lover*, and take this, abstractly, as the situation, we may think that it sounds sufficient to justify any extremity of sympathetic emotion. But this abstracted theme is nothing in itself, and might be the basis of any one of as many different developments as there are kinds of girls. It cannot in itself be an excuse for any emotion. If the mere fact that some girl somewhere is thus lamenting were an occasion for emotion, into what convulsions ought not the evening paper to throw us nightly ? This is obvious, but there is reason to think that very many people are ready to react emotionally to a ' pathetic ' situation merely at this level of abstractness, provided it is put before them in some kind of metre; and, if so, such reactions are certainly ' sentimental ' in the sense of excessive.

The situation evidently has to be something more concrete. It is the poet's business to present it—not necessarily apart from his presentation of the emotion. He will usually be presenting both together through the same words. Here, since the girl is speaking herself, every word, every cadence, every movement and transition of thought and feeling is part of the situation.

This being so, we may ask two questions. Is the situation so given concrete enough, near enough to us, and coherent enough to justify the vigorous emotional response invited from us? And is it, in its concreteness, nearness and coherence so far as they go, of the kind to which *this* response is appropriate? (I am not saying that nearness, concreteness and coherence are required in all poetry—this would be an illegitimate technical presupposition. But I am saying that if certain effects are aimed at, certain methods are thereby prescribed.)

On the first question 4·23, 4·25 and 4·31 forcibly present the adverse opinion, though as we have seen in Chapter IV we must be careful in applying the rhythm test. (4·25 seems, however, here to be justified in the rhythm he ascribes to the verses.) These writers, in contrast to 4·11, 4·24 or 4·52, seem to be responding to the situation as actually presented by the poet—not to situations they have imagined for him or to the ' trappings and catchwords of romance ' in which he has decked out the verses. These decorations by their conventional quality raise all the problems reviewed in the last chapter. That they were the source of the poem's great popularity is not to be doubted. Equally evident is the great danger of snobbery whenever such questions arise. That a metaphor is conventional and familiar is not, of course, *in itself* sufficient ground for objection, though it is often enough the whole explanation of the complaint. Similarly, if the situation and emotion were ordinary, simple and familiar (as 4.3 suggests), that in itself would be no bar to merit, provided the emotion were properly *founded in* the situation. (Compare Gray's *Elegy*.) To suppose otherwise would be a very stupid kind of emotional snobbery. Or if lack of skill in the author were the cause of the conventional metaphors, that again would be no ground for indignation. But if the borrowed, second-hand, quality of the expression

> In slavish habit, ill-fitted weeds
> Oreworn and soild

reflects, not merely neediness or carelessness, but a similar second-hand, reach-me-down, quality in the thing expressed, then the vigour of some of the rejections is excused.

These reflections apply to the concreteness and nearness we are looking for in the poem. Conventional metaphors tend to fail in both characters, a tendency not avoided here. But they apply still more to the coherence that is required. Borrowed decorations—and here is the gravest objection to their use—are almost always irrelevant. The various items do not hang together, and their combined effect, if any, is likely to be crude in the sense discussed above. Here, for example, the sunshine and dog-roses of verse three have somehow to adjust themselves to the winter and the wailing of the wind in verse two, and the idly circulating 'wind of the years', which has possibly blown in from the pages of Swinburne,[1] has to 'whisper' above this wailing. (Such incoherences are characteristic of conventional verse ; only a very intent concentration of the poet's imaginative faculties can prevent them. In themselves they *need* not be destructive (cf. Ch. II), but

---

[1] It may also be suggested that the phrase 'life lies dead' is possibly an echo of Swinburne's *A Forsaken Garden*.

they are a very useful corroboration if we suspect on other grounds that the central impulse of a poem is weak.) By the time these incoherent items have pooled their effects the response can hardly here be anything but crude—an undirected, objectless feeling of pathos that will attach itself to anything that will give it an excuse—to the caravan bells of Hassan (4·52), for example.

The emotion, in fact, which this poem can excite (and on which its popularity depends) is easily enjoyed for its own sake, regardless of its object or prompting situation. Most people will not find it difficult, if they so desire, to sit down by the fireside and concoct a precisely similar emotion without the assistance of any poem whatever—merely by saying Oh! to themselves in various tones of sadness, regret and tremulous hope. It is an emotion that we tend, if we indulge it at all, to luxuriate in, as 4·1 remarks. Hence the power of these verses to divide readers sharply into two camps.

Passing now to *Poem VIII*, accusations of senti-mentality in the first and third of our senses appear most instructively. The charge of excessive emotional response, too light a trigger adjustment for the feelings, is coupled with the suggestions that the poet is ' revelling in emotion for its own sake ' (8·1), ' positively wallowing in a warm bath of soapy sentiment ' (8·12), that he ' seems to love feeling sobby ' (8·41), and that he is ' trying to get effects the whole time ' (8·44)—as explanations of this excess of feeling. As a rule the complainants demonstrate satisfactorily that they have mistaken the situation to which the emotion is a response. It is music in general for 8·12, ' the poet's miseries ' for 8·11, his ' pure, spotless childhood ' and his present state as a ' world-worn wretch ' for 8·41. And as a result of these mistakes the characters of the emotions these writers attributed to the poem are equally irrelevant. The moral again is that before we can decide whether a poem is or is not sentimental in this sense we must be sure that we know both what the presented situation is and what response is invited. Only the very closest reading will tell us enough about either to make judgment worth while.

The charge of sentimentality in our third sense raises a more complicated issue, for the poem is itself clearly a study of a border-line case, and, if not read more carefully than, for example, by 8·3, or 8·31, is likely to be disastrous in its emotional effects. There is, it is true, a ' mawkish sentiment with which we so often think of childhood '; and ' one's loose emotion ' does as easily attach itself to ' old Sunday evenings at home ', ' the cosy parlour ' and ' the vista of years ' as to ' the chimney-nook ' or ' the wind of the years '. But the danger, ' the appalling risk ' (8·5) of arousing only these emotions need not frighten the poet away from such topics if he can give enough nearness, concreteness and coherence [1] to the situation to support and *control* the response that ensues. Or if he can build these dangerous elements into a whole response which completes and frees them. For what is bad in these sentimental responses is their confinement to one stereotyped, unrepresentative aspect of the prompting situation.

This brings us to the subject of inhibitions. Most, if not all, sentimental fixations and distortions of feeling are the result of inhibitions, and often when we discuss sentimentality we are looking at the wrong side of the picture. If a man can only think of his childhood as a lost heaven it is probably because he is afraid to think of its other aspects. And those who contrive to look back to the War as ' a good time,'

---

[1] I am not recommending nearness, concreteness and coherence as specifics for the avoidance of sentimentality. All depends upon what it is that is brought near, what is concrete and what coheres.

are probably busy dodging certain other memories. The mind is curiously quantitative in some of its operations; undue curtailment in one direction seems to imply excess in an opposite direction. Inhibition, in due place and degree, is, of course, a necessity for mental activity—quite as much a necessity as exercise. It was Bergson, I think, who once described Time as resistance—the resistance namely against everything happening at once! Without inhibition everything in the mind *would* happen at once, which is tantamount to saying that nothing would happen or that Chaos would return. All order and proportion is the result of inhibition, we cannot indulge one mental activity without inhibiting others. Therefore the opinion sometimes emitted that all inhibition (or repression) is bad, is at the least an overstatement. What is unfortunate is the permanent curtailment of our possibilities as human beings, the blanking out, through repeated and maintained inhibition, of aspects of experience that our mental health requires us sometimes to envisage.

As a rule the source of such inhibitions is some painfulness attaching to the aspect of life that we refuse to contemplate. The sentimental response steps in to replace this aspect by some other aspect more pleasant to contemplate or by some factitious object which flatters the contemplator. There are innumerable cross-currents of motive here which may conceal from us what we are doing. The man who, in reaction to the commoner naïve forms of sentimentality, prides himself upon his hard-headedness and hard-heartedness, his hard-boiledness generally, and seeks out or invents aspects with a bitter or squalid character, for no better reason than this, is only displaying a more sophisticated form of sentimentality. Fashion, of course, is responsible for many of these secondary twists. Indeed the control of Society over our sentiments, over our publicly avowable sentiments, is remarkably efficient. Compare, for example, the attitudes to tears (especially to masculine tears) approved by the eighteenth and twentieth centuries. Very little reflection and inquiry will show conclusively that the eighteenth century in regarding a profuse discharge of the lachrymal glands as a proper and almost necessary accompaniment of tender and sorrowful emotion was much more representative of humanity in all ages than are our contemporary wooden-eyed stoics. The current attitude naturally appeared in the protocols (8·52, 8·6, 8·61). Even *Poem VIII* itself shows it, for an eighteenth-century writer would have felt no need to fight against such an emotion.

A widespread general inhibition of all the simpler expansive developments of emotion (not only of its expression) has to be recognised among our educated population. It is a new condition not easily paralleled in history, and though it is propagated through social convention its deeper causes are not easy to divine. To put it down, as many have done, to the excesses of the Victorians, is only to show an ignorance of the generations that preceded them. Possibly it is due to the increasing indefiniteness of our beliefs and disbeliefs, to the blurring of the moral background of our lives, but such speculations would take us too far.

Whatever its cause, the fact that so many readers are afraid of free expansive emotion, even when the situation warrants it, is important. It leads them, as *Poem VIII* showed, to suspect and avoid situations that may awaken strong and simple feeling. It produces shallowness and trivial complexity in their response. And it leaves those ' sentimental ' overgrowths that escape the taboo too free a field for their semi-surreptitious existence. The only safe cure for a mawkish attachment to an illusory childhood heaven, for example, is to take the distorted sentiment and work it into close and living relation with some scene concretely and truthfully realised, which may act as a standard of reality and awaken the dream-infected object of the sentiment into actuality. This is the treatment by expansion, and *Poem VIII* may stand as an example of how it may be done. The other, more practised, form of treatment which we apply to sentimentalists—treatment through sneers, through ' realism ', through caustics, the attempt by various means not to enlarge the canalised response, but to destroy it or dry it up—is ineffective, and may lead only to increased impoverishment. For the curse of sentimentality in the third sense is not that its victims have too much feeling at their disposal, but that they have too little, that they see life in too specialised a fashion and respond to it too narrowly. The sentimentalist, in brief, is not distributing his interest widely enough, and is distributing it in too few forms.

CHAPTER VII

DOCTRINE IN POETRY

Logic is the ethics of thinking, in the sense in which ethics is the bringing to bear of self-control, for the purpose of realising our desires.
CHARLES SAUNDERS PIERCE.

WITH most of our critical difficulties what we have had to explain is how mistakes come to be so frequent. But here we are in the opposite case, we have to explain how they come to be so rare. For it would seem evident that poetry which has been built upon firm and definite beliefs about the world, *The Divine Comedy* or *Paradise Lost*, or Donne's *Divine Poems*, or Shelley's *Prometheus Unbound*, or Hardy's *The Dynasts*, must appear differently to readers who do and readers who do not hold similar beliefs. Yet in fact most readers, and nearly all good readers, are very little disturbed by even a direct opposition between their own beliefs and the beliefs of the poet. Lucretius and Virgil, Euripides and Aeschylus, we currently assume, are equally accessible, given the necessary scholarship, to a Roman Catholic, to a Buddhist and to a confirmed sceptic. Equally accessible in the sense that these different readers, after due study, may respond in the same way to the poetry and arrive at similar judgments about it. And when they differ, their divergencies will commonly not be a result of their different positions with regard to the doctrines[1] of the authors, but are more likely to derive from

[1] I am not accusing these authors of doctrinal poetry in the narrow sense of verse whose sole object is to teach. But that a body of doctrine is presented by each of these poets, even by Virgil, can hardly escape any reader's notice.

other causes—in their temperaments and personal experience.

I have instanced religious poetry because the beliefs there concerned have the widest implications, and are the most seriously entertained of any. But the same problem arises with nearly all poetry ; with mythology very evidently ; with such supernatural machinery as appears in *The Rime of the Ancient Mariner :*

> The horned Moon, with one bright star
> Within the nether tip,

with Blake's manifestoes ; but equally, though less obtrusively, with every passage which seems to make a statement, or depend upon an assumption, that a reader may dissent from without, thereby giving proof of mental derangement.

It is essential to recognise that the problem [1] is the same whether the possible stumbling-block, the point of dissent, be trivial or important. When the point is trivial, we easily satisfy ourselves with an explanation in terms of ' poetic fictions '. When it is a matter of no consequence whether we assent or dissent, the theory that these disputable statements, so constantly presented to us in poetry, are merely *assumptions* introduced for poetic purposes, seems an adequate explanation. And when the statements, for example, Homer's account of ' the monkey-shines of the Olympian troupe ', are frankly incredible, if paraded solemnly before the bar of reasoned judgment, the same explanation applies. But as the assumptions grow more plausible, and as the consequences for our view of the world grow important, the matter seems less simple. Until, in the end, with Donne's Sonnet (*Poem III*), for example, it becomes very difficult not to think that *actual*

---

[1] A supplementary and fuller discussion of this whole matter will be found in *Principles of Literary Criticism*, Ch. XXXII-XXXV, where difficulties, which here must be passed by, are treated in detail.

belief in the doctrine that appears in the poem is required for its full and perfect imaginative realisation. The mere assumption of Donne's theology, as a poetic fiction, may seem insufficient in view of the intensity of the feeling which is supported and conveyed to us by its means. It is at least certain, as the protocols show (3·15, 5·42, 5·37, 5·38, 7·21), that many who try to read religious poetry find themselves strongly invited to the beliefs presented, and that doctrinal dissent is a very serious obstacle to their reading. Conversely, many successful but dissenting readers find themselves in a mental attitude towards the doctrine which, if it is not belief, closely resembles belief.

Yet if we suppose that, beyond this mere ' poetic ' assumption, a definite state of belief in this particular doctrine of the Resurrection of the Body is required for a full reading of Donne's poem, great difficulties at once arise. We shall have to suppose that readers who hold different beliefs incompatible with this particular doctrine must either not be able to read the poem, or must temporarily while reading it abandon their own beliefs and adopt Donne's. Both suppositions *seem* contrary to the facts, though these are matters upon which certainty is hazardous. We shall do better, however, to examine the ' poetic fiction ', or assumption, theory more closely and see whether when fully stated it is capable of meeting the complaint of inadequacy noticed above.

In the first place the very word ' assumption ' is unsuitable here. Ordinarily an assumption is a proposition, an object of thought, entertained intellectually in order to trace its logical consequences as a hypothesis. But here we are concerned very little with logical consequences and almost exclusively with emotional consequences. In the effect of the thought upon our feelings and attitudes, all its importance, for poetry, lies. But there are

S

clearly two ways in which we may entertain an assumption : intellectually, that is in a context of other thoughts ready to support, contradict, or establish other logical relations with it ; and emotionally, in a context of sentiments, feelings, desires and attitudes ready to group themselves around it. Behind the intellectual assumption stands the desire for logical consistency and order in the receptive side of the mind. But behind the emotional assumption stands the desire or need for order of the whole outgoing emotional side of the personality, the side that is turned towards action.

Corresponding to this distinction there are two forms of belief and similarly two forms of disbelief. Intellectual belief more resembles a weighting of an idea than anything else, a loading [1] which makes other, less heavily weighted, ideas, adjust themselves to it rather than *vice versa*. The loading may be legitimate ; the quantity of evidence, its immediacy, the extent and complexity of the supporting systems of ideas are obvious forms of legitimate loading : or it may be illegitimate ; our liking for the idea, its brilliance, the trouble that changing it may involve, emotional satisfactions from it, are illegitimate—*from the standpoint of intellectual belief* be it understood. The whole use of intellectual belief is to bring *all* our ideas into as perfect an ordered system as possible. We disbelieve only because we believe something else that is incompatible, as Spinoza long ago pointed out. Similarly, we perhaps only believe because it is necessary to disbelieve whatever is logically contradictory to our belief. *Neither belief nor disbelief arises*, in this intellectual sense, *unless the logical context of our ideas is in*

---

[1] To introspection this loading seems like a feeling of trust—or trustworthiness. We 'side' with the belief intellectually, and though traditionally belief has been discussed along with judgment it is, as William James pointed out, more allied to choice.

question. Apart from these logical connections the idea is neither believed nor disbelieved, nor doubted nor questioned ; it is just present. Most of the ideas of the child, of primitive man, of the peasant, of the non-intellectual world and of most poetry are in this happy condition of real intellectual disconnection.

Emotional belief is a very different matter. In primitive man, as innumerable observers have remarked, any idea which opens a ready outlet to emotion or points to a line of action in conformity with custom is quickly believed. We remain much more primitive in this phase of our behaviour than in intellectual matters. Given a need [1] (whether conscious *as a desire* or not), any idea which can be taken as a step on the way to its fulfilment is accepted, unless some other need equally active at the moment bars it out. This acceptance, this use of the idea— by our interests, desires, feelings, attitudes, tendencies to action and what not—is emotional belief. So far as the idea is useful to them it is believed, and the sense of attachment, of adhesion, of conviction, which we feel, and to which we give the name of belief, is the result of this implication of the idea in our activities.

Most beliefs, of course, that have any strength or persistence are mixtures of intellectual and emotional belief. A purely intellectual belief need have little strength, no quality of conviction about it, for unless the idea is very original and contrary to received ideas, it needs little loading to hold its own. When we find a modern physicist, for example, passionately attached to a particular theory, we may suspect

---

[1] I use 'need' here to stand for an imbalance mental or physical, a tendency, given suitable conditions, for a movement towards an end-state of equilibrium. A swinging pendulum might thus be said to be actuated by a need to come to rest, and to constantly overdo its movements towards that end. We are much more like pendulums than we think, though, of course, our imbalances are infinitely more intricate.

illegitimate loading, his reputation is perhaps involved in its acceptance. Conversely, a very strong emotional belief may have little persistence. Last night's revelation grows dim amid this morning's affairs, for the need which gave it such glamorous reality was only a need of the moment. Of this kind are most of the revelations received from poetry and music. But though the sense of revelation has faded, we should not suppose that the shaping influence of such experiences must be lost. The mind has found through them a pattern of response which may remain, and it is this pattern rather than the revelation which is important.

The great difference between these two kinds of belief, as I have defined them, appears most plainly if we consider what *justification* amounts to for each. Whether an intellectual belief is justified is entirely a matter of its logical place in the largest, most completely ordered, system of ideas we can attain to. Now the central, most stable, mass of our ideas has already an order and arrangement fixed for it by the facts of Nature. We must bring our ideas of these facts into correspondence with them or we promptly perish. And this order among the everyday facts of our surroundings determines the arrangement of yet another system of our ideas : namely, physical theory. These ideas are thereby weighted beyond the power of irreconcilable ideas to disturb them. Anyone who understands them cannot help believing in them, and disbelieving *intellectually* in irreconcilable ideas, provided that he brings them close enough together to perceive their irreconcilability. There are obviously countless ideas in poetry which, if put into this logical context, must be disbelieved at once.

But this intellectual disbelief does not imply that emotional belief in the same idea is either impossible or even difficult—much less that it is undesirable.

For an emotional belief is not justified through any logical relations between its idea and other ideas. Its only justification is its success in meeting our needs—due regard being paid to the relative claims of our many needs one against another. It is a matter, to put it simply, of the *prudence* (in view of *all* the needs of our being) of the kind of emotional activities the belief subserves. The desirability or undesirability of an emotional belief has nothing to do with its intellectual status, provided it is kept from interfering with the intellectual system. And poetry is an extraordinarily successful device for preventing these interferences from arising.

Coleridge, when he remarked that ' a willing suspension of disbelief ' accompanied much poetry, was noting an important fact, but not quite in the happiest terms, for we are neither aware of a disbelief nor voluntarily suspending it in these cases. It is better to say that the question of belief or disbelief, in the intellectual sense, never arises when we are reading well. If unfortunately it does arise, either through the poet's fault or our own, we have for the moment ceased to be reading poetry and have become astronomers, or theologians, or moralists, persons engaged in quite a different type of activity.

But a possible misconception must be noted here The intellectual exploration of the *internal* coherence of the poem, and the intellectual examination of the relations of its ideas to other ideas of ordinary experience which are *emotionally* relevant to it, are not only permissible but necessary in the reading of much poetry, as we saw in connection with the sea-harp in *Poem IX*, and in connection with the sentimentality and stock-response problems of *Poems IV, VIII* and *XIII*. But this restricted intellectual inquiry is a different thing from the all-embracing attempt to systematise our ideas which alone brings up the problem of intellectual belief.

We can now turn back to *Poem III*, to the point from which this long analysis started. There are many readers who feel a difficulty in giving to Donne's theology just that kind of acceptance, *and no more*, that they give to Coleridge's ' star within the nether tip '. They feel an invitation to accord to the poem that belief in its ideas which we can hardly help supposing to have been, in Donne's mind, a powerful influence over its shaping. These readers may, perhaps, be content if we insist that the fullest possible *emotional* belief is fitting and desirable. At the same time there are many who are unable to accord *intellectual* belief to these particular theological tenets. Such readers may feel that a threatened liberty is not thereby denied them. The fact that Donne probably gave both forms of belief to these ideas need not, I think, prevent a good reader from giving the fullest emotional belief while withholding intellectual belief, or rather while not allowing the question of intellectual belief to arise. The evidence is fragmentary upon the point, largely because it has been so strangely little discussed. But the very fact that the need to discuss it has not insistently arisen—seeing how many people from how many different intellectual positions have been able to agree about the value of such doctrinal poems—points strongly in this direction. The absence of intellectual belief need not cripple emotional belief, though evidently enough in some persons it may. But the habit of attaching emotional belief only to intellectually certified ideas is strong in some people ; it is encouraged by some forms of education; it is perhaps becoming, through the increased prestige of science, more common.[1] For those whom it conquers it means ' Good-bye to poetry '.

---

[1] I have discussed this danger at length in *Science and Poetry*. There is reason to think that poetry has often arisen through fusion (or confusion) between the two forms of belief, the boundary between

For the difficulty crops up, as I have insisted, over all poetry that departs, for its own purposes, from the most ordinary universal facts of common experience or from the most necessary deductions of scientific theory. It waylays the strict rationalist with Blake's ' Sunflower ', Wordsworth's ' River Duddon ', and Shelley's ' Cloud ', no less than with their more transcendental utterances. Shakespeare's Lark is as shocking as his Phœnix. Even so honest a man as Gray attributes very disputable motives to his Owl. As for Dryden's ' new-kindled star ', the last verse of Keats' *Ode to Melancholy*, or Landor's *Rose Aylmer*—it is very clear where we should be with them if we could not give emotional assent apart from intellectual conviction. The slightest poetry may present the problem as clearly (though not so acutely) as the greatest. And the fact that we solve it, in practice, without the least difficulty in minor cases shows, I think, that even in the major instances of philosophic and religious issues the same solution is applicable. But the temptation to confuse the two forms of belief is there greater.

For in these cases an appearance of incompleteness or insincerity may attach to emotional acceptance divorced from intellectual assent.[1] That this is

what is intellectually certified and what is not being much less sharply definited in former centuries and *defined in another manner*. The standard of *verification* used in science to-day is comparatively a new thing. As the scientific view of the world (including our own nature) develops, we shall probably be forced into making a division between fact and fiction that, unless we can meet it with a twofold theory of belief on the lines suggested above, would be fatal not only to poetry but to all our finer, more spiritual, responses. That is the problem.

[1] The most important example of this divorce that history provides is in the attitude of Confucius towards ancestor-worship. Here are the remarks of his chief English translator, James Legge, upon the matter. ' It will not be supposed that I wish to advocate or defend the practice of sacrificing to the dead. My object has been to point out how Confucius recognised it, without acknowledging the faith from which it must have originated, and how he enforced it as a matter of form or ceremony. It thus connects itself with the most serious charge that can be brought against him—the charge of

simply a mistake due to a double-meaning of ' belief '
has been my contention.   To ' pretend to believe '
what we ' don't really believe ' would certainly be
insincerity, if the two kinds of believing were one and
the same ; but if they are not, the confusion is
merely another example of the prodigious power of
words over our lives.   And this will be the best place
to take up the uncomfortable problem of ' sincerity ',
a word much used in criticism, but not often with
any precise definition of its meaning.

The ideas, vague and precise, for which ' sincere '
stands must have been constantly in the reader's
mind during our discussion both of Stock Responses
and of Sentimentality.   We can set aside at once the
ordinary ' business ' sense in which a man is insincere
when he deliberately attempts to deceive, and sincere
when his statements and acts are governed by ' the
best of his knowledge and belief '.   And we can deal
briefly with another sense, already touched upon in
connection with *Poem VII* (see p. 95), in which a man
is insincere when ' he kids *himself* ', when he mistakes
his own motives and so professes feelings which are
different from those that are in fact actuating him.
Two subtle points, however, must be noted before
we set this sense aside.   The feelings need not be
stated or even openly expressed ; it is enough if they
are hinted to us.   And they need not be actual
personal ' real, live feelings ' ; they may imagined
feelings.   All that is required for this kind of insin-
cerity is a discrepancy between the poem's claim
upon our response and its *shaping* impulses in the
poet's mind.   But only the shaping impulses are
relevant.   A good poem can perfectly well be
written for money or from pique or ambition,
provided these initial external motives do not interfere

insincerity', *The Chinese Classics*, Vol. I, Prolegomena, Ch. V, p. 100.
How far Legge was qualified to expound the Confucian doctrine of
sincerity may perhaps be divined from this passage.

with its growth. Interferences of all kinds—notably
the desire to make the poem ' original ', ' striking ',
or ' poetic '—are, of course, the usual cause of
insincerity in this sense. A sense which ought not,
it may be remarked, to impute blame to the author,
unless we are willing to agree that all men who are
not good poets are therefore blameworthy in a high
degree.

These subtleties were necessary to escape the
conclusion that irony, for example—where the feeling
really present is often the exact contrary to that
overtly professed—is as insincere as simple readers
often suppose it must be.

A more troublesome problem is raised if we ask
whether an emotion, by itself and apart from its
expression, can be sincere or insincere. We often
speak as if this were so (witness 4·2, 4·23 and 8·51),
and though sometimes no doubt this is only an
effective way of saying that we approve (or dis-
approve) of the emotion, there are senses in which
a fact about the emotion, not about our feelings about
it, is meant. Sincere emotions, we say, are genuine
or authentic, as opposed to spurious emotions, and
the several senses which we may imply thereby are
worth examining. We may mean that the emotion
is genuine in the sense that every product of a perfect
mind would be genuine. It would result only from
the prompting situation *plus* all the relevant experience
of that mind, and be free from impurities and from
all interferences, from impulses that had in any way
got out of place and become disordered. Since such
minds are nowhere obtainable in this obstructive
world, such a sense is useful only as an ideal standard
by which to measure degrees of relative insincerity.
' There is not a just man on earth that doeth good
and sinneth not '. Some great poetry, we might
say, represents the closest approach to sincerity that
can be found. And for extreme degrees of insin-

cerity we should look in asylums. Possibly however, the perfect mind, if it ever appeared among us, might be put there too.

But this is plainly not a sense of sincerity which we often use, it is not what people ordinarily mean. For we would agree that stupid people can be very sincere, though their minds may be very much in a muddle, and we might even suggest that they are more likely to be sincere than the clever. Simplicity, we may think, has something to do with sincerity, for there is a sense in which ' genuine ' is opposed to ' sophisticated '. The sincere feeling, it may be suggested, is one which has been left in its natural state, not worked over and complicated by reflection. Thus strong spontaneous feelings would be more likely to be sincere than feelings that have run the gauntlet of self-criticism, and a dog, for example, might be regarded as a more sincere animal than any man.

This is certainly a sense which is frequent, though whether we should praise emotions that are sincere in this sense as much as most people do, is extremely doubtful. It is partly an echo of Rousseau's romantic fiction, the ' Natural Man '. Admiration for the ' spontaneous ' and ' natural ' tends to select favourable examples and turns a very blind eye to the less attractive phenomena. Moreover, many emotions which look simple and natural are nothing of the kind, they result from cultivated self-control, so consummate as to seem instantaneous. These cases, and an attractive but limited virtue in some children's behaviour, explain, I believe, the popularity of sincerity in this sense. So used, the word is of little service in criticism, for this kind of sincerity in poetry must necessarily be rare.

It will be worth while hunting a little longer for a satisfactory sense of ' sincerity '. Whatever it is, it is the quality we most insistently require in poetry.

It is also the quality we most need as critics. And, perhaps, in the proportion that we possess it we shall acknowledge that it is not a quality that we can take for granted in ourselves as our inalienable birthright. It fluctuates with our state of health, with the quality of our recent companions, with our responsibility and our nearness to the object, with a score of conditions that are not easy to take account of. We can *feel* very sincere when, in fact, as others can see clearly, there is no sincerity in us. Bogus forms of the virtue waylay us—confident inner assurances and invasive rootless convictions. And when we doubt our own sincerity and ask ourselves, ' Do I *really* think so ; do I really feel so ? ' an honest answer is not easily come by. A direct effort to be sincere, like other effects to will ourselves into action, more often than not, frustrates its intention. For all these reasons any light that can be gained upon the nature of sincerity, upon possible tests for it and means for inducing and promoting it, is extremely serviceable to the critic.

The most stimulating discussion of this topic is to be found in the *Chung Yung*[1] (The Doctrine of the Mean, or Equilibrium and Harmony), the treatise that embodies the most interesting and the most puzzling part of the teachings of Confucius. A more distinct (and distinguished) word than ' stimulating ' would be in place to describe this treatise, were the invigorating effect of a careful reading easier to define. Sincerity—the object of some idea that seems to lie in the territory that ' sincerity ' covers—appears there as the beginning and end of personal

---

[1] As might be expected, no translation that entirely commends itself is available. Those to whom Legge's edition of *The Chinese Classics*, Vol. I, is not available, may consult the translation by L. A. Lyall and King Chien Kün, *The Chung Yung or The Centre, the Common* (Longmans), very literal, but perhaps slightly too much tinctured with a Y.M.C.A. flavour. Here what is translated by others 'sincerity' or 'singleness' is rendered by 'to be true and 'being' true'.

character, the secret of the good life, the only means to good government, the means to give full development to our own natures, to give full development to the nature of others, and very much more. This virtue is as mysterious as it is powerful ; and, where so many great sinologues and Chinese scholars have confessed themselves baffled, it would be absurd for one who knows no Chinese to suggest interpretations. But some speculations generated by a reading of translations may round off this chapter.

The following extracts from the *Chung Yung* seem the most relevant to our discussion.

' Sincerity is the way of Heaven. The attainment of sincerity is the way of men. He who possesses sincerity, is he who, without an effort, hits what is right, and apprehends, without the exercise of thought ; he is the sage who naturally and easily embodies the right way. He who attains to sincerity, is he who chooses what is good, and firmly holds it fast ' (Legge, XX, 18). ' Sincerity is that whereby self-completion is effected, and its way is that by which man must direct himself ' (Legge, XXV, 1). ' In self-completion the superior man completes other men and things also . . . and this is the way by which a union is effected of the external and the internal ' (XXV, 3). ' In the Book of Poetry, it is said, " In hewing an axe-handle, in hewing an axe-handle, the pattern is not far off ". We grasp one axe-handle to hew the other, and yet, if we look askance from the one to the other, we may consider them as apart ' (XIII, 2). ' There is a way to the attainment of sincerity in one's self ; if a man does not understand what is good, he will not attain sincerity in himself ' (XX, 17). ' When we have intelligence resulting from sincerity, this condition is to be ascribed to nature ; when we have sincerity resulting from intelligence, this condition is to be ascribed to instruction. But given the sincerity, there shall be the intelligence, given the intelligence there shall be the sincerity ' (XXI). How far apart any detailed precise exposition in English, or in any modern Western language, must be from the form of thought of the original, is shown if we compare a more literal version of this last passage : ' Being true begets light, we call that nature. Light leads to being true, we call that teaching. What is true grows light ; what is light grows true ' (Lyall and King Chien-Kün, p. 16).

Meditating upon this chain of pronouncements we can perhaps construct (or discover) another sense of sincerity. One important enough to justify the stress so often laid upon this quality by critics, yet not compelling us to require an impossible per- fection or inviting us to sentimental (Sense 3) indiscriminate over-admiration of the ebullitions of infants. And it may be possible, by apprehending this sense more clearly, to see what general con- ditions will encourage sincerity and what steps may be suggested to promote this mysterious but necessary virtue in the critic.

We may take self-completion as our starting-point. The completed mind would be that perfect mind we envisaged above, in which no disorder, no mutual frustration of impulses remained. Let us suppose that in the irremediable default of this perfection, default due to man's innate constitution and to the accidents to which he is exposed, there exists *a tendency towards increased order*,[1] a tendency which

---

[1] I have in several other places made prolonged and determined efforts to indicate the types of mental order I have in mind (*The Foundations of Æsthetics*, § XIV ; *Principles of Literary Criticism*, Ch. XXII ; *Science and Poetry*, § II), but without escaping certain large misunderstandings that I had hoped to have guarded myself against. Thus Mr Eliot, reviewing *Science and Poetry* in *The Dial*, describes my ideal order as ' Efficiency, a perfectly-working mental Roneo Steel Cabinet System', and Mr Read performing a similar service for *Principles* in *The Criterion*, seemed to understand that where I spoke of ' the organisation of impulses' I meant that kind of

takes effect unless baffled by physical interferences (disease) or by fixations of habit that prevent us from continuing to learn by experience, or by ideas too invested with emotion for other ideas that disturb them to be formed, or by too lax and volatile a bond between our interests (a frivolousness that is perhaps due to the draining off of energy elsewhere) so that no formations firm enough to build upon result.

There is much to be said in favour of such a supposition. This tendency would be a need, in the sense defined above in this chapter—deriving in fact from *the* fundamental imbalance[1] to which biological development may be supposed to be due. This development with man (and his animal neighbours) seems to be predominantly in the direction of greater complexity and finer differentiation of responses. And it is easy to conceive the organism as relieving, through this differentiation, the strain put upon it by life in a partly uncongenial environment. It is but a step further to conceive it as also tending to relieve internal strains due to these developments imposed from without. And a re-ordering of its impulses so as to reduce their interferences with one another to a minimum would

deliberate planning and arrangement which the controllers of a good railway or large shop must carry out. But 'organisation' for me stood for that kind of interdependence of parts which we allude to when we speak of living things as 'organisms'; and the 'order' which I make out to be so important is not tidiness. The distinguished names cited in this foot-note will protect the reader from a sense that these explanations are insulting to his intelligence. A good idea of some of the possibilities of order and disorder in the mind may be gained from Pavlov's *Conditioned Reflexes*.

[1] Whether we can profitably posit a primal imbalance in certain forms of matter for which the appearance of living substances and their development in increasingly complex forms right up to Shakespeare would be, as it were, the swings of the pendulum 'attempting' to come to rest again, is a speculation that has perhaps only an amusement value. The great difficulty would be to get round the separation of the reproductive functions, but that is a difficulty for any cosmologist.

be the most successful—and the ' natural '—direction which this tendency would take.

Such a re-ordering would be a partial self-completion, temporary and provisional upon the external world remaining for the individual much what it had been in the past. And by such self-completion the superior man *would* ' effect a union of the external and the internal '. Being more at one within itself the mind thereby becomes more appropriately responsive to the outer world. I am not suggesting that this is what Confucius meant. For him ' to complete other men and things too ', is possibly the prerogative of the force of example, other men merely imitating the conduct of the sage. But he *may* have meant that freedom calls out freedom ; that those who are ' most themselves ' cause others about them to become also ' more themselves ' ; which would, perhaps, be a more sagacious observation. Perhaps, too, ' the union of the external and the internal ' meant for him something different from the accordance of our thoughts and feelings with reality. But certainly, for us, this accordance is one of the fruits of sincerity.

This tendency towards a more perfect order, as it takes effect, ' enables us, without effort, to hit what is right, and, without the exercise of thought, to apprehend '. The ' exercise of thought ' here must be understood as that process of deliberately setting aside inappropriate ideas and feelings, which, in default of a sufficient inner order—a sufficient sincerity—is still very necessary. Confucius has enough to say elsewhere in the *Chung Yung* (Ch. XX, 20) of the need for unremitting research and reflection *before* sincerity is attained to clear himself from any charge of recommending ' intuition ' as an *alternative* to investigation. ' Intuition ' is the prerogative only of those who have attained to sincerity. It is only the superior man who ' naturally and easily embodies the right way '. And the superior man will know when his sincerity is insufficient and take ceaseless steps to remedy it. ' If another man (more sincere) succeed by one effort, *he* will use a hundred efforts. If another man succeed by ten efforts, he will use a thousand ' (*Chung Yung*, XX, 20). It is the sincerity to which the superior man has already attained which enables him to know when it is insufficient ; if it does not yet enable him to embody the right way, it at least enables him to refrain from embodying the wrong, as those who trust intuition too soon are likely to do. Indeed, looking back over the history of thought, we might say, ' are certain to do ', so heavy are the probabilities against the success of guess-work.

Sincerity, then, in this sense, is obedience to that tendency which ' seeks ' a more perfect order within the mind. When the tendency is frustrated (*e.g.*, by fatigue or by an idea or feeling that has lost its link with experience, or has become fixed beyond the possibility of change) we have insincerity. When confusion reigns and we are unable to decide what we think or feel (to be distinguished sharply from the case when *decided* thoughts or feelings are present, but we are unable to define or express them) we need be neither sincere nor insincere. We are in a transitional stage which may result in either. Most good critics will confess to themselves that this is the state in which a first reading of any poem of an unfamiliar type leaves them. They know that more study is needed if they are to achieve a genuine response, and they know this in virtue of the sincerity they have already attained. It follows that people with clear definite ideas and feelings, with a high degree of practical efficiency, may be in-sincere in this sense. Other kinds of sincerity, fidelity to convictions for example, will not save them, and indeed it may well be this fidelity which is thwarting the life of the spirit (*Chung Yung*, XXIV) in them.

Any response (however mistaken from other points of view) which embodies the present activity of this tendency to inner adjustment will be sincere, and any response that conflicts with it or inhibits it will be insincere. Thus to be sincere is to act, feel and think in accordance with ' one's true nature ', and to be insincere is to act, feel or think in a contrary manner. But the sense to be given to ' one's true nature ' is, as we have seen, a matter largely conjectural. To define it more exactly would perhaps be tedious and, for our purposes here, needless. In practice we often seem to grasp it very clearly ; and all that I have attempted here is to sketch the state of affairs which we then seem to grasp. ' What heaven has conferred is man's Nature ; an accordance with this is the Path ' (*Chung Yung*, I). Sometimes we can be certain that we have left it.[1]

On the ways in which sincerity may be increased and extended Confucius is very definite. If we seek a standard for a new response whose sincerity may be in doubt, we shall find it, he says, in the very responses which make the new one possible. The pattern for the new axe-handle is already in our hand, though its very nearness, our firm possession of it, may hide it from us. We need, of course, a founded assurance of the sincerity of these instrumental responses themselves, and this we can gain by comparison. What is meant by ' making the thoughts sincere ' is the allowing no self-deception ' *as when we hate a bad smell*, and as when

---

[1] But see *Chung Yung*, I, 2. 'The path may not be left for an instant. If it could be left, it would not be the path.' Possibly we can escape this difficulty by admitting that all mental activities are, to some degree, the operation of the tendency we have been speaking of. Thus all are the Path. But the Path can be obstructed, and may have loops. 'The regulation of (what keeps trim) the path is instruction' (*Chung Yung*, I, 1).

T

we love what is beautiful ' (*The Great Learning*, VI, i). When we hate a bad smell we can have no doubt that our response is sincere. We can all, at least, find *some* responses beyond suspicion. These are our standard. By studying our sincerity in the fields in which we are fully competent we can extend it into the fields in which our ability is still feeling its way. This seems to be the meaning of ' choosing what is good and firmly holding fast to it,' where ' good ' stands not for our Western ethical notion so much as for the fit and proper, sane and healthy. The man who does not ' hate a bad smell ' ' does not understand what is good ' ; having no basis or standards, ' he will not attain to sincerity '.

Together with these, the simplest most definite responses, there may be suggested also, as standards for sincerity, the responses we make to the most baffling objects that can be presented to our consciousness. Something like a technique or ritual for heightening sincerity might well be worked out. When our response to a poem after our best efforts remains uncertain, when we are unsure whether the feelings it excites come from a deep source in our experience, whether our liking or disliking is genuine, is *ours*, or an accident of fashion, a response to surface detail or to essentials, we may perhaps help ourselves by considering it in a frame of feelings whose sincerity is beyond our questioning. Sit by the fire (with eyes shut and fingers pressed firmly upon the eyeballs) and consider with as full ' realisation ' as possible :—

i. Man's loneliness (the isolation of the human situation).

ii. The facts of birth, and of death, in their inexplicable oddity.

iii. The inconceivable immensity of the Universe.

iv. Man's place in the perspective of time.

v. The enormity of his ignorance,

not as gloomy thoughts or as targets for doctrine, but as the most incomprehensible and inexhaustible objects for meditation there are ; then in the glow of their emotional reverberation pass the poem through the mind, silently reciting it as slowly as it allows. Whether what it can stir in us is important or not to us will, perhaps, show itself then. Many religious exercises and some of the practices of divination and magic may be thought to be directed in part towards a similar quest for sanction, to be rituals designed to provide standards of sincerity.

These are serious steps, it may be thought, to take in such a matter as the reading of poetry. But though sometimes the irresolute tide of impulses, whose hesitation has been our difficulty, is shallow, sometimes it is deep. And whether deep or shallow the sincerity of our response is all-important. It might be said, indeed, with some justice, that the value of poetry lies in the difficult exercise in sincerity it can impose upon its readers even more than upon the poet.

CHAPTER VIII

TECHNICAL PRESUPPOSITIONS AND CRITICAL PRECONCEPTIONS

Man lives that list, that leaning in the will
No wisdom can forecast by gauge or guess,
The selfless self of self, most strange, most still,
Fast furled and all foredrawn to No or Yes.
GERARD HOPKINS.

' My children ', said Confucius once, ' why does no one of you study the *Odes?* They are adapted to rouse the mind, to assist observation, to make people sociable, to excite indignation. They speak of duties far and near ; and it is from them that one becomes conversant with the names of many birds, beasts, plants and trees '.[1]

In addition to these benefits many other advantages may be expected from the reading of poetry. It is these expectations, and their varying degrees of legitimacy and importance, that are the subject of this chapter. Few people approach poetry without expectations—explicit or, more often, implicit. ' It is supposed that by the act of writing in verse an author makes a formal engagement that he will

---

[1] *Analects*, XVII, 9.

The Odes: a compilation arranged and edited by Confucius himself, so that the philosopher's plaintive tone is intelligible.

Observation: be used for purposes of self-contemplation (Legge). Very true and in more than one sense.

Sociable: no longer true in England, distinctly so in America.

To excite indignation: virtuous indignation (Jennings) ; to regulate feelings of resentment (Legge) ; possumus jure indignari (Zottoli). All these interpretations, too, seem justified by our protocols.

Duties far and near: Cf. *Treasure Island:* ' " Dooty is dooty," says Captain Smollett, and right he is. Just you steer clear of the Cap'n." '

Birds: especially noteworthy in view of twentieth-century English Poetry. And surely fishes should be added.

gratify certain known habits of association ', said Wordsworth in his famous Preface. The reader need not know what he is expecting ; it is enough that he expects it. He will be gratified or annoyed accordingly.

We may sort these expectations under two headings as they concern the means employed by the poet and the ends that he endeavours to attain ; but so much confusion exists between the two that they must first be considered together. Often a reader will not know in the least whether the demand he makes concerns the one or the other, and without a good deal of evidence it may be difficult to decide the point for him. There is nothing surprising in this, for in no complex field of human activity is the distinction between means and ends easy to draw. And in the case of poetry an imposing doctrine of Formal Virtues has lately been in vogue, whose effect is simply to deny the distinction. If ' Art for Art's Sake ', or ' Pure Poetry ', is in the background of our minds [1] we may well despair of reaching any clarity in this matter.

Before we begin again to dip for examples among the protocols a danger already mentioned in Part I may be recalled. We must not suppose that bad critical principles imply bad reading. A good reader *may* allege the most inept reasons for a judgment which in every other way is entirely to the point. It is not so much the stated reasons that we have to examine, as the actual influence of prior expectations, for good or ill. An illegitimate expectation, however, is always a threat to the reader ; it waits until his sensitiveness, his ' neural vigilance ', ebbs enough to leave him at its mercy.

[1] See *Principles*, Chs. II, X, XVIII, where the confusions which are responsible for such doctrines are discussed. The distinction between means and ends is not, of course, normally clear to the poet in the act of composition, or to the reader at the climax of his reading. But when the reader attempts to discuss the poem he ought at least to try to draw the distinction.

Technical presuppositions, though they may trap even intelligent readers, are not a very interesting subject and may be dealt with briefly. They interfere whenever we make the mistake of supposing either that the *means* a poet uses are valuable for their own sake, or that they can be prescribed without reference to his aim, so that by mere inquiry into the means we can conclude as to the value. Put in this form the mistake may seem too silly to be frequent, but in fact it is extremely insidious, for the language of criticism and many of its current assumptions invite us constantly to commit it. If we wish, as critics, to write what the cultivated unspecialised world will accept as a tolerable prose, we are often compelled, for example, to say things about the poem, or the words in it, which are only true of the effects of the poem upon the minds of its readers. We use a shorthand which identifies the ascribed rhythm of the poem with its actual sounds, the various meanings of the words with the words themselves, and our response to the whole poem with a character of the poem itself. We speak of the poem's beauty instead of entering upon elaborate and speculative analyses of its effect upon us. (We may, perhaps, be trusting that our more intelligent and informed readers will decode and expand our shorthand, but in fact few of them will do so.) And because we write in this way very ancient mental habits are restored to power in our own minds and we come temporarily ourselves to think that the virtues of a poem lie not in its power over us, but in its own structure and conformation as an assemblage of verbal sounds. With this recrudescence of an attitude to language, which has long been obsolete and discredited for reflective persons, we become at once exposed to every kind of mistake and confusion.

The frequency and variety of these dogmatic pronouncements upon detail, irrespective of the final result, are amply demonstrated in the protocols. Many were commented upon, as they appeared, in Part II ; but here may be listed some of the chief occasions for this blunder, if only to point a moral. No other critical moral, perhaps, deserves more insistence. The blunder in all cases is the attempt to assign marks *independently* to details that can only be judged fairly with reference to the whole final result to which they contribute. It is the blunder of attempting to say how the poet shall work without regard for what he is doing. I shall proceed from the more obvious to the more debatable instances.

First among these representative occasions for folly may come Imperfect Rhymes (2·1–2·22, 3·1, 3·41) and Metrical Irregularities (2·2, 3·44, 8·44, 12·51, 13·61, 13·62), the Line-end Stop (8·33, 8·43) and Sonnet Form (3·1, 3·4, 3·41, 5·56, 6·4, 9·82, 12·51). Next, perhaps, should come Cacophony (2·23, 3·4, 6·33, 10·42, 10·44) and Euphony (4·22, 7·57), and the Intrinsic Qualities of Words (10·4, 10·55). Then demands for Descriptive Accuracy (2·22, 8·15, 9·2) deserve mention, along with Vividness (11·22), Logic (2·24), Unmixed Metaphor (6·41, 10·61) and the various problems of figurative language discussed in Part III, Chapter II.

More doubt may be felt about insistence upon Clarity (5·51, 6·37), Conciseness (13·65), Majesty in Epitaphs (11·43) and the demand for a Serious Subject or Message (2·3, 11·42, 13·8). But with this we pass to a border-line case where a Technical Presupposition may be indistinguishable from a critical preconception as to the aim of poetry.

The writer of 2·3, for example, may be combining, along with his two other technical presuppositions, a requirement that the *sense* of the poem be important when taken by itself. The verb ' to say ', when used of poetry, is always ambiguous. It may be equivalent to ' communicate '—in which case, of course, every poem worthy of attention ' says ' something of importance. But it may be equivalent to ' state ', and many great poems state nothing. Even when something important is stated, we should beware of considering the statement in isolation from its place in the poem. But on this enough has been said in the last chapter.

In contrast to 2·3, the two writers who follow (2·4 and 2·41) seem to be showing a concern, not with the technique or detail of the poem, but with its general nature or with the result. Their demand for a serious subject may be a demand for an end, not for a means. And a serious subject may be only their name for a serious result. If so, we pass over to the more interesting question of the views that may be held as to the value of poetry and the influence of these views, whether they are held implicitly or explicitly, upon our reading and judgment.

Technical presuppositions, as a rule, are not products of reflection. The man who supposes that rhymes *must* be perfect, that lines *must* not run over, that sonnets *must* have a definite division, that strict descriptive accuracy *must* be achieved, would usually, if challenged, admit that he saw no conclusive reason why these things should be so. Accidents of teaching, bad inductive inferences from a few salient examples, expectations we slip into without reflection, are responsible for most of this technical dogmatism. But general preconceptions as to the value of poetry are theories, that is to say, they are due to reflection ; and the sincerity and intelligence of this reflection can, it fortunately happens, be tested. *The test is whether the values of poetry are described in a way which pretends to be directly serviceable in criticism.*

I can make this rather cryptic assertion clearer by a few examples. Let us take first the common theory that the value of poetry is in the value of its subject. It can be, and usually is, framed in such a way that we can very easily decide for ourselves, according to our tastes and temperament, about the value of the subject. A reader approaching *Poem X* or *Poem XII*, for example, may say to himself, ' Ah, this is a description of the experience of lying and looking at clouds ! ' He picks out something he can call the subject. Usually he has little difficulty in deciding about the value of this subject. He can then argue ' It is good to lie and look at clouds ; this poem conveys the experience of lying and looking at clouds ; therefore, this poem is good '. (See 10·2.) Or conversely : ' Lying and looking at clouds is a commonplace and trivial activity ; this poem represents such an activity ; therefore, this poem is commonplace and trivial '. (See 2·3, 4·24.) One might as well argue that a faithful portrait of a bad man is therefore a bad picture.

Similarly, with the very frequent ' message ' theories. Half the readers of *Poem I*, especially 1·181 and 1·21, will serve us as examples ; or 4·13, 4·24, 4·28, 4·5 ; or 5·3, 5·32, 5·35, 5·38 ; or 7·2, 7·34, 7·5 ; or 9·5, 9·51 ; the list might have been made much longer. The reader finds, or fails to find, something in the poem which seems to him ' an inspiring message ', and argues from the presence or absence of this ' inspirational bit ' to the value or lack of value of the poem. It can hardly be doubted that this quest for a message, this preconception that the value of poetry is in its power to inspire us, is a strong influence in most readers' approach to poetry, and that it determines their reading and judgment in a high degree. What then is wrong with it ?

It may help us to make the fundamental error of this approach clearer if we compare it with another case in which a similar preconception leads to similar indiscrimination and loss of values : the preconception in favour of 'lilt' in poetry (4·16, 4·22, 8·43, 12·41). Lilt is an excellent thing in its due place, but it does not give value to poetry unless the rest of the poem requires it, accords with it, conditions it and justifies it. (See Chapter IV above.) As an independent demand and a test for value, the quest for lilt makes us insusceptible to other more important movements which may be present in its place. It blinds us to more important things which the poet may be doing. So it is with the quest for 'inspiring thoughts'. Sometimes they are in place— who would deny it?—but to expect them is to grow blind to better things that poetry may offer. And, as we may observe if we watch one another, the 'thirst for inspiration' is as capable of refinement or crudity as any other thirst.

The more refined and discriminating our preconception of poetry is, the more impossible any *direct* application becomes. A crude 'subject-theory' or 'message-theory' *can* be applied directly. It will enable us to conclude quickly and easily (and mistakenly) whether the poetry is good or bad. So too will theories that poetry must be 'vivid', 'simple', 'musical', 'stirring', 'passionate', 'sensuous', 'impersonal', or 'sincere',[1] in fact so will any theory that gives us a definite character that we can look for in a poem and decide is present or absent. An enormous amount of trouble has been devoted to the discovery of such keys, and to making them more and more complex. This trouble, if what we are seeking is a key, is wasted. But if what we are seeking is not a key, but an understanding of the whole matter, and particularly of the reasons why no such keys can be used, then the trouble is very

---

[1] It may be thought that, on my own showing in the preceding chapter, I should make an exception of sincerity. But it is only in the conjectural Confucian sense that we could take sincerity as a criterion of excellence in poetry; and on this see p. 301 below. Some kinds of insincerity are perhaps useful *negative* indications.

well rewarded. For the more thoroughly we work out our account of the differences between good and bad poetry the more intricate and complex the account becomes. Alternatives, conditions, qualifications, compensating conditions . . . and the rest, force themselves into it under the pressure of the facts, until it becomes evident that a direct practical application of an adequate account to any poem is impossible. It is much easier to decide that a poem is good or bad than to frame a description of its merits and decide whether this description applies to it.

We might be tempted to conclude from this that inquiry into the differences between good and bad in poetry is futile, and that indulgence in it is an example of academic fatuity. But this conclusion will be seen, I hope, to be a mistake. The physical sciences offer innumerable parallels. It is much easier, for example, to tell whether a falling stone on a mountain is likely to hit you or not than to collect the necessary data and calculate its trajectory. None the less the mathematical and physical theories that here seem so useless have innumerable *indirect* and roundabout applications. (Not two of my readers in a hundred would be alive without them. Such has been the effect of the steamship, itself a result of Galileo, upon civilisation !) And though all the theory in the world does not make it possible to be sure that we shall not be hit, it can at least satisfy us that the stone is not a hostile magician in disguise, and that incantations will not appreciably divert it from its course.

Most critical dogmas, preconceptions of the kind that can be and are applied to poetry, have almost exactly the intellectual standing and the serviceableness of primitive ' superstitions '. They rest upon our desire for explanation, our other desires, our respect for tradition, and to a slight degree upon faulty induction. Sometimes, by good fortune, they are useful ; on the whole they make us much more stupid than we would be without them. Only such an experiment as that which produced the protocols (a small selection only of the harvest and not, in this respect, a selection of extreme examples) can convince anyone of the extent of their interference.

They interfere in two different ways. By blinding the reader to what else is in the poem, so that he *forces* his predilection, if he can, upon the poem—rejecting, comparatively unread, poems that will not allow it. Secondly, by blurring and disabling his judgment. Any general theory that we may be tempted to apply to poetry and continue to apply, must—unless we are very Napoleonic readers—be of the kind which disguises great vagueness and ambiguity behind an appearance of simplicity and precision. Most critical key-words excel in this duplicity, as we have seen with ' sentimental ' and with ' sincere '. Supplied with one of these words—' sincere ' is a great favourite in its primitive un-analysed condition—we have the poem up before us and apply the test. There will probably be from seven to eleven senses, more or less important, all confusedly among the possibilities of the word in the context. The word is the meeting-point of these senses, which without this common outlet of expression might never run any risk of being confused. Such words, like blunderbusses, cover much ground ; yet it is quite easy to suppose that only one unambiguous (though, of course, ' subtle ') meaning is present. Words like ' sincerity ', ' truth ', ' sentimentality ', ' expression ', ' belief ', ' form ', ' significance ', and ' meaning ' itself, seem to those who rely on them to hit the mark repeatedly in an almost miraculous fashion. But this is only because a cloud of heterogeneous missiles instead of a single meaning is discharged on each occasion, and the marksmanship is no more notable than the similar exploits at a Buffalo Bill's Wild Western Show. What is wonderful is the naïvety of the spectators, and of the performers, who here have no suspicion that with such words a total miss is almost an impossibility. But to discover which missile hit what on any occasion is not at all an easy matter.

The result of a highly ambiguous though simple-seeming doctrine, when it collaborates with our well ascertained capacity to read poems much as we wish to read them, is to disable our judgment to a point well below its normal unindoctrinated level. Or rather, to put the point in a better way—a way that more clearly reflects the operations of our minds—the result of doctrine is to transform what was choice into judgment. Judgment *in these matters* is not a refinement upon choice (as it is in legal matters), but a degradation ; it is a disguise which hampers and confuses an activity of choice which to the end remains the animating spirit beneath all the trappings of judgment.

All critical doctrines are attempts to convert choice into what may seem a safer activity—the reading evidence and the application of rules and principles. They are an invasion into an inappropriate sphere of that modern transformation, the displacement of the will by observation and judgment. Instead of *deciding* that we are too cold or too warm we hang up a thermometer. Perhaps wisely, for our feelings here are not altogether to be trusted since the invention of central heating. But in poetry our feelings (in the large sense which makes them as much currents in our will as objects to introspection) are in the end the whole matter. We cannot substitute for them any poetic-thermometer in the form of any doctrine whatsoever without being betrayed. The only exception would be some doctrine—such as the account of sincerity fathered on Confucius in the last chapter—which amounts to making the discernment of what is good a matter of choice. But it must be an essential not an arbitrary choice, one which expresses the needs of the being as a whole, not a random gust of desire or the obstructing capacity of some dead member.

Thus no theory, no description, of poetry can be trusted which is not too intricate to be applied This may be what Blake meant by saying that ' Virtue resides only in minute particulars '. Value in poetry turns nearly always upon differences and connections too minute and unobtrusive to be directly perceived. We recognise them only in their effects. Just as the differences of phase through which we locate sounds in space are too slight in their auditory effects to be discriminated,[1] yet through their ocular reflexes perfectly fulfil their function ; so the differences between good and bad poetry may be indiscernible to direct attention yet patent in their effects upon feeling. The choice of our whole personality may be the only instrument we possess delicate enough to effect the discrimination.

When we have the poem in all its minute particulars as intimately and as fully present to our minds as we can contrive—no general description of it but the very experience itself present as a living pulse in our biographies—then our acceptance or rejection of it must be *direct*. There comes a point in all criticism where a sheer choice has to be made without the support of any arguments, principles, or general rules. All that arguments or principles can do is to protect us from irrelevancies, red-herrings and disturbing preconceptions. They may remind us perhaps, that every poem has many more aspects than are presented on one occasion. They may help us to bring more of our personality to bear upon the poem than we otherwise might do. They certainly

[1] See Piéron, *Thought and the Brain*.   Part II, ch. iv.

can prevent us from judging by the detail rather than by the whole. They may preserve us from bad arguments but they cannot supply good ones. So complex is poetry. And in general if we find ourselves, near this crucial point of choice, looking for help from arguments, we may suspect that we are on the wrong track. The point is critical in the secondary sense too, for it is in these moments of sheer decision that the mind becomes most plastic, and selects, at the incessant multiple shifting cross-roads, the direction of its future development.

The critical act is the starting-point, not the conclusion, of an argument. The personality stands balanced between the particular experience which is the realised poem and the whole fabric of its past experiences and developed habits of mind. What is being settled is whether this new experience can or cannot be taken into the fabric with advantage. Would the fabric afterwards be better or worse? Often it must be the case that the new modification of experience would improve the fabric if it could be taken in, but too much reconstruction would be needed. The strain, the resistance, is too great, and the poem is rejected. Sometimes nothing essential in the fabric prevents the incorporation of the poem. Only some slight unnecessary fold or twist or crumple, or some piece of adventitious scaffolding stands in the way, a result of clumsy thinking rather than a flaw or malformation in the self. Yet these obstructions may cut us off from the thing we most need. Among these accidents inadequate critical theories, withholding what we need and imposing upon us what we do not need, are sadly too frequent in our minds.

The critic himself, of course, in the moment of choice knows nothing about all this. He may feel the strain. He may notice the queer shifts of emotional perspective—that may affect all his other thoughts—as his mind tries, now in one way now in another, to fit itself to the poem. He will sense an obscure struggle as the poem's secret allies and enemies manœuvre within him. When these internal parties in dispute cannot escape their deadlock, or sit down to a war of attrition, he will know, if he is sincere, that any decision he takes about the poem is merely a postponement. For it is not only his opinion about it which is unsettled, but the form and order of his personality itself. He will do well to make a temporary decision however, and persuade himself provisionally either of its excellence or its demerits. The experiment often stirs the internal dispute into a healthy movement. And the oppression which follows the forced acceptance of a bad poem may give its enemies their chance for a revolution. But when the conflict resolves itself, when the obstruction goes down or the crumple is straightened out, when an old habit which has been welcoming a bad poem is revivified into a fresh formation, or a new limb which has grown to meet a good poem wakes into life, the mind clears, and new energy wells up ; after the pause a collectedness supervenes ; behind our rejection or acceptance (even of a minor poem) we feel the sanction and authority of the self-completing spirit.

This amounts, perhaps, to a claim that a certain kind of critical choice is infallible. We know only too well what to expect when a man *begins* by saying ' Of course, we are all fallible. . . '. We are in for some impudent affirmation or other. What ought we to divine in an author who *ends* by announcing that we are all infallible ? Doubt, presumably ; doubt in every direction and to the extremest degree.

I am anxious not to disappoint this expectation. Indeed I would infect these last pages, if I could, with such a virulent culture of doubt that all *critical* certainties, except one, would wither in the minds of all their readers. Points of analysis would remain unaffected, since these are but tentative explorations of a subject-matter which future inquiries will penetrate far more deeply. But *critical* certainties, convictions as to the value, and kinds of value, of kinds of poetry, might safely and with advantage decay, provided there remained a firm sense of the importance of the critical act of choice, its difficulty, and the supreme exercise of all our faculties that it imposes. Mere acquiescent immersion in good poetry can give us, of course, much that is valuable. Acquiescent immersion in bad poetry entails a corresponding penalty. But the greater values can only be gained by making poetry the occasion for those momentous decisions of the will. The alluring solicitancy of the bad, the secret repugnancy of the good are too strong for us in most reading of poetry. Only by penetrating far more whole-mindedly into poetry than we usually attempt, and by collecting all our energies in our choice, can we overcome these treacheries within us. That is why good reading, in the end, is the whole secret of ' good judgment '.

U

PART FOUR

SUMMARY AND RECOMMENDATIONS

Mencius said : ' The son of the K'ung Clan (Confucius) climbed the Eastern Hillock and thought the State of Lu looked small ; he climbed the Great Mountain and found All-below-the-sky inconsiderable. He who has gazed upon the ocean scorns other waters ; and he who has entered in at the gate of enlightened men is critical of words.'

SUMMARY

The uncontrollable mystery on the bestial floor.

W. B. YEATS.

THREE tasks remain, and this final part is accordingly divided under three heads. Under the first, I discuss the current state of culture, as it is indicated in the protocols, and some inferences to be drawn from it ; under the second, the services that psychological theory may afford us here, its uses and limitations ; under the third, the practical measures that seem advisable and possible. It is *not* inevitable, or in the nature of things, that poetry should seem such a remote, mysterious, unmanageable thing to so large a majority of readers. The deficiencies so noticeable in the protocol writers (and, if we could be franker with ourselves, in our own reading) are not native inalterable defects in the average human mind. They are due in a large degree to mistakes that can be avoided, and to bad training. In fact, does anyone ever receive any useful training in this matter ? Yet, without asking more from average humanity than even a misanthrope will grant, something can be done to make men's spiritual heritage more available and more operative. Though I may seem to be traversing, in what follows, ground with which every teacher (and every person thrust into close contact with humanity) is familiar to the point of desperation, I am confident that the last word in this matter has not been spoken. A better technique, as we learn daily in other fields, may yield results that the most whole-hearted efforts fall short of if misapplied. And the technique of the approach to poetry has not yet received half so much serious systematic study as the technique of pole-jumping. If it is easy to push up the general level of performance in such ' natural ' activities as running or jumping (not to insist upon the more parallel examples of mountaineering, fly-fishing and golf) merely by making a little careful inquiry into the best methods, surely there is reason to expect that investigation into the technique of reading may have even happier results. With this not extravagant hope to encourage us, let us try to see what exactly is needed, and what is within our power to do.

I

§ 1. The standing of the men and women who supplied the protocols has been described in Part I (p. 3). With few exceptions they are products of the most expensive kind of education. I would like to repeat, with emphasis, that there is no reason what-ever to suppose that a higher capacity for reading poetry will be manifested by any similar group any-where in the world. Sons and daughters of other Universities who are tempted to think otherwise may be invited to bring experimental evidence collected under the same conditions. But no experienced teacher will be surprised by any of the protocols ; no teacher, at least, who has refrained from turning his pupils into sounding-boards that reflect his own opinions. And, candidly, how many of us are con-vinced, with reason, that we would have made a better showing ourselves under these conditions ?

§ 2. *Immaturity.*—Thus the gaps in these readers' equipment are very significant. First may be placed the general immaturity of the readers. Their average age would be between nineteen and twenty. Yet with several of the poems (notably *Poems I, II and*

XIII) one important reason for erratic opinions seems undeniably to be lack of general experience. I wish very much that I could include as a frontispiece a good group photograph of the protocol-writers. It would help us to realise, better than pages of discussion, the concrete significance of some of these revelations. Statistics as to the proportion of the writers who are going later to be teachers would also assist this realisation. Yet it may be doubted whether any large proportion of those who showed themselves to be under age—not in intelligence alone but in emotional development also—are destined to become much more mature with the passage of time. In some respects the years will do their work, for good and ill, but in others (cf. Ch. V, p. 291) there is little reason to expect any essential change. Much though there is to be said, on general anthropological grounds, in favour of a delayed maturity, an educational and social system which encourages a large proportion of its most endowed and favoured products to remain children *permanently* is exposing itself to danger. The point is a familiar one ; I merely bring my mite of evidence.

§ 3. *Lack of Reading.*—A strong suspicion that I developed in looking over the protocols, that the women-writers were of higher average discernment than the men, is perhaps relevant in this connection. For the young woman of nineteen is generally supposed to be nearer to her final settled character, in most respects, than the equivalent young man. A better explanation would be the greater familiarity with poetry that is certainly possessed by the average girl. A lack of experience with poetry must be placed next to general inexperience of life in this list of deficiencies. A large number of writers showed clearly (a fact which one knew well enough already) that they had hardly any reading at all to serve them as a background and means of orientation. And those readers who did try to use their background often proved the naïvety of their outlook and the poverty of their literary experience by the comparisons and identifications they made. Apart from this wide experience it is hard to see how any but the most gifted readers can help being impressed, for example, by work which is merely a feeble echo of something else. We may sometimes say, then, that it is the original work which is at second-hand the source of the impression. We must acknowledge that very much of the worship that a more experienced and better reader may condemn as too facile is merely *faute de mieux* worship. Also, but more rarely, the condition of poetic starvation appears. The reader, having discovered some value in poetry, swallows all he can of it for a while, hoping that it will do him good, and improve his taste, even when he does not really like it. But there is not a great deal of this in our examples. We could have safely inferred from the protocols that the relatively cultivated youth of our age spends extremely little of its time over poetry.

§ 4. *Construing.*—Partly to this well-recognised fact, but partly to more interesting causes, we may trace the widespread inability to construe meaning, which is perhaps the deficiency made most apparent in my selections. But it is not only those with little experience of poetry who fail in this. Some who appear to have read widely seem to make little or no endeavour to understand, or, at least, to remain strangely unsuccessful. Indeed, the more we study this matter the more we shall find ' a love for poetry ' accompanied by an incapacity to understand or construe it. This construing, we must suppose, is not nearly so easy and ' natural ' a performance as we tend to assume. It is a craft, in the sense that mathematics, cooking, and shoemaking are crafts.

It can be taught. And though some gifted individuals can go far in the strength of their own sagacity alone, instruction and practice are very necessary for others. The best methods of instruction remain to be worked out. At present, apart from not very satisfactory exercises in translation from other languages and some still less satisfactory experiments with *précis* writing and paraphrasing, this instruction ceases at too early a stage. No attempt at imparting a reasoned general technique for construing has yet been made. Perhaps because the need for it has not been sufficiently realised. Two problems for reflection, suggested by this low capacity in construing, may be noted. (1) What is the worth of poetry for readers who cannot make out what it means ? (2) How far can we expect such readers to show themselves intelligent, imaginative and discriminating in their intimate relations with other human beings ? Neither question can be answered summarily, certainly not the second (see § 10, below). But it is not doubtful that certain ' sentimental ' addictions to poetry are of little value, or that this poor capacity to interpret complex and unfamiliar meanings is a source of endless loss, for those whose lives need not be narrowly standardised at a low level. If anything *can* be done, educationally, that is not already being done to improve it, the attempt would be worth much trouble. This defect in our equipment is so essential a point for any student of poetry to realise, and so neglected, that I need not apologise for the emphasis laid upon it in what follows.

§ 5. *Stock Responses.*—Closely connected with this incapacity to apprehend unusual meanings is the fatal facility with which usual meanings reappear when they are not wanted. Great stress was laid in Part III upon this tendency of our acquired responses to intervene in situations to which they are not appropriate, and little need be added here. If we wish for a population easy to control by suggestion we shall decide what repertory of suggestions it shall be susceptible to and encourage this tendency except in the few. But if we wish for a high and diffused civilisation, with its attendant risks, we shall combat this form of mental inertia. In either case, since most of the protocol writers would certainly regard themselves as belonging to the few, rather than the many, were such a division to be proposed, we shall do well to recognise how much of the value of existence is daily thrust from us by our stock responses, necessary though a substratum of stable and routine mental habits may be.

§ 6. *Preconceptions.*—As special cases of these inappropriate acquired responses : certain tests, criteria and presuppositions as to what is to be admired or despised in poetry proved their power to hide what was actually present. A pretension to knowledge of such criteria is sometimes linked with a certain temptation, never lurking far below the surface, to teach the poet his business. But, apart from this motive, a serious but less arrogant reader, unprovided with any such criteria, theories and principles, often feels himself distressingly at a loss before a poem. Too sheer a challenge to his own unsupported self seems to be imposed. The desire to condense his past experience, or to invoke doughty authority, in the form of a critical maxim, is constantly overwhelming. Without *some* objective criteria, by which poetry can be tested, and the good distinguished from the bad, he feels like a friendless man deprived of weapons and left naked at the mercy of a treacherous beast. We decided that the treacherous beast was within him, that critical weapons—unless too elaborate to be employed—would only hurt him, that his own experience—not as represented in a

formula but in its available entirety—was his only
safeguard, and that if he could rely sufficiently upon
this, he could only profit from his encounter with the
poem.

§ 7. *Bewilderment.*—But this advice, however well
meant, can perhaps only further perplex that great
body of readers whose first and last reaction to poetry
(it is hardly a response) is bewilderment. An over-
tone of despairing helplessness haunts the protocols
in a degree that my selections do not sufficiently
display. I omitted a great mass of sit-on-the-fence
opinion. Without further clues (authorship, period,
school, the sanction of an anthology, or the hint of a
context) the task of ' making up their minds about
it ', or even of working out a number of possible
views from which to choose, was felt to be really
beyond their powers. The extraordinary variety of
the views put forward, and the reckless, desperate
character of so many of them, indicate the difficulty
that was felt, and how unprepared for such a testing
encounter the majority of the readers were. It
should surely be possible, even without devoting
more time or trouble to the reading of English than
is given at present, to prepare them better, and make
them more reasonably self-reliant.

§ 8. *Authority.*—The protocols show, equally, how
entirely a matter of authority the rank of famous
poets, as it is accepted and recognised by public
opinion, must be. Without the control of this rather
mysterious, traditional authority, poets of the most
established reputations would very quickly and sur-
prisingly change their places in general approval.
This is, if we pursue it, a disturbing reflection, for it
should lead us to question very closely the quality
of the reading we ordinarily give to authors whose
rank and character have been officially settled. There
cannot be much doubt that when we know we are

reading Milton or Shelley, a great deal of our approval and admiration is being accorded not to the poetry but to an idol. Conversely, if we did not know that we were reading Ella Wheeler Wilcox, much of our amusement or patronising condescension might easily be absent. Far more than we like to admit, we take a hint for our response from the poet's reputation. Whether we assent or dissent, the traditional view runs through our response like the wire upon which a climbing plant is trained. And without it there is no knowing at what conclusion we might not have arrived.

The attempt to read without this guidance puts a strain upon us that we are little accustomed to. Within limits it is a salutary strain. We learn how much we are indebted to the work of other minds that have established the tradition, at the same time that we become aware of its dangers. And we discover what a comparatively relaxed and inattentive activity our ordinary reading of established poetry is. Even those who have won a deserved eminence through their critical ability, who have worthily occupied Chairs of Poetry and taken their part in handing on the torch of tradition retrimmed, would probably admit in their secret souls that they had not read many poems with the care and attention that these anonymous items, under these conditions, invite. But while we become, through such reflections, on the one hand more ready to question tradition, we become on the other more sensible of our dependence upon it.

§ 9. *Variability.*—It was interesting to observe the wide range of quality that many individual readers varied through. They would pass, with contiguous poems, from a very high level of discernment to a relatively startling obtuseness, and often force one to consider very closely whether what appeared to be so stupid did not mask unexpected profundity, and whether the obtuseness was really where one hoped it was. The odds, I know, are much against my having escaped this danger. I have not illustrated these variations, for such studies of individual readers would have taken this book too far from its main path, and made what is already a complex investigation too unwieldy. Nor have I attempted to trace carefully any correlations between approval of one type of poem and disapproval of another, and so forth. I have only a strong impression that such correlations would be difficult to find ; as, indeed, on theoretical grounds—seeing how complex the conditions are—we should expect. But this individual variability in discernment was striking enough to deserve notice. It has the comforting moral attached to it that however baffled we may be by one poem, we may still be extraordinarily acute with another—with a poem perhaps that to most readers proves more difficult. Some of these unevennesses may be put down to fatigue. I am inclined to think that four poems are too many for a week's reading—absurd though this suggestion will seem to those godlike lords of the syllabus-world, who think that the whole of English Literature can be perused with profit in about a year !

But apart from fatigue there are other very evident reasons why critical capacity should vary. ' Making up our minds about a poem ' is the most delicate of all possible undertakings. We have to gather millions of fleeting semi-independent impulses into a momentary structure of fabulous complexity, whose core or germ only is given us in the words. What we ' make up ', that momentary trembling order in our minds, is exposed to countless irrelevant influences. Health, wakefulness, distractions, hunger and other instinctive tensions, the very quality of the air we breathe, the humidity, the light, all affect us. No one at all sensitive to rhythm, for example, will doubt that the new pervasive, almost ceaseless, mutter or roar of modern transport, replacing the rhythm of the footstep or of horses' hoofs, is capable of interfering in many ways with our reading of verse.[1] Thus it is no matter for surprise if we find ourselves often unable to respond in any relevant and coherent fashion.

What is indeed remarkable is that we should pretend that we can even usually do so. We should be better advised to acknowledge frankly that, when people put poems in our hands (point to pictures, or play us music), what we say, in nine cases out of ten, has nothing to do with the poem, but arises from politeness or spleen or some other social motive. It cannot arise from the poem if the poem is not yet there in our minds, and it hardly ever, in fact, is there, under such public and hurried conditions of reading. It would be an excellent thing if all the critical chitchat which we produce on these occasions were universally recognised to be what it is, social gesture, ' phatic communion '. But though people to whom tone is more interesting than either sense or feeling have always treated it as such, the sincere and innocent reader is much too easily bounced into emptying his mind by any literary highwayman who says, ' I want your opinion ', and much too easily laid low because he has nothing to produce on these occasions. He might be comforted if he knew how many professionals make a point of carrying stocks of imitation currency, crisp and bright, which satisfy the highwaymen and are all that even the wealthiest critic in these emergencies can supply.

[1] Mr T. S. Eliot, than whom there could be no more qualified observer, has suggested that the internal combustion engine may already have altered our perception of rhythms. (Preface to *Savonarola*, by Charlotte Eliot.)

§ 10. *General Values.*—It is natural to inquire how far insensitiveness, poor discrimination, and a feeble capacity to understand poetry imply a corresponding inability to apprehend and make use of the values of ordinary life. This is a large and awkward question which we shall answer in different ways as our experience varies. Two answers, however, would certainly be wrong : the view that a man who is stupid with poetry *must* be as stupid with life, and the view that obtuseness in literary matters implies no general disabilities. Doubtless to some degree poetry, like the other arts, is a secret discipline to which some initiation is needed. Some readers are excluded from it simply because they have never discovered, and have never been taught, how to enter. Poetry translates into its special sensory language a great deal that is given in the ordinary daily intercourse between minds by gesture, tones of voice, and expression, and a reader who is very quick and discerning in these matters may fail for purely technical reasons to apprehend the very same things when they are given in verse. He will be in the same sad case as those Bubis of Fernando Po, who need to see one another before they understand what is said. On the other hand, it is sometimes not difficult in reading through the protocols to distinguish those who are incapacitated by this ignorance and *lack of skill in reading* from those whose failure has deeper causes. And, moreover, those who have naturally a fine imagination and discrimination, who have a developed sensibility to the values of life, do seem to find the password to poetry with great ease. For there is no such gulf between poetry and life as over-literary persons sometimes suppose. There is no gap between our everyday emotional life and the material of poetry. The verbal expression of this life, at its finest, is forced to use the technique of poetry ; that is the only essential difference. We cannot avoid the material of poetry. If we do not live in consonance with good poetry, we must live in consonance with bad poetry. And, in fact, the idle hours of most lives are filled with reveries that are simply bad private poetry. On the whole evidence, I do not see how we can avoid the conclusion that a general insensitivity to poetry does witness a low level of general imaginative life. There are other reasons for thinking that this century is in a cultural trough rather than upon a crest. I need not expatiate here upon them. But the situation appears sufficiently serious to force us to consider very carefully what influences are available as remedies. When nature and tradition, or rather our contemporary social and economic conditions, betray us, it is reasonable to reflect whether we cannot deliberately contrive artificial means of correction.

It is arguable that mechanical inventions, with their social effects, and a too sudden diffusion of indigestible ideas, are disturbing throughout the world the whole order of human mentality, that our minds are, as it were, becoming of an inferior shape —thin, brittle and patchy, rather than controllable and coherent. It is possible that the burden of information and consciousness that a growing mind has now to carry may be too much for its natural strength. If it is not too much already, it may soon become so, for the situation is likely to grow worse before it is better. Therefore, if there be any means by which we may artificially strengthen our minds' capacity to order themselves, we must avail ourselves of them. And of all possible means, Poetry, the unique, linguistic instrument by which our minds have ordered their thoughts, emotions, desires . . . in the past, seems to be the most serviceable. It may well be a matter of some urgency for us, in the interests of our standard of civilisation, to make this highest form of language more accessible. From

the beginning civilisation has been dependent upon
speech, for words are our chief link with the past
and with one another and the channel of our spiritual
inheritance. As the other vehicles of tradition, the
family and the community, for example, are dis-
solved, we are forced more and more to rely upon
language.
Yet, as the protocols show, such reliance as we
place in it at present is quite unjustified. Not a
tenth of the power of poetry is released for the
general benefit, indeed, not a thousandth part. It
fails, not through its own fault, but through our
ineptitude as readers. Is there no means to give the
' educated ' individual a better receptive command
of these resources of language ?

II

§ 11. *Abuse of Psychology.*—The psychologist is
properly suspect to-day when he approaches these
topics. A shudder is a likely, and to some degree a
justified, response to the suggestion that he can be
called in to assist us in reading poetry. Statistical
inquiries into the ' efficiency ' of different forms of
composition, into types of imagery, into the relative
frequency of verbs and adjectives, of liquids, sibilants
and fricatives in various authors ; classifications of
literary ' motives ', of ' drives ' that may be employed
by writers ; inquiries into the proportions of ' sex-
appeal ' present ; measurements of ' emotional re-
sponse ', of ' facility in integration ', of ' degree of
retention of effects ' ; or gradings of ' artistically
effective associations ' ; such things will make any
reader of poetry feel curiously uncomfortable. And
it is worse still with the efforts of some psycho-
analysts to elucidate masterpieces which they are
clearly approaching for the first time and only for

x

this purpose. Poetry has suffered too much already from those who are merely looking for something to investigate and those who wish to exercise some cherished theory. The best among the experimentalists and the analysts will agree over this.

But between these two extreme wings of the psychological forces there is the comparatively neglected and unheard-of middle body, the cautious, traditional, academic, semi-philosophical psychologists who have been profiting from the vigorous manœuvres of the advanced wings and are now much more ready than they were twenty years ago to take a hand in the application of the science. The general reader, whose ideas as to the methods and endeavours of psychologists derive more from the popularisers of Freud or from the Behaviourists than from students of Stout or Ward, needs perhaps some assurance that it is possible to combine an interest and faith in psychological inquiries with a due appreciation of the complexity of poetry. Yet a psychologist who belongs to this main body is perhaps the last person in the world to underrate this complexity. Unfortunately, the subject-matter of psychology—to a centrist—is so immense that few have been able to devote much attention to literature. Thus this field has been left rather too open to irresponsible incursions.

§ 12. *Profanation.*—If we propose to look closely into the mental processes active in the reading of poetry a certain reluctance or squeamishness will often be felt. ' We murder to dissect ', someone will murmur. This prejudice must be countered. No psychological dissection can do harm, except to minds which are in a pathological condition. The fear that to look too closely may be damaging to what we care about is a sign of a weak or ill-balanced interest. There is a certain frivolity of the passions that does not imply a greater delicacy, a more perfect sensibility, but only a trifling or flimsy constitution. Those who ' care too much for poetry ' to examine it closely are probably flattering themselves. Such exquisites may be pictured explaining their objections to Coleridge or to Schiller.

But we should recognise how grim the prospect would be if these scruples were justified. For it is as certain as anything can be that in time psychology will overhaul most of our ideas about ourselves, and will give us a very detailed account of our mental activities. I am not prepared to argue that the acceptance of inept ideas about ourselves will not prove damaging. Damage is very likely already being done, in America and elsewhere, by elementary courses in Behaviourism, and by a too simplified stimulus-response psychology. Yet it is not the inquiry which is harmful, but the stopping short of inquiry. It would be better, no doubt, for the immediate prospects of poetry that we should content ourselves with our traditional notions than accept in their place ideas too simple to mark any of the distinctions which matter—the ' spiritual ' distinctions. But this is not the only option we are allowed. A naturalistic psychology that observes these finer distinctions is possible, though civilisation is perhaps in for a bad time before it arrives, and has become generally accepted. Watson in place of the Bible, or in place of Confucius or Buddha, as a source of our fundamental conceptions about ourselves is an alarming prospect. But the remedy of putting the clock back is impracticable. Inquiry cannot be stopped now. The only possible course is to hasten, so far as we can, the development of a psychology which will ignore none of the facts and yet demolish none of the values that human experience has shown to be necessary. An account of poetry will be a pivotal point in such a psychology.

§ 13. *Prudential Speech.*—The understanding of speech is an art which we are supposed to acquire chiefly by the light of nature—through the operation of sundry instincts—and to perfect by dint of practice. That in most cases it remains very imperfect indeed is the principal contention of this book. During the earlier stages of the acquisition of language—in childhood and early years at school—it is possible that nature works well enough, though the researches of Piaget[1] suggest that considerable assistance might be given. But after a certain stage, when the individual has become fairly competent, the pressure of the need to understand ever more and more finely relaxes. Errors and failures no longer so clearly entail the penalty of being left out. Nor are they so easily exposed. A child of eight is constantly made to feel that he is not understanding something. At eighteen he may misunderstand nearly as often, but the testing instance, which makes him realise that this is so, infrequently arises. Unless either his company or his studies are exceptional, he will rarely be forced to face any such disagreeable facts. For he will have acquired enough skill in the reproduction of more or less appropriate language to disguise most of his failures both from the world and from himself. He can answer questions in a way which may convince everybody, himself included, that he understands them. He may be able to translate difficult passages with every sign of discernment, write passable essays and converse with great apparent intelligence upon many subjects. Yet in spite of these acquirements he may be making at innumerable points, what Mr Russell once called, in connection with the words *number* and *two*, ' a purely prudential use of language.' That is, he may be using words not because he knows with any precision what he means by them, but because he knows how they are

---

[1] *The Language and Thought of the Child.*

ordinarily used, and does with them what he has
heard other people do with them before. He strings
them together in suitable sequences, manœuvres
them aptly enough, produces with them pretty well
the effects he intends, yet meanwhile he may have
not much more inkling of what he is really (or should
be) doing with them than a telephone-girl need have
of the inner wiring of the switchboard she operates
so deftly. He may merely be in the condition that
Conrad ascribed to those Russians who pour words
out ' with such an aptness of application sometimes
that, as in the case of very accomplished parrots, one
can't defend oneself from the suspicion that they
really understand what they say '.[1]

It may make this accusation seem less unjustifiable
if we underline *really*, and then ask ourselves how
often, even in our most enlightened, most conscious
and most vigilant moments, we would be prepared
to claim such understanding ourselves. Under-
standing is very evidently an affair of degree, never
so consummate as to be insusceptible of improve-
ment. All we can say is that the masters of life—the
greater poets—sometimes seem to show such an
understanding and control of language that we
cannot imagine a further perfection. And judged,
not by this exalted standard, but by a much humbler
order of perceptions, we can be certain that most
' well-educated ' persons remain, under present-day
conditions, far below the level of capacity at which,
by social convention, they are supposed to stand.
As to the less ' well-educated '—genius apart—they
inhabit chaos.

Few sincere minds will perhaps, in their private
councils, be prepared to dispute this, however much
the pretensions which are socially imposed upon us
may force us to deny it. But to fathom the implica-
tions of this situation we shall need to make some

---

[1] *Under Western Eyes*, p. 3.

distinctions. What do we understand here by
' understanding ' ? Various senses of this loose and
ambiguous word invite our attention.

§ 14. *Understanding*.—To take the most primitive
sense first, we shall agree that when nothing whatever
happens in our minds beyond the mere perception
of the sound or shape of words *as words*, we do not
understand them. Comparatively, any thoughts or
feelings or impulses stirred into activity by the words,
and seemingly directed towards something which the
words represent, are a beginning of understanding.
In this primitive sense it is possible that a dog or a
horse may come to ' understand ' a few words and
phrases. In a more developed instance we under-
stand when the words prompt in us action or emotion
appropriate to the attitude of the person who speaks
them. Animals achieve this level also, and much
of the conversation we address to infants asks only
for this degree of understanding. (This aim—a
blend of tone and intention—continues in some
degree perhaps through all human intercourse right
up to the highest utterances of the philosopher.) At
a third level ' understanding ' implies some degree
of intellectual discrimination. We are required to
distinguish the thought invited by the words from
other thoughts more or less like it. The words may
mean ' *This* not *That* ', the nearness of *This* to *That*
corresponding to the precision of the thought invited.

Here we meet with our first opportunity for
deceiving ourselves as to the quality of our under-
standing. For as soon as we pass out of the realm
of immediate action or naïve emotional expression,
as soon as pointing and touching, seeing and trying
can no longer be applied as a test of our under-
standing, we have to fall back upon other words. If
we wish to prove to other persons that we have really
discriminated the *This* from *That*, our only method

will be to produce some description of *This* and *That* to make their difference clear. Now a ' purely prudential ' use of such descriptions is not difficult to acquire. It need not be accompanied by any precise thoughts of either *This* or *That*. If we are asked, ' What do you mean by so and so ? ' —by *understanding*, for example, we can usually reply by giving a few other words that experience has taught us can be used in its place. We reply, ' I mean comprehending, grasping the sense, realising the significance, seizing the meaning, that's what I mean ', and it does not follow in the least that because we can supply these alternative locutions we have any precise ideas upon the matter. This *dictionary understanding*, as it may be called, has long been recognised as an insidious substitute for more authentic kinds of understanding in the elementary stages of all those sciences in which definitions are required. But its operation is really much more extensive. No one with experience of philosophical discussion will confidently set bounds to it, and we are all in danger of becoming philosophers as soon as we attempt to explain our use of words or draw distinctions between our thoughts.

The real danger of *dictionary understanding* is that it so easily prevents us from perceiving the limitations of our understanding ; a disadvantage inseparable from the advantage it gives us of concealing them from our friends. A parallel disguise with similar disadvantages is available for the other chief form of communication. In addition to directing a fairly precise thought, most language simultaneously endeavours to excite some refinement of feeling. As we have seen above, this function of language fails at least as often as the communication of sense. And our means of discovering for ourselves whether we have or have not understood this feeling correctly are even less satisfactory than in the case of thought.

As a rule, only close contact with persons who are exacting in this respect can give us the necessary training. They must be exacting in the sense of noticing with discrimination what feeling we apprehend, not, of course, in the sense of constantly demanding certain definite feelings from us. Most of our devices for exhibiting feeling through words are so crude that we easily convince ourselves and others that we have understood more perfectly than is, in fact, the case. Humanity's pathetic need for' sympathy also encourages this illusion. Thus *dictionary understanding* of feeling, though less glib, is as treacherous as with sense.

Similar considerations apply to the other two forms of understanding—the apprehension of tone and of intention.[1] Subtleties of tone are rarely appreciated without some special training. The gift reaches its heights perhaps only in certain favourable social settings.[2] In the same way the man engaged all his days in intricate (and preferably shady) negotiations most easily becomes an expert in divining other people's intentions. Natural shrewdness and sensibility (a phrase which covers deep mysteries) sometimes compensate for these specially favourable settings.

§ 15. *Confusions.*—Even for a reader who has a good ability in all these four kinds of understanding yet further dangers lie in wait. Pre-eminently the danger of mistaking one function of language for another, of taking for a statement what is merely the expression of a feeling, and *vice versa*, or of interpreting a modification due to tone as an indication of irrelevant intention. These confusions to which all complex

---

[1] Yet other senses of 'understanding' can, of course, be constructed —a sense in which 'understanding' is contrasted with 'knowledge,' for example. But I am anxious here to keep my treatment as simple and unspeculative as possible.

[2] As an example, consider the social development of Julien in *Le Rouge et le Noir.*

or subtle writing is much exposed have been illustrated and discussed above. As soon as metaphorical or figurative uses of speech are introduced, and such writings can rarely avoid them, these dangers become much increased. I have made, since the bulk of this book was prepared, some further experiments with the paraphrasing of fairly simple figurative and semi-allegorical passages. They more than corroborate what was shown by the protocols here given. Not nearly thirty per cent. of a University audience are to be trusted not to misinterpret such language. The facts are such that only experienced teachers would credit a statement of them apart from the evidence.[1] I hope to be able to give it, and discuss the theory of interpretation further in a future work.

This separation or disentanglement of the four language functions is not an easy matter. Even to state the distinctions between them clearly—if we are to go beyond dictionary understanding—is difficult. What is thought? What is feeling? How are we to separate a writer's attitude to us (or to a hypothetical listener) from his intention? And what is an attitude or what an intention? To be able to answer these questions is not, of course, necessary for the good understanding of a phrase involving these four functions. All that is required is that the mind should actually receive each separate contributory meaning without confusion. It is not even desirable, as a rule, that it should *think of* the feeling, the tone and the intention. It is sufficient if it think of the sense. The other meanings are best received, when possible, each in its appropriate more direct and immediate manner. But when difficulty arises, thought may come to the rescue.

---

[1] But when the root and stem (in our nurseries, preparatory schools and public schools) are as we know them to be, ought we to be surprised that the flower and crown are imperfect?

§ 16. *Further Dissection.*—Thought,[1] to put these distinctions rather simply, is a direction of the receptive side of the mind, a sort of mental *pointing* to one kind of object or another. We may think *by means of* images, or words, or by other less describable means, but what is important is not the means but the result. We *turn our attention* this way or that to perceive or contemplate something. Thought thus implies something else, not itself, which is what the thought is ' of ' [2]—its object.

In contrast, a feeling does not imply an object. It is a state of the mind. It is not necessarily directed to anything, or ' of ' anything. It is true that we can speak of ' a feeling of pity ' or ' of anger ', but this is clearly a different use of the word ' of '. No confusion should arise, although sometimes we may use the word in both ways at once, as when we speak of a ' sensation of blue '. (' Feeling ', too, we use in all kinds of ways. ' I feel chilly ', ' I feel you ought to ', ' I feel doubtful '. It is the Jack-of-all-trades in the psychologist's vocabulary.)

So far as ' feeling ', in the sense I am giving it here, seems to have an object, to imply something *towards which* it is directed, it gets this direction either from an accompanying thought or from an accompanying intention. For intentions, too, have objects, though the relation of an intention to its object is not the same as that between a thought and its object. An intention is a direction of the active

---

[1] These definitions are merely those which seem to me, for my purpose here, most convenient . Like all similar definitions they can neither be right nor wrong, but only more or less serviceable. They are not identical with those I should use for other purposes, and have, in fact, used elsewhere. All that is needed is that they should be intelligible and should correspond with the facts in nature to which attention is to be directed.

[2] The kind of relation for which this word 'of' here stands is discussed at length in *The Meaning of Meaning*, Second Edition, Ch. III, and *Principles of Literary Criticism*, pp. 85-91. See also Appendix A, Note 5.

(not the receptive) side of the mind. It is a pheno-
menon of desire not of knowledge. Like a thought,
it may be more or less vague, and it is exposed to
analogous forms of error. Just as a thought may be
actually directed to something other than it professes
to be directed to, so with an intention. We may, in
fact, be trying to do something different from what
we seem to ourselves to be aiming for. (I intend by
this to indicate a different case from that common
form of error in which we persuade ourselves by
thinking that we desire something that, in fact, we
do not at all desire.)

A feeling is thus an innocent and unfallacious
thing in comparison with thoughts and intentions.
It may arise through immediate stimulation without
the intervention of either thought or intention.
Musical sounds, colours, odours, the squeaking of
quill-pens, the skins of peaches, scissor-grinding, all
these can excite feelings without our minds being
directed thereby to anything. But incipient attention
and action ordinarily accompany even the slightest
arousal of feeling. The most elaborate feelings
develop in us, however, only through thought and
intention. Thought turns the mind to certain objects
(presents them to us), or some intention is furthered
or thwarted, and feeling ensues.

There are two important senses in which we can
' understand ' the feeling of a passage. We can
either just ourselves *undergo* the same feeling or we
can *think of* the feeling. Often in witnessing a play,
for example, we think of the feelings of the char-
acters, but undergo the feeling the whole action
conveys. Obviously we can and do make mistakes
in both forms of understanding. Much the same is
true of the apprehension of tone, our appreciation
of the speaker's attitude towards us. His attitude
invites a complimentary attitude from us. So we
can either simply adopt this attitude (thereby in one

sense ' recognising ' his attitude), or think of his attitude (perceive it, thereby ' recognising ' it in quite another sense).

The actual arousal in ourselves either of the feeling or of the complimentary attitude may take place directly or through our awareness of sense or intention. An alarmed chimpanzee utters a peculiar cry which instantly throws his fellows in the group into a state of sympathetic alarm. So it is with humanity, too. The cadence of a phrase may instigate a feeling without any intermediaries. Tone, also, we seem to understand sometimes directly. Biologically, there is good reason to expect us to have this capacity. The same may be true of simple cases of intention—especially intentions which regard ourselves, but more complex cases require (as we saw in Part III, Ch. II) careful study of the sense, if grotesque mistakes are to be avoided. But here again to ' recognise ' an intention is not quite the same thing as to think of it.

§ 17. *Order.*—Innumerable cross influences and complications between these four kinds of meaning are possible, and frequently present, in what may appear a quite simple remark. A perfect understanding would involve not only an accurate direction of thought, a correct evocation of feeling, an exact apprehension of tone and a precise recognition of intention, but further it would get these contributory meanings in their right order and proportion to one another, and seize—though not in terms of explicit thought—their interdependence upon one another, their sequences and interrelations.

For the value of a passage frequently hangs upon this *internal order* among its contributory meanings. If feeling, for example, too much governs thought, or, in another case, if thought too much controls feeling, the result may be disastrous, even though thought and feeling in themselves are as good as can be. More obviously perhaps, a proper feeling, presented not in its own right or in right of the thought, but in undue deference to the reader (tone), or to cajole him (intention), will lose its sanction, unless the author saves the situation either by successfully concealing this fact or by a suitable avowal. But the exact tone of this avowal will be all-important.

It would be tedious to continue upon this aspect of meaning without giving examples, and these would take up too many of these pages. If a mind is valuable, not because it possesses sound ideas, refined feelings, social skill and good intentions, but because these admirable things stand in their proper relations to one another, we should expect this order to be represented in its utterances, and the discernment of this order to be necessary for understanding. Once again, however, this discernment is not the same thing as an *intellectual* analysis of the Total Meaning into its contributories. It is an actual formation in the receptive mind of a whole condition of feeling and awareness corresponding, in due order, to the original meaning which is being discerned. Without some discernment analysis would plainly be impossible. We have now to consider whether practice in such analysis could possibly lead to improvement in the capacity to discern.

III

§ 18. *The Teaching of English*.[1]—I am not aware that any work has been done that would test this sugges-

---

[1] Those who wish to acquaint themselves with the methods employed in schools could hardly do better than to consult the Report of the Departmental Committee appointed by the President of the Board of Education into the position of English in the educational system of England, entitled *The Teaching of English in England* (H.M. Stationery Office, 1921, 1s. 6d.); and the *Memorandum on the Teaching of English*, issued by the Incorporated

tion. Exercises in parsing and paraphrasing are not the kind of analyses I have in view. And I have not heard of any schoolmaster who may have attempted to make a *systematic* discussion of the forms of meaning and the psychology of understanding part of his teaching. I have met not a few, however, who would treat the suggestion with an amused or indignant contempt. ' What ! Fill the children's heads with a lot of abstractions ! It is quite hard enough already to get them to grasp *one* meaning—THE MEANING— let alone four or sixteen, or whatever it is ! They couldn't understand a word you were talking about.' I have been the less discouraged by such remarks, however, by the perception that some of the speakers were in precisely the same case. But even if any teacher should have wished to experiment in this way, it is difficult to see where he would have obtained his intellectual instruments from. Neither the critics nor the psychologists as yet have provided them in any serviceable form. Indeed, it is the oddest thing about language, whose history is full of odd things (and one of the oddest facts about human development) that so few people have ever sat down to reflect systematically about meaning.[1] For no daring or original steps are needed to carry our acquaintance with these matters at least a step further than the stage at which it usually remains. A little pertinacity and a certain habit of examining our intellectual and emotional instruments as we use them, is all that is required. From the point of view thus attained one would expect that our libraries would be full of works on the theory of interpretation, the

Association of Assistant Masters in Secondary Schools (Cambridge University Press, 1927, 3s. 6d.). But Mr George Sampson's *English for the English* should on no account be overlooked. It says some plain things in a plain way, with passion and with point.

[1] Cf. *The Meaning of Meaning*, Ch. II, where evidence is brought to show that the ground for our reluctance to inquire too closely into language lies deep in the early beliefs of the race.

diagnosis of linguistic situations, systematic am-
biguity and the functions of complex symbols ; and
that there would be Chairs of Significs or of General
Linguistic at all our Universities. Yet, in point of
fact, there is no respectable treatise on the theory of
linguistic interpretation in existence, and no person
whose professional occupation it is to inquire into
these questions and direct study in the matter. For
grammatical studies do not trespass upon this topic.
Surely systematic investigation of the uses of language
may be expected to improve our actual daily use
of it, at least in the same measure that the study of
plant-physiology may improve agriculture or human
physiology assist medicine or hygiene. There is no
other human activity for which theory bears so small
a proportion to practice. Even the theory of football
has been more thoroughly inquired into. And if we
ask what is most responsible for this neglect, the
answer should probably be ' Vanity '. We are with
difficulty persuaded that we have much to learn
about language, or that our understanding of it is
defective. And this illusion re-forms whenever it is
shattered, though any efficient educational procedure
ought to have no trouble in shattering it as often as
is needed. The first condition for improvement in
the adult's use of language must be to disturb this
ludicrous piece of self-deception.

§ 19. *Practical Suggestions.*—There is little room
for doubt that some progress in this direction can
be made through such experiments as the one upon
which this book is based. We are quicker to detect
our own errors when they are duplicated by our
fellows, and readier to challenge a pretension when
it is worn by another. But the logic of the situation
can be made in time too strong even for the vainest.
And when a systematic publicity is given to these
ordinary phenomena of misinterpretation that usually

remain so cunningly hidden, the stoutest self-confidence is shaken. Language is primarily a social product, and it is not surprising that the best way to display its action is through the agency of a group. The only way perhaps to change our attitude to language is to accumulate enough evidence as to the degree to which it can be misunderstood. But the evidence must not only be accumulated, it must be pressed home. The wild interpretations of others must not be regarded as the antics of incompetents, but as dangers that we ourselves only narrowly escape, if, indeed, we do. We must see in the mis-readings of others the actualisation of possibilities threatened in the early stages of our own readings. The only proper attitude is to look upon a successful interpretation, a correct understanding, as a triumph against odds. We must cease to regard a misinter-pretation as a mere unlucky accident. We must treat it as the normal and probable event.

But this distrustful attitude takes us but a little way towards a cure. We must, if possible, gain some power of diagnosis, some understanding of the risks that interpretations run, and some capacity to detect what has occurred. This may be considered too abstruse and baffling a matter, bad enough for the determined adult, and self-condemning as an educa-tional suggestion. The reply is that those who think so have probably forgotten how abstruse and baffling every subject is—until it has been studied and the best methods of learning it and of teaching it have been worked out. It would have seemed fairly absurd if somebody in the seventeenth century had suggested that the Method of Fluxions (though with an improved notation) could be profitably studied by schoolboys, and not very long ago Elementary Biology would have seemed a very odd subject to teach to children. With innumerable such in-stances behind us, we ought to hesitate before deciding that a Theory of Interpretation in some slightly more advanced and simplified form (with perhaps a new notation and nomenclature to help it) may not quite soon take the foremost place in the literary subjects of all ordinary schools. No one would pretend that the theory as it is propounded in this book is ready, as it stands, for immediate and wide application. But a very strong case can, I think, be made out, both for the need and the possibility of practical steps towards applying it. No one who considers the protocols closely, or considers with candour his own capacity to interpret complex language, will, I think, deny the need. As to the possibility, the only improvements in training that can be suggested must be based upon a closer study of meaning and of the causes of unnecessary misunderstanding.

This, then, may be made a positive recommendation, that an inquiry into language—no longer confused with the grammarian's inquiry into syntax and into comparative linguistic morphology, or with the logician's or the philologist's studies—be recognised as a vital branch of research, and treated no longer as the peculiar province of the whimsical amateur.

But it is possible without too much rashness to go further. However incomplete, tentative, or, indeed, speculative we may consider our present views on this subject, they are far enough advanced to justify some experimental applications, if not in the school period then certainly at the Universities. If it be replied that there is no time for an additional subject, we can answer by challenging the value of the time at present spent in extensive reading. A very slight improvement in the capacity to understand would so immensely increase the value of this time that part of it would be exchanged with advantage for direct training in reading. This applies quite as much to such studies as economics, psychology, political

Y

theory, theology, law or philosophy, as to literature. For though the material handled in this book has not allowed me to demonstrate it (except perhaps in ways which I should deplore), quite as many readers blunder unnecessarily over intricate argumentation and exposition as over poetry. And a direct study of interpretation here can be made quite as useful. The incidental training that every one is supposed to receive in the course of studying other subjects is too fragmentary, accidental and unsystematic to serve this purpose. Sooner or later interpretation will have to be recognised as a key-subject. *But only the actual effort to teach such a subject can reveal how it may best be taught.*

There is this to be added in favour of the subject. It enlists at once a natural interest, a cousin belonging to that family of interests which govern the crossword puzzle, acrostics and detective fiction. And a type of curiosity about words and their meanings that infants and primitive savages share with sophisticated philologists (very different from a psychological interest in the problem of meaning, and sometimes in conflict with it), can also be engaged—with discretion. Thus, although it would probably be wisest to begin with advanced classes in the Universities, it would be rash to say how far from the Elementary School we need in the end stop.

§ 20. *The Decline in Speech.*—My suggestion is that it is not enough to learn a language (or several languages), as a man may inherit a business, but that we must learn, too, how it works. And by ' learning how it works ', I do *not* mean studying its rules of syntax or its grammar, or wandering about in its lexicography — two inquiries that have hitherto diverted attention from the central issue.[1] I mean

---

[1] There is no intention here to diminish the importance of grammar, which is nowadays not overestimated by teachers, but rather to insist that grammar does not cover the whole subject of interpretation.

by ' learning how it works ', study of the kinds of
meaning that language handles, their connection
with one another, their interferences ; in brief, the
psychology of the speech-situation. The parallel
with the case of a man inheriting a business can be
followed a little further. Some generations ago,
when businesses were simpler and more separate,
the owner could carry one on by rule of thumb or
by a mere routine proficiency without troubling
himself much about general industrial or economic
conditions. It is not so now. Similarly, when man
lived in small communities, talking or reading, on
the whole, only about things belonging to his own
culture, and dealing only with ideas and feelings
familiar to his group, the mere acquisition of his
language through intercourse with his fellows was
enough to give him a good command of it. A better
command, both as speaker and listener, than any but
a few happy persons can boast to-day. For a decline
can be noticed in perhaps every department of
literature, from the Epic to the ephemeral Magazine.
The most probable reasons for this are the increased
size of our ' communities ' (if they can still be so
called, when there remains so little in common), and
the mixtures of culture that the printed word has
caused. Our everyday reading and speech now
handles scraps from a score of different cultures.
I am not referring here to the derivations of our
words—they have always been mixed—but to the
fashion in which we are forced to pass from ideas
and feelings that took their form in Shakespeare's
time or Dr Johnson's time to ideas and feelings of
Edison's time or Freud's time and back again. More
troubling still, our handling of these materials varies
from column to column of the newspaper, descending
from the scholar's level to the kitchen-maid's.

The result of this heterogeneity is that for all kinds
of utterances our performances, both as speakers (or

writers) and listeners (or readers), are worse than those of persons of similar natural ability, leisure and reflection a few generations ago. Worse in all four language functions, less faithful to the thought, less discriminating with the feeling, cruder in tone and more blurred in intention. We defend ourselves from the chaos that threatens us by stereotyping and standardising both our utterances and our interpretations. And this threat, it must be insisted, can only grow greater as world communications, through the wireless and otherwise, improve.

§ 21. *Prose.*—If this decline and its explanation are accepted, and I do not think many students either of literary history or of current sociology will deny them, the moral is clear. A more conscious and deliberate effort to master language is imperative. Since mere practice under these conditions is insufficient, we must look to theory to help us. We must make ourselves more aware of how the language we so much depend upon works. It is important to realise that these deficiencies in our use of words cripple prose quite as much as poetry. Poetry, with its direct means of conveying feelings and its metaphorical modes, suffers especially from certain types of misinterpretation, but prose, the prose of discussion, reflection and research, the prose by which we try to grapple intellectually with a too bewildering world, suffers quite as much from other confusions. Every interesting abstract word (apart from those that have been nailed down to phenomena by the experimental sciences) is inevitably ambiguous—yet we use them daily with the pathetic confidence of children. A few terms in these pages have had some of their ambiguities displayed—*meaning, belief, sincerity, sentimentality, rhythm, understanding,* and so forth—but scores of others which deserve the same treatment have been used in apparent innocence,

and no fully satisfactory account of poetry can be
forthcoming until their ambiguities have been ex-
posed.

But a more considered technique of discussion has
a wider importance. Our opinions about poetry do
not much differ in type from our opinions about
many other topics ; and all such opinions are very
liable to ambiguity. The methods I have here tried
to apply to critical questions, have to be applied to
questions of morals, political theory, logic, economics,
metaphysics, religion and psychology, both for pur-
poses of research and in higher education. Only by
comparing a given opinion, or its verbal formula if
you like, as it is applied by many minds to many
different matters, do we get an opportunity to
observe its ambiguities and analyse them systematic-
ally. But this is an opportunity that we need no
little hardihood to embrace. Dread of the bewilder-
ment that might ensue if we recognised and investi-
gated the inevitable ambiguity of almost all verbal
formulæ is probably a strong reason for our general
reluctance to admit it. For this is one of the most
unpopular truths that can be uttered.

Therefore, we hide it away as often as is possible,
and make the most of those occasions in which the
ambiguity of our speech is reduced to the minimum.
So long as we stay in the realm of things which can
be counted, weighed and measured, or pointed to,
or actually seen with the eyes or touched by the
fingers, all goes well. And beyond this realm, such
things as can be inferred from observations of
measurable and touchable things, as the physicist
infers his molecules and atoms, such things lend
themselves to unambiguous discussion. And in yet a
third region, the region of ordinary conversation,
with its vague meanings that are ruled by social
conventions—talk about sport, literature, politics,
news, personalities and the rest—we manage moder-

ately well, because our meanings are so large and
vague that they can hardly help engaging with one
another. But let such conversation improve (or
degenerate, the point of view varies), let an attempt
at precision be made—let the question be mooted
whether so and so really is an ' intelligent ' or
' intuitive ' person, and in what his intelligence or
intuitiveness precisely consists ; or the question
whether it really is ' right ' or not to pay different
kinds of work with different wages ; or the question
whether this or that poem is ' romantic ' ; or the
question whether this or that composition is poetry ;
or almost any of the questions discussed in these
pages—and another state of affairs soon appears.
Before long we begin ' mistaking one another's
points ', ' failing to understand one another's posi-
tions ', ' seeing. no justification whatever for one
another's assertions ', ' quite misconceiving one an-
other's arguments ', ' utterly misrepresenting per-
fectly obvious matters of fact ', ' introducing bare-
faced equivocations into the discussion ', ' saying
things that no honest and sensible person could
possible mean ', and generally behaving like a mixed
assembly of half-wits and scamps. The full situation,
however, only develops if we are serious, sincere and
pertinacious persons who are determined to ' see the
discussion through to the end '—the only end which
such discussions unfortunately can as yet attain.

Ordinarily some degree of mental youth is needed
if the full harvest of mutual misunderstanding is to
be garnered. More mature intelligences tend to
retreat at an earlier stage and reserve the more exact
statement of their opinions for other occasions. Even
then, at a course of lectures, for example, or before
the pages of a monograph, the ironical student of
communication finds occasion to indulge his per-
verted tastes. Let the listeners or the readers be
suitably questioned, and again the old story has to

be told. There can be few who have ever attempted
by word or pen to expound any general subject with
precision who have not had ample opportunity to
admit that the satisfaction they gained from saying
what they had to say must be offset by the pain of
contemplating the other things which they have been
supposed to have said.

If I am overrating these difficulties it is to a less
degree than they are customarily and conventionally
underrated. They increase in proportion as our
effort towards wide and precise communication in-
creases, and it is very necessary to find a means of
avoiding them. I have written at length about this
necessity elsewhere, and will not labour the point
further here. The escape does not lie through the
avoidance of abstract discussion or the relegation
of such matters to specialists, for it is precisely the
specialists who most indulge in mutual misunder-
standing (cf. *The Meaning of Meaning*, Chs. VI
and VIII). It does not lie in stricter definition of
leading terms and a more rigid adherence to them—
this is the ' militarist ' solution of the problem raised
by the fact that people's minds do not all work alike.
It fails, because the other people cannot really be so
easily persuaded to adopt our point of view. At the
worst they will *seem* to. The only way out does, in
fact, lie in the opposite direction, not in greater
rigidity but in greater suppleness. The mind that
can shift its view-point and still keep its orientation,
that can carry over into quite a new set of definitions
the results gained through past experience in other
frameworks, the mind that can rapidly and without
strain or confusion perform the systematic trans-
formations required by such a shift, is the mind of
the future. It may be objected that there are very
few such minds. But have we ever attempted to
train them ? The whole linguistic training we
receive at present is in the other direction, towards

supplying us with one or other of a number of frameworks of doctrine into which we are taught to force all the material we would handle.

This omnipresent ambiguity of abstract terms, when we reflect upon it, may well appear to present insuperable difficulties for the speculative apprehension of the world. Even the fundamental terms by which we might seek to define and limit these equivocations betray us. For *mind, cause, thing, event, time, space* and even *datum*, all on inspection reveal varieties of possible and actual meanings. As analysis proceeds, any coherent intellectual outlook will derive more and more from the order we can maintain among distinctions that become increasingly abstract and intangible, and therefore more word-dependent. With a confused or self-conflicting outlook it is not easy to live well, but many good minds are not in health to-day without some general world-picture.

This again, unless we can call in the theory of meanings to our help, is a condition which is more likely to grow worse than to improve, as the conceptions of present-day physics and psychology pass into the stream of general speculation. But certainly for most types of discussion and reflection the theory of meaning can help us. By pointing out the systematic character of much ambiguity or by tracing the process of abstraction, for example, by preparing us to distinguish between those ' philosophical ' utterances, which are really expressions of feeling, and statements that claim to be true, and by accustoming us to look not for one meaning but for a number of related meanings whenever we encounter troublesome words. And even for this puzzling branch of the study of interpretation, exercises not too difficult for practical application in education can be devised.

It may be thought that these equivocations among

abstractions betray only philosophers, amateur or professional, and that, therefore, they are of no great moment. But it is not so. One has only to glance at any controversy proceeding in the correspondence columns of the weeklies and watch the proceedings of men of eminence and intelligence at grips, for example, with the distinction between Prose and Poetry, or between Rhythm and Metre, to see clearly that even in simple discussions a better general technique for handling two or more definitions of the same word is badly needed. Without such a technique, confusion, or at best narrowness of outlook, is unavoidable. The habit of beginning a statement with ' Poetry *is* so and so ', instead of with, ' I am defining " poetry " as " so and so " ', constantly stultifies even the most intelligent and determined efforts towards mutual understanding. It would be interesting to know how many persons who interest themselves in these matters can carry even three mutually incompatible definitions of ' poetry ' in their heads simultaneously. And, at least, three definitions would be needed for a satisfactory discussion of the differences between Prose and Poetry. Yet the trick of analysing them and the effort of memory required to carry them over intact are not more difficult than those involved in mental arithmetic. The difference that we all notice is grounded in the fact that we receive no systematic training in multiple definition, and so the required attitude towards words is hardly ever developed. At the best it remains a temporary, instable, precarious attitude, and we succumb easily to the temptation of supposing our ' adversary ' to be in obvious error when, in fact, he may merely be using words for the moment in another sense from our own.[1] To the eye of an intelligence perfectly emancipated from

[1] This is not to say that error is not frequent. But we must know what is being said before we can convict it of error.

words, most of our discussions would appear like the manœuvres of three dimensional beings who for some reason believed themselves to exist only in two dimensions.

§ 22. *Critical Fog.*—Partly for this reason our current reflective attitudes to poetry contain an undue proportion of bewilderment. It is regarded too often as a mystery. There are good and evil mysteries ; or rather there is mystery and mystery-mongering. That is mysterious which is inexplicable, or ultimate in so far as our present means of inquiry cannot explain it. But there is a spurious form of mysteriousness which arises only because our explanations are confused or because we overlook or forget the significance of what we have already understood. And there are many who think that they are serving the cause of poetry by exploiting these difficulties that every complex explanation presents. They are perhaps under the impression that ' to explain ' must mean ' to explain away '. But this is to show a poor respect for poetry. Since we no longer receive by tradition any proper introduction to it, explanations, when explanation is possible, are needed. At present, gross general misunderstandings are certainly poetry's worst enemies. And these confusions have been encouraged by those who like to regard the whole matter, and every detail of it, as an incomprehensible mystery— because they suppose that this is a ' poetic ' way of looking at it. But muddled-mindedness is in no respectable sense ' poetic ', though far too many persons seem to think so. What can be explained about poetry can be separated from what cannot ; and at innumerable points an explanation can help us both to understand what kind of thing poetry in general is, and to understand particular passages. As to the truly mysterious aspect of poetry—that ' leaning of the will ' in virtue

of which we choose what we shall accept or reject—
we are not likely to approach an explanation within
any foreseeable period. And when the human intellect
does reach a stage at which this problem is solved,
there will perhaps be no need to fear this or any
other result of investigation. We ought by then to
have learned enough about our minds to do with
them what we will.[1]

§ 23. *Subjectivity.*—This distinction between what
can and what cannot be explained is not quite equiva-
lent to the distinction between what can and what
cannot be argued about profitably in criticism. A
difference in opinion or taste may be due to a mis-
understanding of the meaning of a passage—on one
side of the dispute or both. But it may be due to an
opposition of temperaments, to some difference in
the direction of our interests. If so, discussion may
perhaps make this difference clearer, but it is hardly
likely to bridge it. We must admit that when our
interests are developing in opposed directions we
cannot agree in our ultimate valuations and choices.
Unless we are to become most undesirably
standardised, differences of opinion about poetry
must continue—differences, not only between in-
dividuals, but between successive phases in the growth
of the same personality. As any attitude is genuinely

---

[1] It is instructive to conjecture what would be the major interests
of such an infinitely plastic mind. Being, by hypothesis, able to
become any kind of mind at will, the question 'What kind of mind
shall I choose to be?' would turn into an experimental matter ; and
the process of surveying and comparing the possibilities of experience
from all the relevant different 'personalities' (with varying degrees
of dominance of the intellectual, emotional, and active components
perhaps, and with different degrees of projection, self-awareness, etc.)
would occupy much attention. Our present critical activities would
compare with those of such a mind much as the physical conceptions
and experimental technique of an Aristotle compare with these of an
Eddington. We are still far from a General Theory of Critical
Relativity, but at least we are reaching the point of knowing how
much we shall soon come to need one.

and enthusiastically taken up, it inevitably appears to be the right attitude, and the perception that accompanies it seems sagacious, penetrating and illuminating. Until, for obscure reasons, the mind changes, finds itself with different interests and a new outlook. All emotional development, in an active mind that retains any remembrance of its past, must appear a jerky and inconsequent process. What will be thought or felt next year seems uncertain, for what seemed fundamental last year seems to-day hardly worth notice. This is not a description of the neurotic temperament, but of the vigilant, living, growing individual.

But this shifting, because living, basis for all literary responses does *not* force us, as some intellectual defeatists, misled by the word ' subjective ', may suppose, to an agnostic or indifferentist position. Every response is ' subjective ' in the sense that it is a psychological event determined by the needs and resources of a mind. But this does not imply that one is not better than another. We may also grant that what is good for one mind may not be good for another in a different condition—with different needs and in a different situation. Nevertheless the fundamental question of values, the better or worse, does not lose any of its significance. We have only shifted it to a clearer ground. Instead of an illusory problem about values supposed to inhere in poems which, after all, are only sets of words—we have a real problem about the relative values of different states of mind, about varying forms, and degrees, of order in the personality. ' If you look deeply into the ultimate essentials of this art, you will find that what is called " the flower " has no separate existence. Were it not for the spectator who reads into the performance a thousand excellences, there would be no " flower " at all. The Sutra says, " Good and ill are one ; villainy and honesty are of like kind ".

Indeed, what standard have we whereby to discern good from bad ? We can only take what suits the need of the moment and call it good.'[1] One man's need is not another's, yet the question of values still remains. What we take we do indeed judge according to ' the need of the moment ', but the value of this momentary need itself is determined by its place among and its transactions with our other needs. And the order and precedence among our needs incessantly changes for better or worse.

Our traditional ideas as to the values of poetry—given us automatically if poetry is set apart from life, or if poems are introduced to us from the beginning as either good or bad, as ' poetry ' or ' not poetry '—misrepresent the facts and raise unnecessary difficulties. It is less important to like ' good ' poetry and dislike ' bad ', than to be able to use them both as a means of ordering our minds. It is the quality of the reading we give them that matters, not the correctness with which we classify them. For it is quite possible to like the ' wrong ' poems and dislike the ' right ' ones for reasons which are excellent. Here our educational methods are glaringly at fault, creating a shibboleth situation that defeats its purpose. So long as we feel that the judgment of poetry is a social ordeal, and that our real responses to it may expose us to contempt, our efforts, even after passing the gate, will not take us far. But most of our responses are not real, are not our own, and this is just the difficulty.

§ 24. *Humility.*—If the specimens of contemporary judgments given in Part II have no other uses, they will, at least, do us this service : that those who have read carefully through them will be for a little while after less impressionable by literary

---

[1] Seami Motokiyo (A.D. 1363-1444). Quoted from Waley, *The Nō Plays of Japan*, p. 22.

judgments, however confidently or trenchantly expressed, less dogmatic, less uncharitable, less subject also to floating opinion. ' I know not how it is ', wrote Matthew Arnold, ' but their commerce with the ancients appears to me to produce, in those who constantly practise it, a steadying and composing effect upon their judgment, not of literary works only, but of men and events in general. They are like persons who have had a very weighty and impressive experience : they are more truly than others under the empire of facts, and more independent of the language current among those with whom they live '. It would be absurd to compare the effects upon our minds of the masterpieces of antiquity with those that an attentive scrutiny of these scraps of literary opinion may produce. But there is an obverse aspect to every human achievement. And there is in the inner history of every opinion, if we can examine it and compare it with the other opinions it so narrowly missed becoming, a spring of ironical comedy. The confluence of many such rivulets might well have both a cleansing and a ' steadying and composing effect upon the judgment '. We might become less easily imposed upon by our fellows and by ourselves.

Some discipline that will preserve us from these twin dangers we badly need. As the finer parts of our emotional tradition relax in the expansion and dissolution of our communities, and as we discover how far out of our intellectual depth the flood-tide of science is carrying us—so far that not even the giants can still feel bottom—we shall increasingly need every strengthening discipline that can be devised. If we are neither to swim blindly in schools under the suggestion of fashion, nor to shudder into paralysis before the inconceivable complexity of existence, we must find means of exercising our power of choice. The critical reading of poetry is an arduous discipline ; few exercises reveal to us more clearly the limitations under which, from moment to moment, we suffer. But, equally, the immense extension of our capacities that follows a summoning of our resources is made plain. The lesson of all criticism is that we have nothing to rely upon in making our choices but ourselves. The lesson of good poetry seems to be that, when we have understood it, in the degree in which we can order ourselves, we need nothing more.

APPENDIX A

1. *Further Notes on Meaning.*

Function 2 (feeling) and Function 3 (tone) are probably more primitive than either Function 1 (sense), or the more deliberate explicit forms of Function 4 (intention). Originally language may have been almost purely *emotive ;* that is to say a means of expressing feelings about situations (the danger cry), a means of expressing interpersonal attitudes (cooing, growling, etc.), and a means of bringing about concerted action (compare the rhythmical grunts that a number of individuals will utter while pulling together at some heavy object). Its use for *statement*, as a more or less neutral means of representing states of affairs, is probably a later development. But this later development is more familiar to us now than the earlier forms, and we tend, when we reflect upon language, to take this use as the fundamental use. Hence perhaps in a large degree our difficulty in distinguishing clearly between them. And when we are expressing feeling and tone in comparative purity we are usually not in a mood to make abstract inquiries into our uses of language. This is another difficulty.

If Sir Richard Paget's recent views are accepted, sense (the descriptive indication of states of affairs) would however be very primitive in language indeed. If we suppose, that is, that a great deal of speech from the beginning has been an equivalent—by means of gestures (movements) made with the organs of speech— for descriptive gestures earlier made by the hands. Certainly we must admit that the sounds and movements of many words and phrases do seem even still to correspond significantly with their sense. And this correspondence probably gives them an important power of bringing their sense concretely before our minds, of making us 'realise' what they mean—this realisation, however, being very largely an awakening of feelings.

In much poetry—as has often been remarked—language tends to return towards a more primitive condition : a word like *iron*, for example, exciting, in poetry, a set of feelings rather than thoughts of the physical properties of that material, and a word like *spirit* evoking certain attitudes rather than ontological reflections. Hence Function 1, as we know it in its developed form in strict prose discussion, frequently appears to lapse in poetry. Or it returns there to that vaguer kind of reference by which we speak of *This* or *That*, not as objects having the properties by which, if challenged, we might in some science define them, but as objects of a kind towards which we have certain attitudes and feelings, or objects that have this or that effect upon us. This vagueness is very frequently misunderstood in poetry. It is due to a replacement of scientific classifications by emotive classifications. We make use of external properties in place of internal properties—the effects produced by objects on us, instead of qualities inherent in the objects. But these emotive classifications are in their own way very strict and definite. Thus incoherence in the thought of poetry, though it cannot be demonstrated by the same means as incoherence in a logical exposition, can be inquired into once we have grasped the principle at work.

But thought governed by emotive classifications is still thought, and with words so used Function 1 (sense), though not in the most obvious way, may still be dominant. More puzzling situations arise when the whole aspect of words as conveying thought is either abrogated or subordinated. Let us take the case of complete abrogation of thought first. 'How do you do ? ' as uttered on most occasions is an excellent example. It has ceased to be an inquiry and become a social ritual, its function being to adjust the tone of intercourse between two people. It is analogous on a small scale to the spirit-calming ceremonies with which the Japanese begin some of their greater rites. So is it with 'Dear Sir ' and ' Yours sincerely '. To a less degree, weather-talk and much conversation about current affairs fill the same need. In poetry, Function 2, rather than Function 3, is usually responsible for this abrogation, this reduction of what looks like sense to nonsense. The ' meaningless ' refrains of many ballads are the obvious example—subtler forms of *Hurrah !* and *Alas !* More usually the sense is *negligible* rather than nonsense— such that though a scheme of sense could be given to the words it is not sufficiently relevant to make the effort worth while. Much diction in songs is of this kind, and it is not a demerit.

Subordination (as opposed to abrogation) of sense is nearly omnipresent in poetry. The poet makes a statement about something, not in order that the statement may be examined and reflected upon, but in order to evoke certain feelings, and when these are evoked the use of the statement is exhausted. It is idle and irrelevant to consider the statement further. This is a hard saying for those whose habit it is to look for inspiring messages in poetry, but this habit frequently leads to a profanation of poetry.

The frequent independence of poetry from what it *says* (Function 1) is clearly shown in many odes, elegies and celebrations. Perhaps very little that is said in Dryden's *Ode to the Pious Memory of the Accomplished Young Lady, Mrs Anne Killigrew*, is true ; perhaps Dryden himself had in fact no such opinion of these accomplishments as he there expressed. Perhaps Milton was not thinking very closely about Edward King in composing *Lycidas*. Perhaps Burns when writing *Ae Fond Kiss* was only too glad to part from the lady for whom it was written. Perhaps neither Shelley nor Victor Hugo deserved in fact half what Swinburne wrote about them. But whether what was written was good or bad is unaffected by these doubts. The identity of the addressee is irrelevant to the poetry *as poetry*. As biography or as criticism it would be all important. This is not to say that a certain amount of knowledge about the addressees may not be *useful* to the reader in understanding the poet, but it ought not to be used to condemn or to exalt the poem. These remarks apply evidently to some of the comments on *Poems IX* and *XI*.

Taking now the converse case—when Function 2 is subordinated to Function 1. Whatever noble, elevated, moral or otherwise admirable sentiments may be explicitly stated by the poet, they are clearly not to be taken *as proof* of his lofty poetic stature. The reception of *Poem I* and some of the comments on *Poems V* and *XI* may help to preserve us from this danger. It is easy to insist that our feelings are interesting, it is less easy to prove it. It is easier to describe them than to present them. For if we are to present them, a natural not an artificial form of utterance must be found. We must not only state our feelings but express them. And the fact that a poet is *stating* them is almost in itself suspicious—at least it is with much Georgian verse of the anecdotal nature-description kind. A poet who is conscious of his feelings in a form in which he can describe them and analyse them is in some danger. Another step and he is mentally inside out, as so many contemporary intellectual emotionalists are. There is a big difference between controlling and conveying feelings and talking about them.

2. *Intention.*

Intention may be thought a more puzzling function than the others. We may admit the distinctions between sense, feeling and tone, but consider that between them they cover the uses of language, and that to speak of intention as a fourth additional function is to confuse matters. There *is* some justification for this. None the less there are plenty of cases, especially in drama, in dramatic lyrics, in fiction which has a dramatic structure, in

z *

some forms of irony, in writings of the detective type—whether of the order of Conan Doyle or of Henry James—when this additional function may assist our analysis. Where conjecture, or the weight of what is left *unsaid*, is the writer's weapon, it seems unnatural to bring this under the heading of sense (or statement). The false trail or misleading hope may be due not to anything the writer has said or to any feelings he has expressed, but merely to the order and degree of prominence that he has given to various parts of his composition. And when we have admitted this, it is no long step to admitting that the form or construction or development of a work may frequently have a significance that is not reducible to any combination of our other three functions. This significance is then the author's intention.

But there is a better way of showing how constantly intention intervenes. It controls the relations among themselves of the other three functions. We have seen that to read poetry successfully we must constantly distinguish the case where sense is autonomous from the case when it is in subjection to feeling. Sometimes the sense is the most important thing in a line of verse, and our feelings take their quality from it. Verses 1–5 of *Poem X* may be instanced. What is said there, the sense, is the source of the feeling. But with verse 6, distortion, in the form of exaggeration, begins. Feeling is subordinating sense to its own ends. The distortion, provided we realise to some degree what is happening, then produces other reciprocal distortions in the feeling. These alternations in the precedence of sense and feeling we apprehend as a rule automatically, by an acquired tact.[1] We may not explicitly remark them. If we had to describe them we might perhaps say that one verse was ' serious ', another ' not quite serious ' or ' extravagant '. But we do certainly interpret them differently, and this subtle, extremely delicate variation in our modes of interpreting different passages of poetry is what I hope to bring out.

Another example is provided by those worthy people who refuse to leave any utterance of Hamlet or Lear, however ' distraught ', without extracting some recondite philosophical import. Any indication of sense can be compared to a man pointing to something ; and this question can be put by asking whether we are to look at what he is pointing to or concentrate our attention on his gestures. For example, in Pope's *Elegy to the Memory of an Unfortunate Lady*, the poet's eye is very plainly on himself and on his reader rather than on the imaginary

---

[1] Or as some would say, using a word which now has in these connections only an obfuscatory value, 'instinctively.'

object, and the reader should follow him in this, otherwise such lines as

> So flew the soul to its congenial place,
> *Nor left one virtue to redeem her race.*

and

> Cold is the breast *which warmed the world before,*

> Thus, if eternal Justice *rules the ball,*
> Thus shall your wives and thus your children fall ;
> On all the line a sudden vengeance waits,
> And frequent hearses shall besiege your gates . . .

ought certainly to produce effects very unlike those which Pope intended. But examples are innumerable. Whether we proceed from the sense to the feeling or *vice versa*, or take them simultaneously, as often we must, may make a prodigious difference in the effect, altering not only the internal structure of the Total Meaning, but even such apparently unconnected features as the sound of the words.

Of this last fact ' vaporous vitiate air ', the much disputed phrase from the last verse of *Poem XI*, may serve as an instance. What may appear to a first reading as a displeasing and affected piece of mouthing, may—as the first strain put upon the sense by the feeling relaxes, and the return effect of the notion of spiritual climates upon the feeling develops—come to seem not only natural but even inevitable as sound. It may, however, be more obvious that *Poem I* was interpreted by some readers primarily in terms of sense and by others primarily in terms of feeling, the divisions of opinion as to its merits being also determined by the way in which its tone was interpreted. The protocols of *Poem VI* supply further excellent material for tracing these variations. Sense, tone and feeling being there very exquisitely adjusted, clumsy reading has evident effects upon the apprehension both of meaning and form.

3. *Æsthetic Adjectives.*

These æsthetic or ' projectile ' adjectives and their corresponding abstract substantives raise several extraordinarily interesting questions. I can only indicate them here for even an outline discussion would require a whole volume. In so far as they register the projection of a feeling into an object they carry a double function at least and give rise to a systematic series of ambiguities.[1] We may take such a word as *beauty* either as standing for some inherent property (or set of properties) in

---

[1] Hence arise those special difficulties in discussion labelled in *The Meaning of Meaning* (Ch. VI) as due to the Utraquistic Subterfuge.

the object said to be beautiful ; or as standing for an emotive classification (*i.e.*, placing the object in the class of things that affect us in a certain way) ; or, thirdly, as expressing the occurrence of a certain feeling in the speaker. Obviously the word may very well be doing all three simultaneously. Which of them has priority in any case may depend upon the degree of reflection and the direction of sophistication in the speaker.

It may make this linguistic situation clearer if we compare three examples that show different degrees of projection. Let us take *pleasant* first. Few would maintain that all pleasant things possess any peculiar property in common, except that of causing (under suitable conditions) pleasure in suitable persons. The tendency to projection here—though the grammatical form supports it—is slight. We all agree that when we say ' this is pleasant ' we might equally well say ' this is pleasing ' (to me, as I am, and to folk like me in these conditions), without any consciousness of a change of meaning. And correspondingly we agree easily that what may be pleasant on one occasion may not be pleasant on another or to a different person.

Now consider *pretty*. If we say that something or someone is pretty, we do seem to be doing more than merely saying that we are affected by it or her in a certain fashion. Pretty things do seem to have some property in common that is perhaps peculiar to them, though it is extremely hard to discover what it can be that can belong in common to landscapes, kittens, book-bindings, geisha and tunes, and to nothing that is not pretty. Moreover, what seems pretty as a rule goes on seeming pretty to us. If the thing remains the same itself, no very obvious changes in the mere conditions, provided we can still attend to it, suffice to make it seem no longer pretty. All this shows that the projection in this case is much more pronounced and more stable. None the less, if challenged, few people would maintain that there is in fact an objective, inherent quality or property, namely prettiness, which belongs to certain things quite apart from their effects upon our minds, a quality that, as it were, independently *makes* them pretty. The very termination -ness (compare *pleasantness, prettiness, loveliness, ugliness, attractiveness*), is, perhaps, a slight indication too, but not one to be relied upon, of the middle stage at which the projection remains.

A further degree of projection is found with *beautiful*. Half at least of the literature of æsthetics is a proof that we find it exceedingly difficult not to believe that some simple or complex property does in fact reside in all the things—however different in other respects they may be—that we correctly call beautiful. And this inherent property, *Beauty*, is, we tend to think, independent of any effects upon our minds or other minds and unaffected by changes in us. Similarly, though with some slight but curious difference, with *sublime* (*sublimity*) and *holy* (*holiness*). Four stages of relative naïvety or sophistication may be remarked in our handling of this word *beauty*. The least sophisticated view assumes that, of course, things are beautiful or not *in themselves*, just as they are blue or not blue, square or not square A less naïve view plunges to the other extreme and regards beauty as 'altogether subjective', as perhaps merely equivalent to 'pleasing to the higher senses'. A still more sophisticated view reconstructs again—as a counterblast to this 'subjective view'— a doctrine of real inherent objective tertiary qualities, giving it a complex philosophical and logical scaffolding and perhaps venturing some provisional formula as a description of this property—'unity in variety', 'logical necessity in structure', 'proportions easeful to the apprehension', and so forth. Lastly a perhaps still more sophisticated view reduces this formula to something so vague and general that it ceases to be useful as an instrument for investigating differences between what is said to be beautiful and what is not. For example, if we define *beautiful*, as I suggest for this purpose we might, as 'having properties such that it arouses, under suitable conditions, tendencies to self-completion in the mind' (or something more elaborate of this kind), *beauty* ceases to be the name of any *ascertainable* property in things. It is still objective, it is still the property in virtue of which the beautiful thing does arouse these tendencies. But we cannot take these beautiful things and look to see what they have in common, for in fact they need have nothing *in common* (if the conditions are dissimilar) beyond this purely abstract property of 'being such as to arouse, etc.' In each case there will be some account that can be given as to how the thing is beautiful, but no *general* account will be possible. (Compare the case of the word *lovable*. In each case we can perhaps point to characters which explain why the thing is loved, but we cannot give any general account of the common and peculiar properties that all lovable things possess—those they all share and which nothing not lovable possesses.)

This last view clearly does away with our traditional notion of Beauty as an august embodied principle or power inherent in beautiful things, and those who hold it will be thought by many to be cut off—'by their barren and materialistic logic-chopping'? —from a natural source of inspiration. (Similarly materialists are frequently supposed to be debarred from the appreciation and use of spiritual values.) But this is a result of a mistaken theory of poetry and a confusion of poetry with science. It brings us back to the point at which we started—the use of 'projectile' language.

When we utter the word *Beauty* or when we read it, we may, as we have seen, be making any one of at least three distinct uses. We may be using it for either of two kinds of senses, or to express feeling. Whatever view we take *philosophically* as to the status of beauty as an inherent objective quality or as to the process of projection, we are *not* (this is a fact of observation not a theoretical position) necessarily deprived of our capacity to use it as though it stood for such an objective quality, and to enjoy all the advantages that derive from this usage. It is difficult for those who have long been accustomed to the idea of beauty as a projected quality to recall the chill and dismay with which a first acquaintance with this account may be received. Yet much of the opposition to psychological æsthetics has this emotional origin, and it is important to insist that the first numbing effect wears off. (Similarly with those who feel that it is more ' poetic ' to regard poetry as a mystic, inexplicable power ; the feeling can be retained after the obscurantism has been rejected.) Even though we hold firmly that there is no inherent general quality ' beauty ' we can still use the word as though there were. The effects upon our feelings will be the same, once the initial shock of the mental operation by which we recognise the fact of projection has passed away. And it is the same with all the rest of our projectile language. Happily—for otherwise the effect of investigation here would be not only to destroy poetry but to wreck our whole emotional life.

In some minds, perhaps some such danger is to be feared—minds in which too close a dependence of feelings upon notions has developed, minds without sufficient intellectual suppleness, and cut off from the natural sources of emotion and attitude. But this problem has been discussed in Chapters V and VII.

4. *Rhythm and Prosody.*

In a recent authoritative work (*What is Rhythm?* by E. A. Sonnenschein) the following definition of rhythm is recommended:

' Rhythm is that property of a sequence of events in time which produces in the mind of an observer the impression of proportion between the durations of the several events or groups of events of which the sequence is composed.' (p. 16.)

A serious objection may be brought against this type of definition. The property so defined may not be an *internal property* of the sequence at all. The impression of proportion may be due to no character of the object which is regarded as rhythmical but to some other cause. As some of the phenomena of opium, nitrous oxide and hashish dreams show, a single stimulus may give rise to a most definite impression of rhythm. And, to take a less extreme example, it is a common phenomenon, noticeable constantly in connection with verse, for the rhythm attributed to a sequence to be determined less by the configuration of the sequence than by other factors external to it—in poetry the meanings of the words. It may be granted that usually when a rhythm is attributed to a sequence by some observer ' some proportion between the durations of the several events in the sequence ' can be found. But it is doubtful, to say the least, whether study of the details of these proportions is very useful if the ' impressions of proportion ' they produce are only in part due to them.

Professor Sonnenschein seems himself to go some way towards admitting this when he says (p. 35) : ' What we are concerned with in all manifestations of rhythm is not so much a physical fact as a psychological fact—*i.e.*, the impression made by the physical fact upon the mind of man through the organs of sense '. My objection is that he does not make the fact we are concerned with psychological enough. The processes we have discussed under the heading—The Apprehension of Meaning—enter, I believe, as important factors in the formation of the impression, though, of course, they do not wholly determine it. The impression is a compromise.

In any case it is surely the relations of the ascribed rhythm to the meaning (in its various forms) that is of interest to the student of poetry, not the characters of the ascribed rhythms in this respect or that. And though these relations can be felt (they are, of course, psychological relations, correspondences between different systems of activity in the mind), and in all good reading of good poetry they are felt continuously, it is hard to see how any description of the characters of rhythms, such as prosodists could supply, could be of any assistance in the matter. To suppose that we can ever *intellectually observe* the relation of a rhythm to a meaning in any example that is poetically interesting, and with the degree of nicety that would be required if our observations were to be useful or provide a basis for a scientific generalisation, is, I believe, to be unwarrantably optimistic. For apart from the difficulties of measuring the ascribed rhythm, we should need also in some way to measure the meaning.

To study rhythm in poetry apart from meaning, since meaning is undoubtedly the controlling factor in the poet's choice of the rhythmical effects he will produce, seems from this point of view an enterprise of doubtful value. None the less, certain *general* effects of rhythms, mentioned in *Principles*, Ch. XVII, seem worth attention. And as a means of indicating to absent persons how certain verses may be read, prosody has an obvious function. But even this will soon perhaps be made obsolete by wireless and the gramophone. And to distinguish the differences in the

rhythms to be ascribed, for example, to different types of blank
verse is, of course, a valuable accomplishment ; but whether
instruction in prosody can really enable anyone to do this who
could not do it without (or with only the most obvious notation)
is also questionable. If prosody is only a means of directing
a reader's attention to the formal features of verse, then clearly
it long ago reached a stage of development sufficient for this
purpose, and further researches are not required. But if it is
hoped that some correlation may be established, we may ask
' Between what is this correlation to hold and what reasons are
there to expect it ? ' This question seems to have been strangely
neglected, and there has perhaps here been a confusion between
the two senses of *law*. Indeed it seems possible that the terribly
laborious studies of modern prosodists may in time to come be
placed among the curious displays of misdirected intelligence
and great ability that the history of science so often presents.

' Cette page nuira de plus d'une façon au malheureux auteur,'
as Stendhal was fond of saying. There may however be other
persons as much in need of instruction as the writer—instruction
as to the precise goal or purport of the labours of so many
distinguished men.

5. *Visual Images.*

The word ' visualise ' has been given a metaphorical extension
so that it is often used for ' to think of something in *any* concrete
fashion '. There is no harm in this, of course, *unless* it leads us
to suppose that we cannot think concretely without using visual
or other images. But in fact it is possible, for many people, to
think with the utmost particularity and concreteness and yet to
make no use of visual images at all. Sometimes other, non-visual,
imagery is being used instead. Many people think they are
using visual imagery when, in fact, if they examined the matter
more closely, they would discover that kinæsthetic imagery of
movements of the eyeballs has taken its place. But it is also
possible to think concretely without any imagery of any kind, or
at least (for this point is disputed) without imagery corresponding
at all closely to what is being thought of. (This point is not
disputed.) The imagery we use (if we do use any) may be very
sketchy, vague and incoherent, yet our thought may be rich,
detailed and coherent.[1]

---

[1] Dogmatic assertions to the contrary are common. 'Thus in
reading poetry one of the first necessities is to visualise, to see clearly
every picture as it is presented by the poet. Without visualising the
poet's words the reader in no sense has before him that which the
poet had at the time of writing. Nor can he in any full sense share

Confusion and prejudice on this point are chiefly due to a too simple idea of what is necessary for mental *representation*. Images, we may think (and traditionally psychologists, too, have thought) must be required, if absent sights and sounds and so forth are to be represented in our minds ; because images are the only things sufficiently *like* sights and sounds and so forth to represent them. But this is to confuse representation with resemblance. In order that *a* may represent *A* it is not necessary for *a* to resemble *A* or be a copy of *A* in any respect whatever. It is enough if *a* has the same effect upon us, in some respect, as *A*. Obviously *a* and *A* here have both the effect of making us utter the same sound if we read them out—and they have other effects in common.

This is in outline the way in which words represent things. In order that a word should represent a thing—the word *cow* represents a cow—it is not necessary that it should call up an image of a cow that is like a cow ; it is enough if it excite any considerable set of those feelings, notions, attitudes, tendencies to action and so forth that the actual perception of a cow may excite.[1] This clearly is a more general sense of ' representation ' which includes ' representation ' in the sense of ' being a copy ' as a special case.

Words on the whole *now*, however it may have been in the

his emotion.' J. G. Jennings *Metaphor in Poetry*, p. 82. The writer's intention here is excellent, we must read poetry receptively, but his knowledge of psychology is insufficient.

[1] The most fundamental sense of representation (or meaning) is, I believe, different from this, which may, however, serve sufficiently well to indicate the case against the copy theory of representation. (And against Wittgenstein's principle, for example.) What is given above is, roughly, Mr Bertrand Russell's (1921) view of representation. *The Analysis of Mind*, pp. 210, 244. My own view is that a word represents a thing, not by having similar effects to the thing, but by having things of that kind among its causes. His view, in brief, was in terms of ' causal efficacy,' mine in terms of causal origin. In his *Outline of Philosophy* (1927), however, Mr Russell combines both theories (p. 56) with a distinction between *active* meaning, that of a man uttering the word, and *passive* meaning, that of a man hearing the word. He suggests that Mr Ogden and myself in writing *The Meaning of Meaning* neglected passive meaning. I think this is a misunderstanding, but we do consider active meaning the more fundamental of the two, since it explains much in passive meaning and because consideration of it throws more light upon the growth and development of language. Incidentally we cannot accept Mr Russell's summary of our view : ' It says that a word and its meaning have the same causes '. It says, on the contrary, that the meaning is the cause of the word, in a not quite usual sense of ' cause '. (Cf. *The Meaning of Meaning*, 2nd Ed., p. 55.) The two accounts need not be incompatible. They yield, however, two distinct kinds of meaning and it may on occasion be very important to separate them.

remote past, do not resemble the things they stand for. None the less traces of resemblance—in the form of onomatopœia and, more important perhaps, tongue and lip gesture—can be noticed. We can grant some part of the effect of words in poetry to these resemblances if we are careful not to overwork them. For the representative and evocative power of words comes to them more *through not resembling* what they stand for than through resembling it. For the very reason that a word is *not* like its meaning, it can represent an enormously wide range of different things. Now an image (in so far as it represents by being a copy) can only represent things that are like one another. A word on the other hand can equally and simultaneously represent vastly different things. It can therefore effect extraordinary combinations of feelings. A word is a point at which many very different influences may cross or unite. Hence its dangers in prose discussions and its treacherousness for careless readers of poetry, but hence at the same time the peculiar quasi-magical sway of words in the hands of a master. Certain conjunctions of words— through their history partly and through the collocations of emotional influences that *by their very ambiguity* they effect— have a power over our minds that nothing else can exert or perpetuate.

It is easy to be mysterious about these powers, to speak of the ' inexplicable ' magic of words and to indulge in romantic reveries about their semantic history and their immemorial past. But it is better to realise that these powers can be studied, and that what criticism most needs is less poeticising and more detailed analysis and investigation.

APPENDIX B

THE RELATIVE POPULARITY OF THE POEMS

THE following figures (given in percentages) are rough estimates only, no precision being, under these conditions, attainable. No reliance should be placed in them and they are intended only as an indication of the voting. In any case, since the reasons for liking and disliking the poems are so various, no numerical estimate could have much significance.

Poem	Favourable.	Unfavourable.	Non-committal.
Poem I	45	37	18
„ II	51	43	6
„ III	30	42	28
„ IV	53	42	5
„ V	52	35	13
„ VI	31	59	10
„ VII	54	31	15
„ VIII	19	66	15
„ IX	48	41	11
„ X	37	36	27
„ XI	31	42	27
„ XII	44	33	23
„ XIII	5	92	3

INDEX

Lightning Source UK Ltd.
Milton Keynes UK
30 September 2010

160593UK00001B/58/P